For Handbells and Handchimes

By Susan Berry

Senior Editor: David Berry

Contributing Editors:
Denise Kinlaw, P.T. and Henry Meinecke, M.D.

Illustrated by Allan Berry

Forward by Dr. William A. Payn

Copyright © 2000, 2012 (Reprint) Susan M. Berry and David W. Berry

Published by Handbell Services, Inc.

ISBN-13: 978-0615603575 (Handbell Services, Inc.)

Includes index.

Printed in the United States of America

Edition 1.1

All rights reserved. No part of this book, including cover design, interior graphics, illustrations and icons may be reproduced or transmitted in any form, by any means (electronic, photocopying, recording or otherwise) without written permission of the copyright owner and the publisher of this book.

The BellMan character and all images found within this publication are copyrighted materials and may not be photocopied or transferred without written permission of the copyright owner and the publisher of this book.

The following are registered trademarks of Handbell Services, Inc.:

This publication is designed to provide accurate and authoritative information with regard to the subject matter covered. It is sold with the understanding that the publisher is not engaged in rendering professional medical advice. If assistance is required, the service of a competent professional person should be sought. Before engaging in any exercise program, it is advisable to consult with a health-care provider.

Illustrations and Cover design: Allan Berry
Book Design: Susan Briggs, Bristol Lake Studio
Calligraphy: Millie Janka
Legal Advisor: Mark J. Craig, Attorney

Handbell Services, Inc.
23500 Park Street, Suite #2, Dearborn MI, 48124
1-800-37-BELLS

Dedication

I dedicate this book to my husband, David, who has inspired in me the willingness to travel down new pathways, to work toward a high standard of excellence, to pursue a dream, and to develop a strong backbone even when the walls were sometimes crumbling.

What doctors and therapists Say about *Healthy Ringing*

"I feel that *Healthy Ringing* is a helpful, concise, and timely publication. In this day when work related injuries occupy a major part of the practice of physical therapy and the medical practice in general, I think that the readers of this book will find helpful information. As music for handbells becomes more challenging, there will be times when ringers will find themselves in some discomfort from the activity of handbell ringing and the use of the variety of techniques that are incorporated into pieces today. This book has many helpful hints for avoiding injuries and what might be done if an injury is sustained. It is important to maintain a level of fitness with any activity that we pursue. Handbell ringing is no different. You must condition yourself for the activity or you risk injury. Follow the principles in this book and you may indeed avoid a trip to the doctor."

Denise Kinlaw
Handbell director and ringer
Physical Therapist, Mayo Clinic, Rochester, MN

"*Healthy Ringing* is about balance and control; developing and coordinating all the parts of your body, from breathing to balance, from foot stance to fingers - for bell ringers and their conductors. There are many parallels between athletic endeavors and bell ringing - e.g. coordination, balance, muscle strength, stress injuries. This book is an excellent resource for the basics of developing good physical habits, recognizing danger signals, and understanding "why". Just as professional (and advanced amateur) football players can, with much hard work and specialized training, go beyond what is "safe" for the weekend football player, the bell ringer can go beyond what is prudent and healthy for the ringer who doesn't work out and practice every day. This book should be required reading for all directors and ringers!"

Henry Meinecke, M.D.
Assistant handbell director and ringer
Surgeon, Murphy, SC

"Over the last few years, there has been increasing interest in whether handbell ringing causes musculoskeletal injury - with a great deal of attention given to carpal tunnel syndrome. Much of what 1 have heard and read seems to be lacking in one key ingredient: common sense! *Healthy Ringing* addresses this matter with a pragmatic and sensible approach, building on the premise that handbell ringing a few hours each week is very unlikely to cause injury in most people who do not already have such problems - especially if a few rudimentary precautions are observed. Some of the activities described in this work are designed for long-term gain and should be carried out on a regular basis in order to maximize their benefit, but other suggestions relate to the immediate enhancement of ringing style and ability. To me, the art of handbell ringing should not be a spectacle of brute force but rather an elegance of finesse - from the lowest bass to the highest treble, and the approach in *Healthy Ringing* is a great stride toward that visual and musical goal."

William L. Waggener, Ph.D.
Professor of Biological Sciences
Mt. San Antonio College, Walnut, CA

What handbell experts say about *Healthy Ringing*

"*Healthy Ringing* is a long-awaited manual for both directors and ringers of handbells. Beyond the excellent physiological information provided in this book, the application of good physical design of all handbell techniques is outstanding. As a massed ringing conductor, I rejoice at the prospect that this written information will be in the hands of inquisitive handbell directors and ringers throughout the world. This careful instruction of ringing techniques will enhance precision, musicality, and healthier ringing throughout the art. Physiological insights presented should transform the conductor's preparation and execution of all rehearsals. The book presents multiple exercises to be used in preparation for rehearsal, mid-rehearsal, and after rehearsals. The emphasis on the use of the breath throughout rehearsal and performance will vastly improve the precision of your performances. Massed Ringing events provide great opportunities for physical abuse and *Healthy Ringing* provides excellent information for both the massed ringing conductor and ringer. I was very pleased to read SECTION 21: Ears. Very good warning is issued here with viable solutions to continued exposure to high decibel exposure. I welcome *Healthy Ringing* to the instruction materials available to handbell directors and ringers and encourage serious consideration of its materials. It will add depth to beginner and advanced handbell ensembles. Thank you Sue Berry for compiling in such a thorough, understandable, and practical manual. *Healthy Ringing* is a must for all college handbell courses."

David R. Davidson
Handbell lecturer, clinician, and conductor
Past President of the American Guild of English Handbell Ringers, Inc., Dallas, TX

"*Healthy Ringing* is an invaluable tool for ringers, directors and clinicians. In an age where the words "carpal tunnel" have become everyday language, it is wonderful to have available such a comprehensive study of the muscles and mechanisms of ringing - from head to toe! This manual is absolutely complete, so that there is now no excuse for EVER losing ringers to the various maladies of the wrists, elbows, and so on that can be easily be prevented by simply following these easy-to-understand exercises. From church, community, or school program to directing to festivals, it's all here - and is clearly and thoughtfully presented. *Healthy Ringing* should be required reading for ALL ringers and directors in the handbell world."

Kevin McChesney
Composer, editor, conductor, clinician
Colorado Springs, CO

"*Healthy Ringing* is an excellent book which brings to light the critical importance of good posture, supportive breath, proper use of muscles, and the physical conditioning required not only for healthy ringing skills but also for ringing musically! With advice from medical professionals and years of her own experience Sue has written a stimulating, easy to read and understand, and challenging treatise for all in the handbell field. As directors we cannot afford to continue to ignore the health of those we lead and *Healthy Ringing* provides the tools to properly achieve success in our musical (and physical!) art."

Beth Watson
Conductor, clinician, director
Grapevine, TX

"As more handbell choirs across the world perform more challenging handbell compositions more regularly on larger and larger sets of bells, it is critical that ringers learn how to ring properly to prevent injuries. This is the first handbell technique book that not only addresses the techniques of ringing bells but also truly provides the details on how to ring bells using healthy techniques. From the topics on the muscles used to ring handbells to the topics on warming up, stress management and nutrition, Susan provides a comprehensive and easy to understand explanation that each ringer should follow to prevent pain. This book should be included in every handbell choir director's library and should be found in every ringer's hands so that we can continue to pursue this wonderful art of ringing handbells."

Scott Harris
Member of Raleigh Ringers
Raleigh, NC

"Susan Berry has provided for us a comprehensive yet extremely understandable text that will benefit handbell directors and ringers for years to come. The technical suggestions and *Healthy Ringing* concepts are in a clear and easily readable text that includes many helpful exercises that we must use to develop and maintain handbell ringing as we know it today. The size and number of handbells and the techniques needed for our current repertoire has changed dramatically over the years. Sue's book offers us a new and closer view of our work that should have positive effects on our ringers' health, directors' health, and the resulting musical effect of our art."

Lee J. Afdahl
Conductor, clinician, composer Director of Music
First Presbyterian Church, Rochester, MN

"I'm delighted to see such a fine resource - *Healthy Ringing* - become available to musicians and conductors in the bell world. In my work, I have long realized that music making, especially with bells, is a whole body endeavor, and having this resource available to guide each step of the ringers' activities makes a difference!

I've enjoyed using *Healthy Ringing* both as a book to read and remind myself of concepts and ideas that I need to include in conducting and as a ready reference for a quick-fix spot from the podium. I take *Healthy Ringing* with me on the stand as I conduct festivals and teach in the classroom.

The section on stress management is particularly helpful to both remind me of working to reduce stress and to give practical and applicable tips to put stress reduction into action.

This resource is the handbell musician's equivalent of the Physician's Desk Reference! I recommend it highly to anyone who is ringing, beginners and veterans alike."

Timothy Waugh
Chair - Division of Fine Arts
Pike View High School, Princeton, WV

"Susan Berry has given handbell ringers and directors a much-needed wake-up call to the physical aspects of our art. As with any activity, we place ourselves at risk when we do not understand the body's functions that are involved. Based on years of research and practical experience, **Healthy Ringing** is an innovative and timely approach to handbell ringing with a comprehensive presentation of the inherent physical processes. Through the use of breathing, warm-ups, physical conditioning and a thorough review of bell technique, Sue's guide to **Healthy Ringing** will prove to be an invaluable tool for the first-time director as well as the seasoned professional who wishes to approach the art of handbell ringing with insight and integrity."

David VanderMeer
Minister of Music - Northwoods Presbyterian Church
Musical Director - Houston Bronze Ensemble, Houston, TX

"By the time I had read through the opening material prior to Section One, I was already sold on this incredible resource for ringers and directors. Susan Berry's credentials, experience and contacts in the world of handbells and music education have uniquely gifted her to present the insights and practical applications necessary for healthy handbell ringing and directing. The manner of presentation allows the director to include one or more "handbell health hints" at each rehearsal. There are even instructions for correctly lifting and carrying handbell cases. Thank you, Susan, for this much-needed addition to the art of handbells."

Tammy Waldrop
Publisher, composer, clinician
Kingwood, TX

"I believe **Healthy Ringing** will be viewed as a seminal work in the continuing evolution of handbell ringing education. Filled with a passion for sharing her knowledge of muscular - efficient ringing methodology, Sue Berry gives the ringer information that is easy to read, understand, and apply, presented with informative illustrations and clever use of icons. This is a massive labor of love - a legacy seeking the perfect combination of bells, body and motion."

Charm Peterman
Solo ringer, clinician, director
Yorktown, VA

Acknowledgements

- I'd like to acknowledge the following individuals and ensembles that have assisted and supported me during the research and writing of this publication:

- My family, which has been there for me during this long road of discovery. I especially thank my husband, David, who has been my main advisor in this eight-year project and my son Allan, who took time after graduating from The University of Michigan to help edit the manuscript and draw all the splendid illustrations. Without their professional and personal support, this book would not have been written.

- My art designer, Susan Briggs, who always adds the creative side to my company's publications. I'm grateful to her for combining my words and Allan's graphics into this extraordinary book.

- Denise Kinlaw, P.T., Mayo Clinic, Rochester, MN, a special "thank you" for her dedication to this project and her continued support throughout the past several years. Combining her work as a therapist and as a handbell director, Denise has willingly offered her expertise to several important areas within *Healthy Ringing*.

- Henry Meinecke, M.D., Murphy, NC, another special "thank you" for his continued medical guidance. His persistence and attention to detail in words and in concepts helped solidify the medical foundation of this publication.

- Doctors and other health specialists (many of them bell ringers) who have willingly volunteered their professional knowledge and time to review and edit the manuscript: William Dickieson, P.C., Norman Hogikyan, M.D., F.A.C.S.; Laurie Long, M.A. CCC-A; James Rogers, M.D.; Lisa Rudnicki; Theresa Smyth, MS, RD; Frank Tarwacki, FNAO; William L. Waggener, Ph.D.; Ralph Younkin, D.O.

- Sport physiologists who have advised and reviewed sections in *Healthy Ringing* important to the general physical fitness of handbell ringers: John Downes, Mary Sue Klink, and Christina Willenborg.

- Members of the Detroit Handbell Ensemble: Lucia Bahorich, Timothy Chanko, Laurie Habedank, Paul Kinney; Fran Loiselle, Carolyn Marengere, Judy Phillips, Nancy Plumley, Larry Pye, Douglas Smith, Sandra Smith, Kimberly Strine, and William Taylor and others who have given me the "laboratory" to test an assortment of ringing styles, to analyze special techniques, and to apply appropriate physical warm-ups to a healthier way to ring.

- Handbell colleagues who provided expert reviews and important suggestions to effectively strengthen sections in *Healthy Ringing*: Lee Afdahl,. Douglas Benton, Edna Clay, Kathy Ebling-Thome, Kim Finison, Louise Frier, David Harris, Scott Harris, Nancy Hascall, Nate Judson, Carolyn Marengere, Kevin McChesney, Margery Moore, Marc Olson, Charm Peterman, Larry Pye, Elizabeth Watson, and David Week.

- Carol Coughenour and William Waggener, whose exceptional proofreading skills helped iron out many of the wrinkles in the text, Ian Moore and Allan Berry for graphic design editing, and Cynthia Weber for indexing the entire book.

- To my staff at Handbell Services – Lucia Bahorich, Janice Berry, and Marjorie Riker – who edited and proofread early drafts of the manuscript, and carried on the work of the company during my final months of researching and writing *Healthy Ringing*.
- A special appreciation to the thousands of ringers and directors that I've met at workshops and/ or ringing festivals. I've appreciated all your positive responses to my healthy way of teaching, your willingness to answer my questionnaires, your continued interest in my work, and your eagerness to learn.

Contributing medical, health and sport advisors

- William Dickieson, D.P.M.; Attended The University of Michigan, Ann Arbor, MI; Medical Training, Illinois College of Podiatric Medicine, Chicago, IL; Staff physician, Oakwood Hospital, Lincoln Park, MI; Private Practice, Dearborn, MI since 1982.
- John Downes; Personal trainer and group exercise leader, Fairlane Club, Dearborn, MI; Attended Michigan Technological University, Houghton, MI and the University of Michigan, Dearborn, MI; Certified ACSM, AFFA-Primary and Weight Room, ISSA-Fitness Therapy.
- Norman D. Hogikyan, M.D., F.A.C.S.; Director, The University of Michigan, Vocal Health Center; Asst. Professor, Otolaryngology-Head and Neck Surgery, University of Michigan Medical School; Asst. Professor, Division of Vocal Arts, The University of Michigan School of Music, Ann Arbor, MI.
- Denise Kinlaw, P.T.; B.S., in Zoology and Pre-Physical Therapy, Ohio University; Graduate, The Mayo Clinic School of Physical Therapy; Asst. Professor, Physical Therapy, The Mayo School of Health-Related Sciences Program in Physical Therapy, Rochester, MN; Specialist in hand therapy; Handbell ringer since 1984; Handbell director since 1995.
- Mary Sue Klink; M.S. from Vanderbilt University, Health Education and Promotion; B.A.A. from Central Michigan University, Healthy Fitness in Preventive and Rehabilitative Programs; Athletic Director, Fairlane Club, Dearborn, MI.
- Laurie Long, M.A. CCC-A; B.S., Communication Disorders, Central Michigan University; M.A. Audiology, Western Michigan University; Clinical Audiologist, E.N.T. Specialists, Farmington, MI.
- Henry Meinecke, M.D., F.A.C.S.; Graduate, The University of Arkansas School of Medicine; Surgical residency, Naval Hospital, Portsmouth, VA; General Surgeon, US Navy, twenty-three years; Private practice, eleven years; Consulting physician, repetitive motion injury for several industrial plants; Handbell ringer and assistant director since 1981.
- James H. Rogers, M.D.; B.A., Chemistry, Florida State University; Medical training, The University of Alabama Medical School, Birmingham, AL; Internal medicine/private practice, thirty-three years, Huntsville Clinic, Huntsville', AL; Retired from active practice since 1998; Church and community handbell director since 1984.

- Lisa Rudnicki; B.S., Physiology, Central Michigan University; Licensed Emergency Medical Services Instructor; Specialist, critical care pre-hospital medicine; Medical instructor, Kellogg Community College, Battle Creek, MI; Handbell ringer since 1974.
- Theresa Smyth, RD.; B.S. Dietetics and M.S., Allied Health Education, The University of Detroit Mercy, Detroit, MI; Registered Dietitian, American Dietetic Association, Fairlane Club, Dearborn, MI.
- Frank Tarwacki, A.B.O.C.; B.S., Ferris State University; Certified Optician, American Board of Opticianary; P.C., Optical Manager, Suburban Eye Care, Livonia, MI.
- William L. Waggener, Ph.D.; B.A., Music, Pomona College, Claremont, CA; M.A. Music, Claremont Graduate University, Claremont, CA; M.S. Biological Sciences, California State Polytechnic University, Pomona, Pomona; Ph.D., Physiology, University of California, Riverside, CA. Professor, Biological Sciences and Chairman, Department of Biological Sciences, Mt. San Antonia College, Walnut, CA; Handbell director since 1974; Festival conductor I clinician.
- Ralph Younkin, D.O.; Medical training, Kansas City College, Kansas City, MO; Graduate, The University of Health Science, Kansas City, MO; Adjunct faculty, Michigan State University; Asst. Professor of Medicine, Dept. of Family Practice, Michigan State University, College of Osteopathic Medicine; Specialist over forty years; Family practice in Redford, MI and Akron, OH; Retired, 1996; Handbell ringer since 1974.

Contents

Foreword by Dr. William Payn 16
An Overview and Short History 18

PART I: ANATOMY OF RINGING 23

SECTION 1: MAJOR MUSCLES USED 24
Arm 24
Hand 26
Neck 26
Shoulder 27
Chest 27
Back 27
Respiration 28
Leg 29
Foot 30

SECTION 2: POSTURE 31
Proper posture for ringing 31

SECTION 3: BREATHING 34
Breathing basics 34
Deep breathing awareness 35
Combining breathing and ringing 37
Breathing for the handbell choir 37
Breathing cues for the director 38

PART II: RINGING BASICS 39

SECTION 4: BASIC GRIP 39
Proper balance 40
Proper grip 40
Proper hand fit 43
Grip adjustment 43
Grip tension 44
Grip strength 45

SECTION 5: BASIC RING 47
Ready-to-ring 47
Basic ring 48
Basic stroke 49
Common ringing concerns 52
Alternative ringing set-ups 53

SECTION 6: BASIC DAMP 55
Shoulder damp 55
Finger damp 58
Table damp 59

SECTION 7: WEAVING 61
- Weaving "in a nutshell" 61
- Weight shifting 61
- Weaving process 62
- Three-bell weave 64
- Four-bell weave 66

SECTION 8: SPECIAL EFFECTS 68
- Stopped techniques 68
  - Plucking 68
  - Thumb damp 69
  - Martellato 69
  - Ring touch 72
  - Mallets 69
- Non-stopped techniques 73
  - Shake 73
  - Toll (Swing) 74
  - LV (Let Vibrate, "Laissez Vibrer") 75
  - Gyro or shimmer 75
  - Belltree 75

SECTION 9: BASS BELL RINGING 77
- Preparation 77
- Proper ringing 79
- Proper damping 81
- Special techniques 82
- Alternative ringing setup 84
- Protecting the body 85
- Director's responsibility 86

SECTION 10: MULTIPLE BELL TECHNIQUES 87
- Basic grip 88
- Basic ring 89
- Basic damp 90
- Shelley 92
- Four-in-hand 93
- Combo-ring 94

SECTION 11: HANDCHIMES 97
- Basic grip 97
- Ready-to-ring position 98
- Ringing 98
- Damping 99
- Weaving 101
- Multiple chimes 102
- Special techniques 102

PART III: EXERCISES FOR RINGING 103
Introduction to healthy exercises 104

SECTION 12: WARM-UPS FOR RINGING 106
- Why are warm-ups important 106
- Benefits of stretching 106
- How do you stretch? 106
- Basic stretching guidelines 107
- A stretching routine 107
- Understanding resistance 108

SECTION 13: SHOULDER AND NECK 110
- The basics 110
- Care when ringing 110
- Shoulder and neck warm-ups 111
- Shoulder and neck stretches 111

SECTION 14: ARM 115
- The basics 115
- Arm warm-ups 115
- Arm stretches 116

SECTION 15: FINGERS, HAND AND WRIST 118
- The basics 118
- How can you avoid muscle strain? 118
- Basic warm-up 119
- Finger stretches 119
- Hand and wrist stretches 123
- Cool down stretches 124

SECTION 16: BACK 125
- The basics 125
- Back stretches 126
- Back care 130
- Back strain 131

SECTION 17: ABDOMEN 132
- The basics 132
- Abdominal stretches 132

SECTION 18: LEGS 134
- The basics 134
- Calf stretches 135
- Hamstring stretches 136
- Quadriceps stretches 137

SECTION 19: FOOT 138
- The basics 138
- Ankle and foot stretches 138
- Foot protection 139

SECTION 20: RESISTANCE TRAINING 141
Developing hand, arm and upper body strength 141
Sets and repetitions..141
Procedure..141
Developing grip strength..141
Guidelines for using free weights..142

PART IV: CARE OF YOUR BODY 145

SECTION 21: EARS 146
Noise/music exposure..146
Hearing protection devices 146

SECTION 22: EYES 148
General eye care 148
Eyeglasses...148
Contact lenses..149
Visual aids...150
Visual support 151

SECTION 23: VOICE 152
For the director..152
Vocal concerns...152
Amplification..153

SECTION 24: STRESS MANAGEMENT 154
Controlling stress..154
Feeling stressed? Here are a few stress relievers.........................154
Prior to performance..155
Dealing with pre-performance anxiety 155
During performance...156
General stgretches in cramped quarters 156

SECTION 25: NUTRITION 158
Water – the essential ingredient!..158
Eating prior to a concert is important!......................................158

SECTION 26: MOVING HANDBELL CASES AND TABLES 160
The basics of lifting 160
Questions about moving handbell cases 162
Alternatives to lifting heavy handbell cases 162

SECTION 27: GLOVES 164
Basic care...166

SECTION 28: SUPPORT DEVICES 168
Muscle overuse 168
Support bands or braces 168

SECTION 29: MEDICAL CONCERNS	171
Common problems	171
Drug pain relievers	173
Non-drug pain relievers	174

PART V: THE MASSED RING ... 177
SECTION 30: THE DIRECTOR ... 179
SECTION 31: THE RINGER ... 184

RESOURCES ... 189
INDEX ... 190

About the Author ... 197
About the Illustrator ... 197

Foreword

by Dr. William Payn

Congratulations! You are now holding a book that can improve your performance as either a handbell ringer or conductor. Most importantly, you hold in your hands a way to gain access to healthy ringing and conducting. Over the years, much study has gone into the effects of improper physical positioning when playing an instrument. It is now a proven fact that one can ultimately cause serious injury to certain muscular groups by holding an instrument in the wrong position or by incorrect body stance. Until now, however, no one has addressed the importance of healthy ringing. In this innovative book, Susan Berry guides you through a program of exercise and body care unique to handbell ringing. By the time you finish this book, you will have learned how to change patterns of behavior that impair healthy ringing. Perhaps you have purchased this book because you worry about shoulder pain every time you ring. Maybe you leave rehearsals with numbness in your fingertips or weakness in your wrist. Possibly, as a low-bell ringer, you can't manipulate the bells without tension and fatigue in your forearm. Or perhaps you are a massed-ringing conductor who experiences fatigue and pain in your upper body following a long day of rehearsals. Regardless of the nature of your symptoms, the information Susan has assembled in this book will help you draw on your body's own resources for healthy ringing/conducting.

After many years as a massed-ring /festival conductor, I have come to realize the importance of a consistently healthy life-style in maintaining energy and vitality on the podium. When I first started conducting festivals thirty years ago I would huff and puff my way through rehearsals and be in agony by the end of the festival, often needing a session on a chiropractor's table or long hours of physical therapy to relieve the aching in my arms and the tension in my lower back. It didn't take me long to realize that, although my conducting technique and gesture were correct, I needed to pay more attention to physical, mental and emotional preparation. I only wish that I could have had the benefit of Susan Berry's many suggestions for warm-ups, stretches, and proper breathing. Because of mistakes I made as a young conductor, I'm now able to teach my own students the benefits of proper breathing, stance and posture, as well as the advantage of physical fitness coupled with a healthy life-style. Every spring at Bucknell University, I teach a course in conducting. One of the main topics I emphasize, especially to beginning students, is the necessity of proper breathing. Susan devotes an entire section to this important fundamental of handbell ringing and to its effect upon performance, stress and energy. Her discussion on nutrition, including the importance of drinking water to stabilize energy, is enormously helpful to ringers and conductors who wonder why they can't maintain a high level of energy during a long rehearsal or concert. This book can keep ringers and conductors from forming bad habits at the crucial early stages of their individual or ensemble development.

My generation grew up in an environment that did not emphasize the importance of physical fitness. As a child, I spent ten months in bed with rheumatic fever, gaining a tremendous amount of weight for my size and frame. Then, following my illness, I was never encouraged to exercise or find ways to strengthen my heart. As a result, I was not in good cardiovascular condition, let alone physically prepared for a demanding career as a conductor. Now, many years later, (by the way, it's never too late to start) I follow a program of weekly physical exercise that includes resistance training, weight-lifting, and walking. As a result, I am able to take on several festival/ rehearsals in a row and walk away without muscle fatigue. I no longer feel that I personally have to "pull" every ringer through a piece of music, nor do I need to use repeated large, jerky beats when a passage actually calls for soft legato ringing. My physical training has given me an understanding of the importance of resistance and balance to the act of conducting. I can allow the ringers to follow me and express themselves, without having to resort to large, swooping motions that can do severe damage to my muscles. Every community in the United States has a nearby fitness center, and the benefits of leading a healthy life are well worth the total average cost of approximately $1.00 per day. I "work out" three times a week, for approximately one hour and fifteen minutes each time, and I walk at least two miles every day. My weekly conducting schedule includes four major ensembles plus an average of two guest-conducting engagements per month. If I didn't demand a regular health and fitness program of myself, I could neither keep up the pace nor so quickly recover from its physical and mental strain.

This book illustrates hundreds of small steps you can take to develop a weekly exercise program and lay the foundation for healthy ringing/ conducting. You can decide how much of this book you want or need to use on a permanent basis. In fact, the creative illustrations, together with clear, concise guides for every aspect of ringing, will allow you to easily choose topics that relate to your own experience. I chose to make positive physical changes in my life at a point when I was able to appreciate the long-range benefits. The rewards have been enormous, because now I can conduct for as long as I want without unnecessary muscular stress, certain that my body won't give out before I'm ready to retire, Obviously you are concerned about changes in your ringing/ conducting style - otherwise you wouldn't be reading this book. Susan Berry has taken her passionate work on this subject and pointed you in the right direction. Now you must be willing to change old habits and dig in!

I suspect there are many ringers/ conductors who take prescribed drugs or over-the-counter pills to relieve pain following a rehearsal or performance. Perhaps this book will help you to discover that a simple adjustment of ringing/ conducting style is all you need. The sound ideas presented in this book will give you all the information you need to change damaging ringing habits and protect your body from the assaults of improper ringing. Throw those pain killers out the window! This book will change the way you think about healthy ringing.

William A. Payn, **Ph.D.** - Professor of Music
Bucknell University, Lewisburg, Pennsylvania

An Overview and Short History

Handbell ringing is currently growing and developing much like school bands and orchestras did earlier in this century and like marching bands and drum corps have in the past thirty years. More and more music is being published for handbells, large festivals are building a diverse handbell community, and schools are including handbells and handchimes in their music programs. More than ever before, people are discovering music through handbells and making it an important part of their lives.

In the early 1960's, handbell choirs in churches began emerging in the United States. Initially, the range of bells manufactured was a 25-note set, and repertoire included simple hymn-tunes, folksong arrangements, and easy original compositions. Handbell ringing and damping was uncomplicated, with a minimum number of changes in technique and style.

As the handbell field grew, handbell manufacturers expanded the available range of handbells. Basic sets extended farther into the treble and bass ranges. Larger (and heavier) bells were created to enhance the sound, making it more orchestral. The largest of these cast bronze bells proved too heavy for average ringers, so aluminum cast handbells were created in an attempt to solve this problem.

Programs expanded into schools, and special ensembles began developing in local communities. Ensembles became more sophisticated, as they found new ways to challenge their members. New techniques were discovered that let fewer ringers play more handbells, and performers and composers began experimenting with more exotic sounds and with exciting percussive techniques.

Recognizing this growth, The American Guild of English Handbell Ringers, Inc. created (January 6, 198 1, Nashville, TN) a committee representing handbell manufacturers, publishers, composers, and directors. Called the Handbell Notational Conference, it meets approximately once every three years, setting standards for all musical notation and technique.

Often, conversations in these meetings have centered on the variety of handbell effects and sounds, encouraging the use of many new techniques. However, little has been mentioned about the physical effects these new techniques could have on the bodies of handbell ringers!

While the goal of a handbell choir - performance of satisfying, meaningful, and beautiful music - has stayed the same for many decades, the expectations placed on ringers has increased dramatically. Ringing now involves a multitude of ambitious techniques, and ringers engage in heavy physical activity without considering the energy it takes and the strain it may cause to their bodies!

Ringers can overexert muscles not often used in the rest of their daily activities. Most people don't realize how much effort goes into playing handbells; fingers, hands, arms, shoulders, back and legs need to be in good condition, ready for a workout when the rehearsal begins. Instead, handbell rehearsals generally occur only once a week - hardly often enough for a handbell ringer to become fit. In addition, rehearsal time often follows busy daily schedules, and ringers are often tired, having come directly from the demands of school, home, family and job. After initial greetings among the group, handbells are quickly removed from cases, music is placed on tables, and rehearsal begins. In most cases, no consideration is given to preparing the ringers physically for rehearsal.

This book is necessary because handbell ringing is a physical workout!

Athletes always warm up! Athletes at any level in any sport such as basketball, dancing, or swimming always prepare by warming up muscles of the body and respiratory system. Athletes must prepare themselves for their activity, and they must execute this activity correctly if they want to remain healthy and injury free. Athletes routinely stretch and condition their muscles, because they know the consequences of not stretching and the strain that may occur. Ringing handbells is also a physically demanding workout and requires attentive warm-ups as well!

Despite injuries increasingly entering the handbell world, preventive measures (such as simple warm-ups) remain incorrectly done or not done at all. Unless individual ringers understand how their muscles work, feel the correct way to ring, and understand the benefits of physical conditioning, they will place great strain on their bodies. The handbell is the only percussion instrument played with its full weight *above* the hand – a potentially awkward and unnatural position. For handbell ringing to become graceful and healthy, this weight must be precisely controlled so that ringing handbells can be a healthy and vibrant musical experience.

This book is entitled ***Healthy Ringing*** to help all once-a-week handbell ringers and directors play in *harmony* with handbells, instead of harming themselves with handbells. My wish is for safe enjoyment and for cautious challenge. If you share my goals, then you'll find that this book offers a wealth of important advice for ringers and directors alike.

The background of writing this book

I've been actively involved in the handbell industry - as a church musician, clinician, conductor, author, and business owner - for thirty years. I've had the opportunity to teach, train, listen to, and observe hundreds of choirs and thousands of individual ringers in rehearsals, festivals, and concerts. Within the last ten years I began hearing concerns from ringers within choirs about physical ailments attributed to handbell ringing. I started considering these recurring problems. Were they caused by handbell ringing, a lack of exercise - or perhaps both?

In 1991 I joined an athletic club and became aware of the benefits of controlled exercise, especially in personal training sessions with a sports physiologist. Created for me was a workout routine including aerobics (to raise my heart fitness) and resistance training with free weights and machines (to strengthen my muscles). I found aspects in my personal training that could be easily carried over into handbell playing; after all, ringers lift weights, they use many muscles when lifting, and suffer similar physical problems common to weight lifters. Transferring this new knowledge to my teaching, a section of warm-ups was added during each clinic or festival I taught. Health-related questions were asked at teaching events, and a personal, non-scientific questionnaire of participants to gather general information was used. Some questions were:

- Do you do any routine physical exercise?
- Do you walk on a daily basis?
- Do you do any type of consistent workout - especially resistance-training?
- Have you incurred any type of strain or injury by handbell ringing?

The feedback from these questions was strangely consistent. Ringers reported finger strain and strain on the top of the hand (near the wrist), aches near the elbow, discomfort in the forearm, soreness in the neck and near the shoulder blade, and lower back trouble. These localized aches and pains occurred during and following handbell rehearsals! I found that most ringers participated in no other regular activities to elevate their heart rate or to strengthen their bell-ringing muscles.

My interest was kindled; observing ringers from this different perspective, I became concerned with the way handbells were rung (and taught). Jerky ringing strained not only the muscles of the ringer, but created unpleasant ringing sounds as well. People were struggling to ring bells much too heavy for their size, twisting their hands to ring three bells in one hand, and incorrectly bending over to pick up handbell cases.

I began paying special attention to the opening minutes of massed handbell festivals, and noticed that most of the conductors neglected physical warm-ups for the assembly. The most ambitious conductors mentioned a few quick superficial arm or neck stretches; however, the large majority, after brief introductions, launched directly into the demanding music.

For the many reasons above, research was compiled to write this book. All of my teaching had a new purpose, with new focus relating directly to *Healthy Ringing*. I started to teach individuals how to sense what their body was telling them, to understand and feel individual muscles as they rang, to know when to take a stretch break, and to know when it was time to stop!

As *Healthy Ringing* is now a reality, it seems obvious to me that it is not an optional piece of handbell instruction; instead, it's an essential prerequisite for ringing, and should be an integral part of any handbell program. This philosophy of teaching a healthy way to ring is the organizing factor of this book; it is laid out sequentially, as I would teach in my workshops.

Fortunately, I've had an excellent pool of experts to draw upon; without their help this book would never have appeared. Highly educated professionals in the medical, musical, and kinesiological fields (many of whom are also regular handbell directors or ringers), were consulted who have provided insight, advice, and editing. Through these connections, as well as my experience with a personal trainer, the information presented here is accurate, up-to-date, and thorough.

The Detroit Handbell Ensemble has given me unconditional support; members have willingly allowed themselves to be part of this discovery. During this eight-year *Healthy Ringing* project, concepts that I developed were evaluated, discussed, accepted or rejected. As a result, these ideas have helped DHE become a polished, cohesive, and healthy ensemble.

Whether you are a casual, once-a-week handbell ringer who rings for pure musical pleasure, a solo ringer who rehearses daily, a weekly ringer in an advanced ensemble that pushes beyond normal ringing, a director deeply involved in the intricacies of performance - or somewhere in between - this book will help you become aware of the demands handbell ringing places on your body. It provides the basic knowledge you need to develop good habits in handbell ringing, to keep you injury free, and to make handbell ringing as fulfilling as possible.

Susan Berry

Icons used in this book

Important!

Thumbs up

Recommended for a healthy way to ring

Thumbs down

Potential for physical harm

Caution!

An idea!

Remember!

Flexibility is the key!

Stretching exercise

Resistance exercise

*These icons are used throughout **Healthy Ringing®** to place emphasis upon certain sections of particular importance. Sometimes they are used to highlight a paragraph, an entire page, or to indicate an exercise for the reader to practice.*

PART ONE

Anatomy of Ringing

- Major Muscles Used

- Posture

- Breathing

SECTION ONE

MAJOR MUSCLES USED

The human body consists of interdependent and complicated systems which control its structure, circulation, respiration, digestion, and movement. The nero-muscular system controls the body's physical movement through the cooperation of groups of muscles throughout the body.

The primary muscles most significant to handbell ringers are included in this publication. The anatomical names are used where applicable, along with any common names they might have. The definition for each muscle is simply stated in user-friendly terms; any additional interest and more explanation will require further individual inquiry.

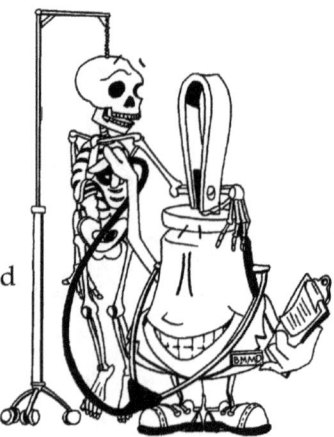

Arm

BICEPS (*biceps brachii*) AND TRICEPS (*triceps brachii*)

The *biceps* bends your elbow and pulls objects closer to your body. The *triceps* is the biceps' opposite; it functions to extend or straighten your elbow to push things away. These two muscles cooperate with each other; when one contracts, the other relaxes. Although the biceps is used most in basic handbell ringing, the triceps works also, especially doing tower swings, martellatos, and pushing tables and cases against a wall or into a cabinet. It is important that **both** biceps be well developed since we ring using both arms. If a biceps muscle is poorly developed, other muscles must compensate (usually the forearm muscles). Strains, aches and pains may develop.

1. Deltoid
2. Triceps
3. Biceps
4. Brachioradialis
5. Brachialis (functions with the biceps)
6. Brachioradialis
7. Extensor carpi radialis longus
8. Pronator teres (rotates the forearm)
9. Flexors (various)
10. Flexor carpi ulinaris
11. Extensors (various)
12-13. Flexor digitorium superficialis
14. Lumbricales

Muscle diagram may include more muscles than are referred to in the text.

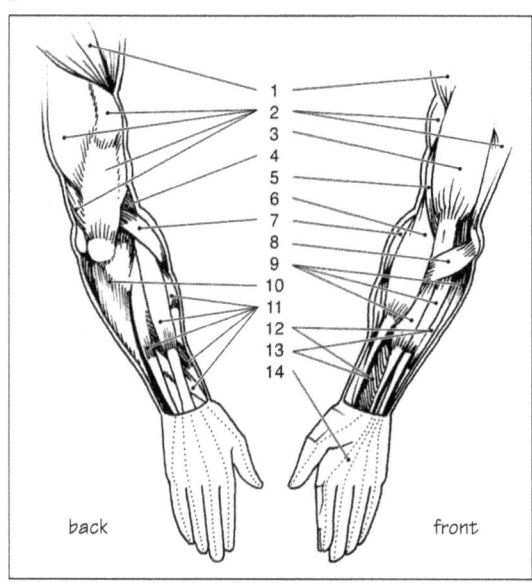

figure 1a

Healthy Ringing

24

MAJOR MUSCLES USED

ANATOMY OF RINGING

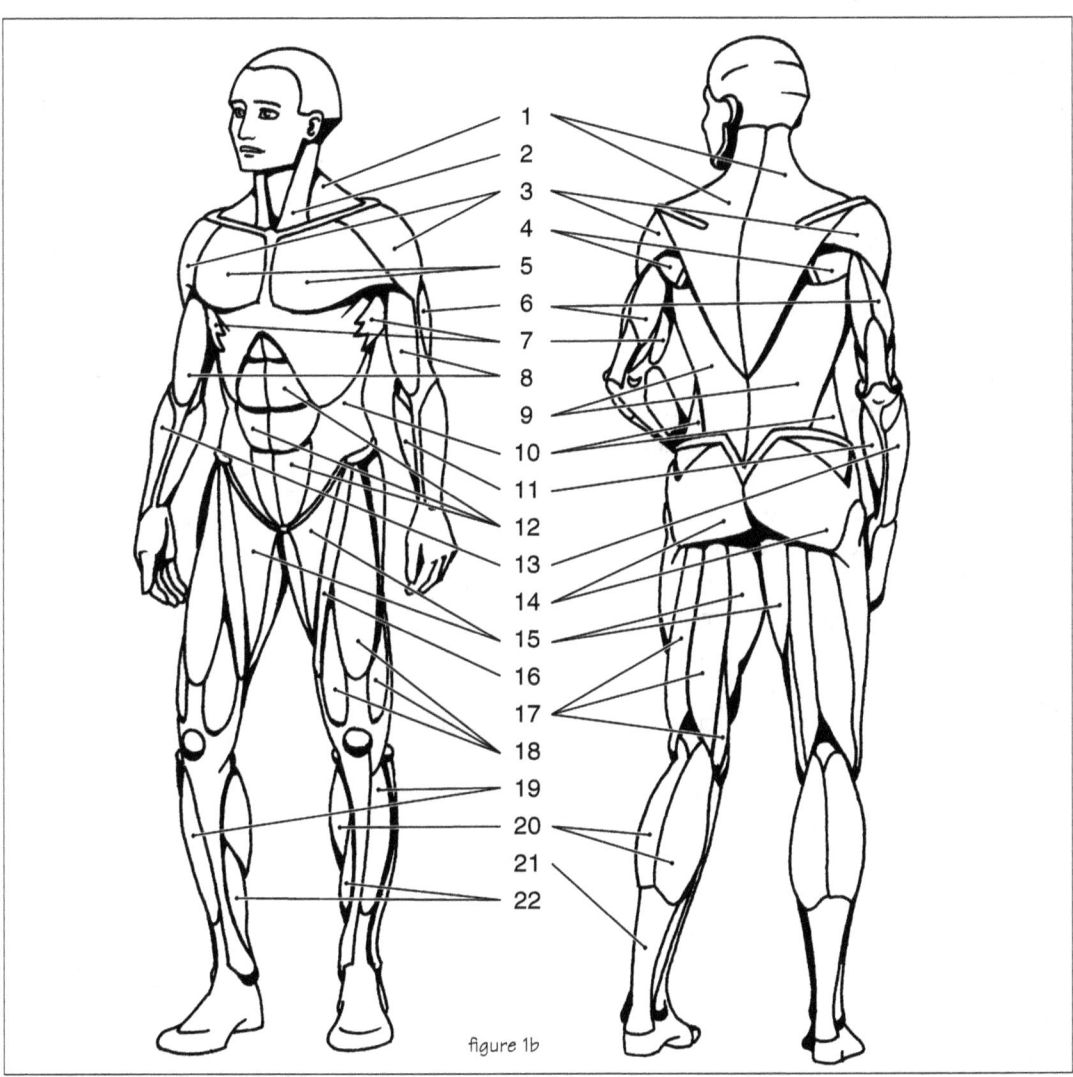

figure 1b

1. Trapezius
2. Sternocleidomastoid
3. Deltoid
4. Rotator cuff
5. Pectoralis major
6. Triceps
7. Serratus anterior
8. Biceps
9. Latissimus dorsi
10. External oblique
11. Forearm flexor group
12. Rectus abdominus
13. Forearm extensor group
14. Gluteus maximus
15. Adductor
16. Sartorius
17. Hamstrings
18. Quadriceps
19. Tibialis anterior
20. Gastronocnemius
21. Achilles tendon
22. Soleus

Healthy Ringing

SECTION ONE

FOREARM
The collection of muscles in your forearm helps support your wrist and hand, and allows you to rotate your wrist, maneuver your hand, and manipulate your fingers via tendons threaded through your wrist.

The muscles that bend your fingers, the *flexor* muscles (*flexor digitorum superficialis*, and the *flexor digitorum profundis*, among others) line the palm-side of your forearm. Their opposite muscles, the *extensors* (*extensor digitorum*) line the back-side of your forearm and function to straighten your fingers. Without conditioned forearm muscles, gripping a bass bell can cause strain to the wrist.

Hand
There are several small muscles in the hand that assist in flexing and extending your fingers and thumb, provide support to the many tendons and bones in the hand, and manipulate your hand in other ways.

Two types of hand muscles help to move our fingers, the *extrinsic* and *intrinsic* muscles. *Extrinsics* originate in the forearm, and manipulate the fingers via tendons threaded through the wrist. They are responsible for the movement of the end and middle finger joints. The *intrinsics* lie entirely in the hand, and help to extend the fingers by manipulating their large first joints, as well as helping to move the thumbs.

The most significant muscles for the bell ringer are the *flexor digitorum profundis*, *flexor digitorum superficialis*, and the *lumbricals*. Combined, they help to close your hand around the bell's handle. The finger *flexors* and *extensors* work together to provide a strong grip.

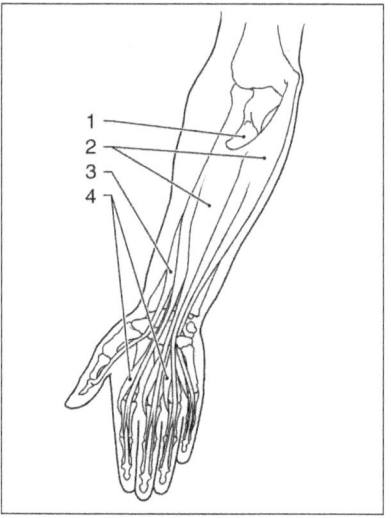

figure 1c

Extrinsic hand muscles
1. Flexor digitorum profundis (extends under superficialis)
2. Flexor digitorum superficialis
3. Flexor pollicis longus

Intrinsic hand muscles
4. Lumbricales

Muscle diagram may include more muscles than are referred to in the text.

Neck
STERNOCLEIDOMASTOIDS
These neck muscles help keep your head on straight and along with the muscles of the spine allow your head to move from side to side. They also work to move your head down. Neck extensors help move your head up and back, and work in combination to move your head up and down.

TRAPEZIUS (traps)
The *trapezius* is the strong upper back, shoulder, and neck muscle that stretches from shoulder to shoulder and from the middle of your spine past your neck to your head. One of the strongest and largest muscles in your body, your trapezius helps raise your

Healthy Ringing

shoulder, and is essential in lifting and in arm movement. It allows you to shrug your shoulders and pinch your shoulder blades together. Your trapezius tends to tense up in stressful situations such as performing, which can cause great tension in your upper back and neck.

Shoulder

DELTOID (delts)
This shoulder muscle is the primary muscle for lifting your arm and moving it in all directions. You cannot reach for things or lift a heavy bell, case, or table without it. Your two deltoids make it possible to give a big hug!

TRAPEZIUS (see *Neck*, page 26)

ROTATOR CUFF (subscapularis, teres minor, supraspinatus and infraspinatus)
This set of shoulder muscles joins your upper arm bones (*humerus*) and your shoulder blades (*scapula*); they help to rotate your arms, to reach for objects, and to keep your shoulders pulled back. They are used constantly when ringing handbells, and can suffer particular abuse from bass bell ringing.

Chest

PECTORALIS MAJOR AND PECTORALIS MINOR (pectorals or pecs)
These chest muscles function to pull your arm across your chest, to push things away from you, and to help lift your arm (and whatever the arm is carrying, like a bass bell or heavy case). The *pectoralis minor* lies underneath your *pectoralis major*. Despite the misleading name, a "shoulder damp" actually happens against your pectoralis major muscle.

Back

TRAPEZIUS (see *Neck*, page 26)

RHOMBOIDS
Your *rhomboid* muscles pull your shoulders back and down and help to maintain good posture. Closely associated with and covered by the *trapezius*, they stretch from your shoulder blades to your spine. You have two pair of rhomboid muscles, the *rhomboideus major* and the *rhomboideus minor*.

ROTATOR CUFF (see *Shoulder*, above)

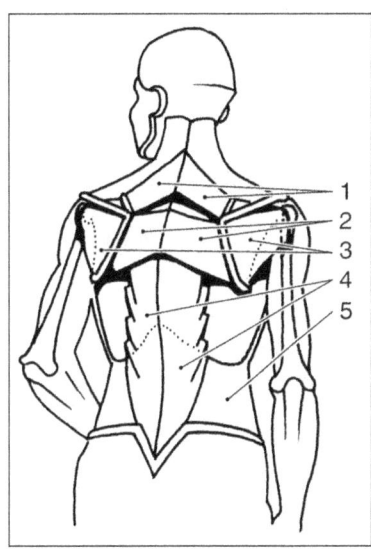

figure 1d

1. Rhomboideus minor
2. Rhomboideus major
3. Rotator cuff
4. Erector spinae
5. Obliques (internal & external)

SECTION ONE

LATISSIMUS DORSI (lats)
This is the largest muscle that runs along the side of your back. It helps you reach behind when paddling a canoe or throwing a ball and helps your arm muscles pull a handbell toward your body for the damp.

ERECTOR SPINAE
These muscles keep your spine erect, help create good posture, and are essential when lifting. Running along your spine from your lower back to the base of your skull underneath the *latissimus dorsi,* they support your torso in everything it does. These muscles can be strained when bending from the waist to pick up handbell cases or bass bells.

Respiration

DIAPHRAGM
This is a double-domed muscle (shaped like two rounded hills) located between the chest organs above and the abdominal organs below. When it contracts, it flattens – pushing the abdominal organs down and pulling air into the lungs through the trachea (windpipe). At the same time, the abdominal muscles relax a bit to accommodate the displaced organs. **This is commonly referred to as "abdominal" breathing.**

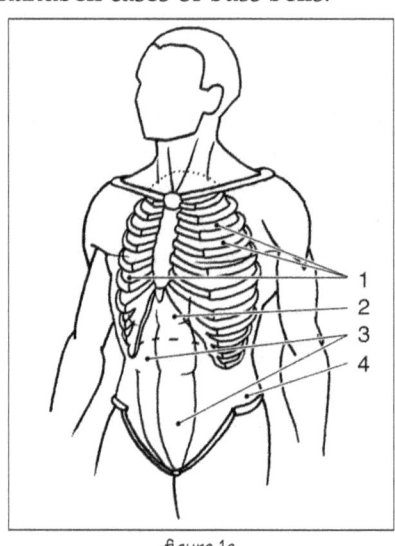

figure 1e

1. Intercoastals
2. Diaphragm
3. Rectus Abdominus
4. Obliques (internal & external)

INTERCOSTALS
These muscles connect each rib with the one above and the one below. The whole rib cage is like a partially collapsed box when relaxed. As the ribs are lifted up by the intercostals (and certain neck muscles), they increase the volume of the chest and "square the box", creating space for the lungs to expand. **This is commonly referred to as "chest" breathing.**

ABDOMINALS (abs)
In combination with the lower back (lumbar) muscles, the *abdominals* help keep the pelvis aligned for erect posture and help you turn from side to side. Working your abdominals gives added strength supporting your upper body, improving posture, and relieving pressure on your lower back.

The abdominal muscles also aid in breathing, pushing air out of the lungs faster than the normal contracting elasticity of the lungs allows. This breathing is assisted by the lumbar muscles, which are over the "back side" of your abdomen (over the kidneys). The abdominal group consists of four muscles: the three flat, layered muscles along the side of the abdomen (*internal obliques, external obliques and transverse abdominis*) and the paired vertical *rectus abdominis* muscles.

Healthy Ringing

MAJOR MUSCLES USED

Leg

GLUTEALS (glutes)

When you stand up from a sitting position, these are the muscles that, along with the quadriceps, do most of the work as they pull your torso over your legs. You cannot stand without them, and they provide your basic support when lifting a bass bell. Your *gluteals* are actually a group of three separate muscles: *gluteus maximus, gluteus medius,* and *gluteus minimus.*

QUADRICEPS (quads)

The *quadriceps* help extend or straighten your knee, giving you the support necessary when lifting a bass bell or heavy case. The *quadriceps* group consists of four separate muscles: *rectus femoris* (the longest muscle in your body), *vastus lateralis, vastus medialis,* and internally, not shown, the *vastus intermedias.*

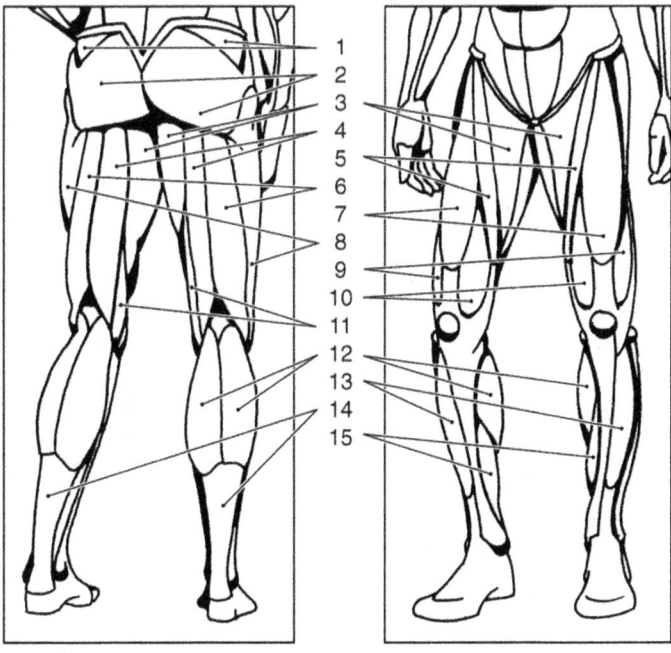

figure 1f

1. Gluteus medius (extends under gluteus maximus, covers gluteus minimus)
2. Gluteus maximus
3. Adductors
4. Semitendinosus
5. Sartorius
6. Biceps femoris
7. Rectus femoris
8. Iliotibial tract
9. Vastus lateralis
10. Vastus medialis
11. Semimembranous
12. Gastrocnemius
13. Tibialis anterior
14. Achilles tendon
15. Soleus

HAMSTRINGS

These flexion muscles help pull your leg back and help bend your knees. The *hamstrings* are composed of three separate muscles: the *biceps femoris,* the *semimembranous* and the *semitendinous.*

LOWER LEG MUSCLES

The *calf* muscles help support your leg when walking, standing, reaching, or pushing off when walking, as well as when maneuvering your foot. The calf group consists of the *gastrocnemeus* and *soleus* which raise you onto the balls of your feet (i.e. "on your toes"), and *tibialis anterior* (along with others) which raise your foot (i.e. "standing on your heels").

SECTION ONE

Foot

Your foot holds and carries the weight of your entire body. This large collection of small bones is held firmly in place by a web of muscles and ligaments that have great power and strength. The top of your foot has a series of extensor muscles (the *extensor digitorum longus* and *extensor hallucis longus*) that help lift your foot and create the extension of your toes. The bottom of the foot has flexor muscles (*flexor digitorum brevis* and the *flexor hallucis brevis*) that help lower your foot. Other flexor muscles, the *tibialis posterior* and the *peroneus longus*, are located in your lower leg. They help flex your foot and stabilize the arch. (Not shown in *figure 1g*; see *Legs*, page 134, *figure 18a*.)

The *Achilles tendon (figure 1f)*, although not a muscle, it is the most important part of your foot. Attached to your calf muscle and heel bone, the Achilles tendon is your foot's shock absorber. It gives the spring to your step when moving from foot to foot as you walk, run, or move from side to side.

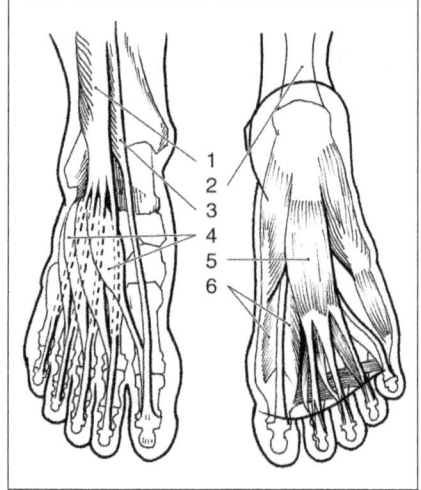

figure 1g

1. Extensor digitorum longus
2. Achilles tendon
3. Extensor hallucis longus
4. Extensor digitorium brevis
5. Flexor digitorum brevis
6. Flexor hallucis brevis

SECTION TWO

POSTURE

Correct posture is the foundation of all handbell ringing!

Standing behind a handbell table – before even picking up a bell – the body must be prepared and properly aligned. This feeling of *planned good posture* is important from the feet up to the head! Train your body to create support for lifting bells.

Good posture and body alignment minimize fatigue and stress throughout your body and are essential to every aspect of handbell playing. For example, allowing your shoulders to slouch places strain on your back and neck and limits the air available to your lungs. When you get less air, you produce less energy, and you'll not play as well as you could otherwise. You might even pull a muscle!

"Proper posture prevents problems"

Proper posture for ringing

STAND UP STRAIGHT (figure 2a)
Stand with your feet evenly spaced, shoulder width apart. The proper *stance* should equalize and support the weight of your body, with your center of gravity balanced midway between your feet, allowing both movement of your feet and shifting of your weight easily from one foot to another. This requires that your knees are not *locked* in the full back position, but are on the "balance point", closer to the balls of your feet than the heels – not flexed, but also not locked.

KEEP YOUR SPINE ERECT
Imagine a string attached to the crown of your head, lifting you upward. This is a common dance technique for teaching balance and good posture; it will help you feel whether your body is in alignment and make you taller as well. If your spine is erect, your pelvis will not be tilted forward, and your rib cage and pelvis will be in alignment.

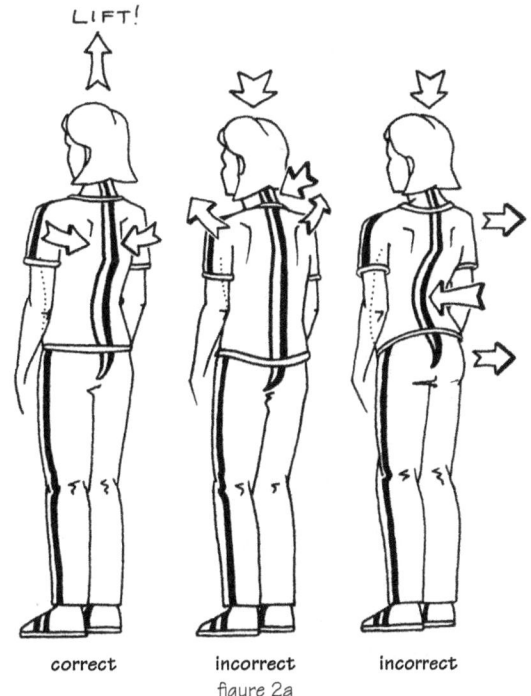

correct   incorrect   incorrect
figure 2a

Healthy Ringing

SECTION TWO

KEEP YOUR HEAD ON STRAIGHT
Your head should look outward – not directly downward – and your ears should be directly over your shoulders. This removes strain from your spine, neck and trapezius muscles – a cause of upper body fatigue. This concept will also strengthen eye contact between director and ringer.

Visualize this with a child's set of building blocks. Each block supports the weight of all the blocks resting on it. If one is out of position, the entire set of blocks will tumble – especially if that one is the top block on the pile!

KEEP YOUR SHOULDER BLADES PULLED BACK AND DOWN
This will allow your lungs more room to expand and consequently give you more air to breathe. Imagine squeezing a pencil between your shoulder blades; if your head is held straight and high, you will find this much easier.

FEEL YOUR LARGE MUSCLES AT WORK
Your erector spinae, abdominal, gluteus and quadriceps muscles are your body's primary support, and you should always be aware of them. These muscles should bear most of the weight of lifting and ringing handbells (as well as lifting handbell cases).

USE ABDOMINAL CONTROL
The abdominal muscles help control breathing and help relieve the strain on your lower back – problems that can be caused by heavy bells. As you raise handbells from the table, consciously tighten your abdominal and gluteus muscles to support this lift. Called the *posterior pelvic tilt*, this practice will become automatic when repeated over time.

KEEP YOUR KNEES UNLOCKED
This will assist your sense of balance and help to take pressure from your lower back; your knees are your body's shock absorbers. This does not mean that your knees should be *bent*, since bending your knees places unnecessary strain on your calf and quadriceps muscles.

LEARN TO SHIFT YOUR WEIGHT
Learn the important difference between *transferring* your weight and *swaying* or twisting your weight. Transferring your weight is merely moving your center of gravity from left to right. *Swaying* and *twisting* place unnecessary strain on your lower back.

Do this exercise: without moving your feet (or lifting your heels), simply shift your weight from one foot to the other, then back to the center. Keep your weight forward toward the balls of your feet, **with knees unlocked**. Repeat this movement several times until it becomes comfortable. Mastering this simple weight shift will allow weaving and other techniques to be controlled, fluid, and accurate. (For additional information, see page 61.)

Healthy Ringing

POSTURE

UTILIZE THE SPACE AROUND YOU
Move and be flexible – keep a little "corner of the world" for yourself, spacious enough to allow movement – a place where you are in control. If you feel cramped, create more space around you. Are there too many bells and not enough room? Table footage may need to be added. Avoid confinement!

USE PROPER FOOTWEAR
Always wear athletic or flat, low heeled shoes with a good arch support – this simple advice may be the best single thing you can do to prevent lower back pain while ringing! Shoes with tied laces – especially for bass bell ringers – will give better ankle support as you lift and move heavier bells.

AVOID FATIGUE
Most church, school, or concert facilities do not have carpeted floors in rehearsal or performance locations. These floor surfaces (most often linoleum or tile) are easy to clean, but are not considerate of the comfort of a ringer standing for long periods of time. Protect your body from these extended playing periods by standing on carpet squares or on an interlocking foam puzzle mat (purchased at an educational supply store or through a pre-school supply catalog).

SECTION THREE

BREATHING

Of course, we all breathe naturally, an involuntary action that supplies our bodies with the oxygen needed to live. Less obvious, perhaps, is the need for handbell ringers to pay attention to their breathing as a fundamental aspect of handbell ringing. Conscious breathing is as important to the beginner as to the advanced ringer; just as our bodies derive energy from the oxygen we breathe, music performance derives much of its energy from breathing. Perhaps most importantly, deep controlled breathing alleviates stress, which our fast modern society provides in huge quantities. Handbell ringing should be exciting, but should also be relaxing; it shouldn't set you on edge like so many other daily events.

TAKE TIME TO BREATHE!

Handbell ringers and directors often fail to think of handbells as an instrument that requires breath control. We don't breathe into a wind chamber or pipe – as do clarinet or trumpet players – nor do we have to control breath like singers. The breath control of a handbell player is more like the breath control of the violinist, for whom breathing acts as an internal metronome. For example, if you were to ring a bell once for every breath you take, then your ringing would surely be regular and even, just as your breath is regular and even. In this way, conscious breathing creates exactness in ringing by regulating the speed of the basic handbell ring.

A group that learns to breathe together creates a common pulse, level of energy, and level of expression. Consider the idea of a group of marathon runners: if they breathe and move their legs in *sync* with one another, then they will stay together as a group. A handbell choir is no different. Breathing as a synchronized group will aid a handbell choir in counting together, executing clean musical entrances, and helping give a cohesive sense of style. In addition, synchronized breathing provides the director with the control necessary to give instant, wordless directions to an ensemble; slight changes in breathing by a director can convey tempo, rhythm and style changes.

Breathing focuses the individual, the group, and the director better than any other technique in ringing.

Breathing basics

BREATHE DEEPLY FROM THE DIAPHRAGM

As you breathe normally, your diaphragm and the intercostal muscles (found between your ribs) expand your ribs and lungs, creating a vacuum that sucks in the air. As you breathe out, the diaphragm relaxes, the rib muscles relax, and the air is pushed out by the elastic lungs (just like a balloon deflating).

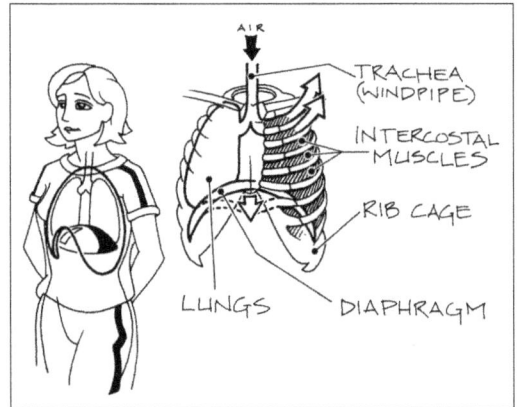

figure 3a

Healthy Ringing

— BREATHING

TRY THIS DEMONSTRATION
- Sit down in a comfortable chair. Shut your eyes, relax, and simply breathe for a minute or so.
- Place your hands on your waist (with your thumbs and index fingers just below your rib cage). Keep your chest erect. Press your shoulders down and backward. Breathe again for another minute. Focus your thoughts on the moving muscles around and below your rib cage. You are breathing as naturally as a newborn baby.

Deep breathing awareness

Inhaling

- Stand or sit up straight with your hands comfortably at your waist. Slowly take a deep breath and feel the expansion of your abdomen as you inhale. If you don't feel this expansion, you are not *relaxing* the abdominal muscles, which is essential for diaphragm breathing. Since diaphragm contraction pushes the abdominal contents (like intestines, spleen and liver) downward, the abdominal muscles *must* be relaxed so the organs have somewhere to go.

INHALE / EXHALE

- Stand with your arms at your sides. Slowly inhale while raising both arms over your head (like making a snow angel). Slowly return your arms down to your sides to rest position as you exhale. If done correctly (without raising your shoulders), you can feel the proper expansion of rib cage, lower chest, and abdomen.

Caution: for persons with recurring back problems, it would be best to avoid the next exercise.

- Sit on a chair with both of your feet on the floor, and breathe deeply. Now bend from the waist as far forward as you comfortably can, and breathe deeply (which should be close to impossible). When bent over, the abdomen (the principle area for deep breathing) is unable to expand, giving you a perfect example of what *not* to do.

Exhaling

- Imagine blowing out a candle. Place your index finger directly in front of your mouth. Then take a deep breath, and, exhaling quickly, blow out the imaginary flame on your fingertip. This will develop a focused, abdominal exhalation.

- Imagine blowing out ten candles. Extend all ten of your fingers in front of you as if they were candles on a birthday cake. Inhale deeply, then exhale slowly to blowout all ten candles with one breath. This is a wonderful exercise for *controlled* exhalation.

SECTION THREE

- Acquire a pinwheel (found in most toy stores). Take in a deep breath and then blow (exhale) into the pinwheel. Try to move the pinwheel's blades as fast as possible. You are using the abdominal muscles correctly if the blades move around quickly, pushed by moving air – they will move more slowly if the exhaling is either slow or weak.

- Acquire a medium sized balloon, and blow it up by taking a deep breath, tightening your abdominals to push air into the balloon. Try this exercise several times, increasing the size of the balloon with each breath.

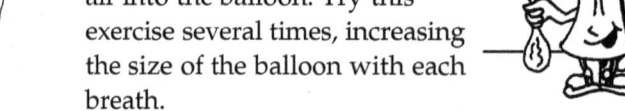

BREATHING TROUBLE

For a good, relaxed performance, this steady, deep diaphragm breathing must be continuous. Watch out for these breathing disruptions:

- Body fatigue – after climbing stairs or moving equipment, for example, you may feel "out of breath".

- Pressure to perform – usually self-induced by not being prepared or by expecting too much from yourself. When a mistake is made or when a comment from the director or another ringer is taken to heart, shallow breathing often results.

- Stage fright – your body may respond by releasing adrenaline into the bloodstream, causing shallow and quick breathing rather than deep and full breathing. In fact, you may completely stop breathing temporarily by holding your breath. Under stresses like these, you tense your neck and shoulder muscles and raise your shoulders, resulting in inefficient shallow breathing, reduced lung capacity and fatigue.

Shallow breathing ruins everything – you can't take in enough oxygen or let out the used air (carbon dioxide) in your lungs. When you don't have enough new air, your body is not getting the energy it needs. Holding your breath is worse – there is no oxygen getting into your lungs at all.

If you feel some performance anxiety, just keep breathing with regular, deep breaths. Remember that your audience *wants* you to play well and probably won't notice the mistakes that you think are obvious. A long sigh, done slowly and softly – perhaps two or three in a row – can also have a calming effect. Handbell ringing should be enjoyable, not stressful.

BREATHING

Combining breathing and ringing
Controlled, synchronized breathing is essential!

THE BASIC STROKE (figure 3b)

- Inhale in tempo as you lift the bell (or chime) from your body and begin to extend your arm. Breathe at the same speed that your arm moves. Now...

- Exhale at the exact moment the clapper makes contact with the casting. Continue to exhale as you return the bell to the damp position.

figure 3b

Slowly repeat the above exercise several times and pay special attention to your body's movements. After a while, this combined breathing and ringing will feel natural and correct.

The breathing and the ringing motion must work together as a unit. It's important to breathe together when beginning a piece, when there is a tempo change, a holding pattern, or at the beginning of a new section in the music. You'll naturally adjust your breathing pattern as you ring a string of sixteenth notes or a series of special techniques.

SLOW AND LEGATO PASSAGES

Use soft and slower breaths – perhaps inhaling only through your nose – and exhale as if blowing out the ten candles in the illustration on page 35. You'll want to imagine the bell floating through the air.

FAST OR STACCATO PASSAGES

Open your mouth slightly and inhale quickly; exhale with a focused air-stream, like blowing out the single candle.

Breathing for the handbell choir

PREPARATORY BREATH

The most dramatic single improvement most handbell choirs can make is to begin to breathe in *sync* with each other! Breathing as a team is the key to a solid and mature ensemble. Breathing as a group also solves problems associated with the inexperienced choir. Breathe as a team on every entrance!!!

A preparatory breath helps improve:

- Tempo and meter changes
- Entrance of a block chord following a fermata
- Martellato exactness
- Combination of chords and martellatos (or other percussive sounds)
- Transitions between musical styles and sections

A preparatory breath – in tempo – avoids a *splatter chord*.

Healthy Ringing

SECTION THREE

Breathing cues for the director

IN GENERAL
Teach proper breathing to your ringers. Talk about proper breathing and use of the respiratory muscles. Many of your ringers may not have formal instrumental or choral training, so the understanding of preparatory breathing may be foreign to them.

Continually remind your ensemble to stand tall with feet shoulder-width apart; head centered, shoulders back. Breathing is easier with proper posture!

Take a few minutes at the beginning of each rehearsal to breathe cooperatively and quietly. This small, seemingly insignificant practice will focus the group, and if necessary, help them reduce the stress of the day.

Help your choir understand how to breathe as a single unit, both at fast and slow tempos. Use conducting patterns and practice controlled, deep breathing entrances (see below).

Talk about performance nerves – inexperienced ringers may freeze in a performance setting and unconsciously hold their breath. You can see it – their bodies become rigid, the bell movements become choppier and closer to the body, and their faces become stern.

CONDUCTING
As the conductor, it's your job to blend the handbell choir members into a unified ensemble. Your conducting cues and your body should control the manner in which the ensemble performs. You must use more than simply a baton to communicate with the ensemble. Quality handbell conducting is a combination of eye contact, baton, and controlled breathing.

Visually scan the entire group for readiness to play and breathe *together* with them as you raise the baton for its preparatory beat. It's natural to slightly raise shoulders and expand the abdomen as your arm is moving into this preparatory position, and slightly opening your mouth helps the ringers breathe with you. Your breathing language is a direct signal that can influence – without words – the sensitive aspects of a performance. The preparatory breath can communicate tempo, meter, and style of the music that is to be rung – and the choir can more accurately follow your leadership.

To prevent splatter chords, anticipate musical entrances with a quick signal breath. Use enough body language to make a visual impact.

Healthy Ringing

PART TWO

Ringing Basics

- Basic Grip
- Basic Ring
- Basic Damp
- Weaving
- Special Effects
- Bass Ringing
- Multiple Handbell Techniques
- Handchimes

SECTION FOUR

BASIC GRIP

There is only one correct way to grip a handbell – the healthy way!

In orchestras and bands, instrumentalists are taught a preferred way of holding and playing their instruments – one that enables the best sound and smoothest operation and causes the least stress on the player's body. Consider the standard bow hold for a violinist, which allows the cleanest and most fluid sound possible. Or, perhaps think of the percussionist's mallet grip, which is as perfect for playing rapid passages on a xylophone as it is for powerful timpani attacks. These grips are strong but relaxed, precise, and standardized after centuries of attentive development. When a musician alters the best physiological and muscular approach to playing his/her instrument, whether from bad habit or poor instruction, the sound suffers and repetitive motion injuries may occur.

Current handbell instructional books and articles have only briefly touched on the basic handbell grip. As handbell notation (and other aspects of handbell ringing) become standardized, we must similarly standardize a correct grip, for the good of handbell music and the health of handbell ringers.

Proper balance

Understanding balance is essential before even picking up a handbell for the proper grip. Balance – as with, for example, a perfectly positioned see-saw or a top spinning on a table – allows a basic ease of movement with little effort. A balanced handbell relies on a *circle of support* (see *figure 4d*, page 42) that allows the rest of the hand and arm the easy freedom to perform further tasks of ringing, whether creating dynamic ranges or executing table-top techniques.

The accurate placement of a handbell, resting it comfortably and evenly on top of the thumb and index finger with a **gentle but supportive** grasp around the handle, creates this proper balance for efficient ringing.

Proper grip

A correct grip aligns all body parts from the thumb through the shoulder, allowing the body to make fluid ringing movements. If done correctly, you'll be able to feel your muscles at work, controlling each movement with confidence.

- **Place a handbell on the table with the manufacturer's logo facing you**
  (figure 4a)

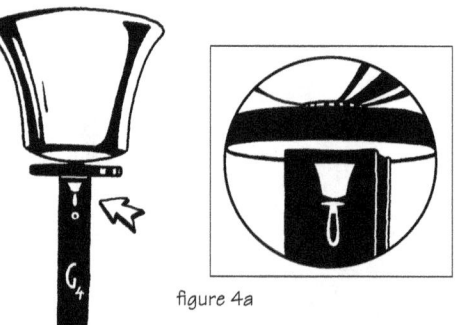

figure 4a

Healthy Ringing

BASIC GRIP

• **Pick up the handbell** (figure 4b)
Wrap your hand and fingers around the handle, **directly** underneath the handguard. Depending on the size of the player's hand and the width of the handle, the thumb should gently overlap the index finger. Your grip should be comfortable, secure, and without strain. Avoid a "death grip"! Instead, think of gently "laying of hands" around the bell. Do not place fingers *through* the handle! This will prevent a flexible grip and will send energy into the handle instead of correctly into the handle block and internal mechanism.

correct
figure 4b

A correct grip position will allow the clapper mechanism to move freely back and forth and will be in alignment with your arm. Bass bells will require a firmer grip based on the size of your hand and the weight of the casting.

• **Point your thumb directly away from you** (figure 4c)
If your thumb is not pointing away correctly (even if off just slightly), then your hand position turns awkwardly, causing strain to the back of your hand and wrist after prolonged ringing.

In special circumstances the position of your thumb may need to be adjusted in those individuals who are unable to assume this position comfortably. A common example is a person troubled with arthritis, who may need to alter the grip to ease pain. If the basic grip is uncomfortable – that is, if any strain is felt in your hand or wrist – you may try simply adjusting the thumb position.

correct
figure 4c

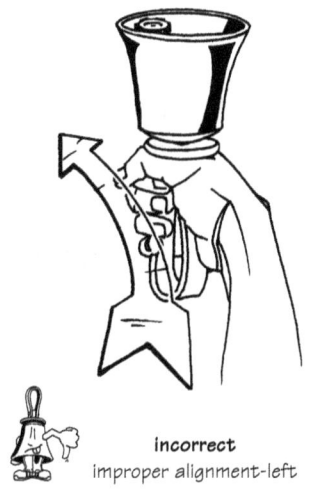
incorrect
improper alignment-left

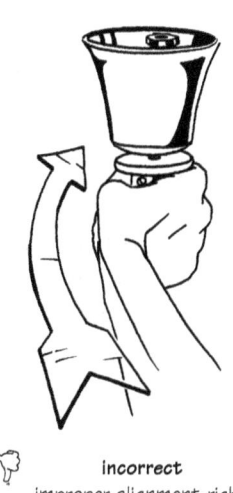
incorrect
improper alignment-right

Healthy Ringing

SECTION FOUR

- **Thumb and index finger (and middle finger for bass bells) provide support when holding the handbell** (figure 4d)

If correct, the handguard should comfortably rest upon the circle of the thumb and index finger (the *circle of support*). The remaining three fingers should wrap gently around the handle, although with bass bells a firmer grip may be necessary.

Physiologically, it has been found that the thumb, index finger, and middle finger provide the grip with precision, and that the ring and little finger provide added strength and added control. If you ring the larger octaves of bells, added strength with these auxiliary fingers becomes necessary.

circle of support
figure 4d

Healthy Hints

Imagine stretching a tightrope from the tip of your thumb to your shoulder. If a miniature acrobat were to fall from this imaginary tightrope, would she fall safely onto your arm, or tumble to the ground? If your grip and thumb are positioned correctly (in alignment with your arm), then the tightrope will extend directly over the line of your forearm and biceps.

A director can monitor proper thumb position in a bell choir by occasionally announcing a **thumb check**. A quick glance down the line of ringers makes it easy to spot thumbs not positioned correctly, and acts as a signal for the choir to remember this vital concept. As in any activity, repetition reinforces retention.

Removing rings from your fingers may also aid flexibility, provide comfort, and prevent swelling.

 **AN INCORRECT HANDBELL GRIP IS OFTEN INDICATED BY ONE OF THE FOLLOWING:**

Non-movement grip:
- Thumb pointed slightly sideways – a definite reason for lack of control and muscle strain.

Movement-oriented grips:
- Tight or locked wrist – results in a punching motion. Instead, relax and feel the muscles easily move back and forth. You should be able to lightly *flick* your wrist.
- Too tight a grip – causes hand and forearm discomfort. The handbell may be too heavy, or your wrist may be over extending through an exaggerated ringing motion.
- A floppy wrist action – allows the casting to drop forward. Your hand and wrist must remain in alignment. If you drop the casting too far below the long axis of your arm you may end up with muscle strain.
- Floppy bell movement (usually by the weaker hand) – you can't hope to have a good handbell grip without support from your forearm. Learn to use all of the muscles throughout your arms, shoulders, and back when you ring. Remember to flex your upper arm as well as your biceps in particular. *Energize* those muscles!
- Stiff or jerky movement of the handbell – causes an awkward punching motion. A good grip promotes strength, not tightness. Control your grip.

Healthy Ringing

BASIC GRIP

Proper hand fit

Each person's hand is unique! Sometimes the larger handles of bass bells prevent ringers with small hands from comfortably gripping a bell, and ringers may compensate by twisting their hands or by positioning their thumbs at an angle. This compensation hampers wrist flexibility, causes cramping, and places stress on the joints of the wrist, elbow, and shoulder. Similarly, a small bell may feel awkward to ringers with large hands. Although the ringer may have all the musical skills necessary to ring upper bells, the size of the handbells may create clumsy playing.

Directors must be careful when assigning handbells to ringers and must notice any complaint of rubbing or soreness around the joints. These are words of concern and should be addressed by assessing the fit of the bell in the ringer's hand and perhaps changing an assignment or a position.

Grip adjustment

All grips discussed in *Healthy Ringing* (SECTION 10, MULTIPLE BELL TECHNIQUES, for example) are modifications of the basic handbell grip, which allows proper dynamic control, greatly reduces tension in your forearm and elbow, and relieves strain on your wrist.

You **must** learn to comfortably adjust the basic handbell grip in order to efficiently ring and execute many different techniques. The ringer with an inflexible handbell grip is often the person with wrist and arm discomfort.

THE "MATCHED" GRIP

In order to perform healthy and effective table techniques (e.g. table damping, martellato, martellato-lift, echo, etc.), you must become familiar and comfortable with the *matched grip* – as the name implies, it's also the proper grip used for holding percussionist's mallets. A slightly altered version of the basic grip, it offers the greatest freedom and flexibility of play for most table damp techniques (table damping, martellato, and martellato-lift).

PRACTICE THIS HAND POSITION

STEP 1: Pick up a mallet or simply find a pencil.

• Hold the mallet horizontally. Unwrap your middle, ring and little fingers from around the mallet handle, relying on your thumb and index finger for support (*figure 4e*). The weight of the mallet should rest directly between your index finger and your thumb pressed lightly alongside (your thumb must also adjust to this new position). Your wrist should be rotated so that your palm faces the table's surface.

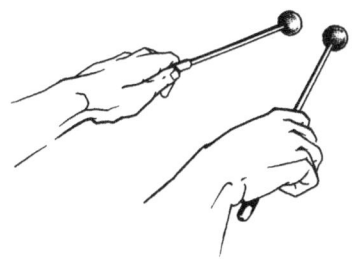

figure 4e

• Tap the table with your mallet a few times for practice (the motion is in your wrist, not your elbow). The mallet must still be in alignment with your wrist and arm. This should always be the case, and is essential to avoid wrist and forearm strain. The hand, wrist, and arm must work as a *single unit* in all handbell ringing if strain is to be avoided!

Healthy Ringing

SECTION FOUR

STEP 2: With your opposite hand, gently remove the mallet and immediately substitute a *small* handbell in its place (*figure 4f*). The manufacturer's logo is now visible.

Simply allow the tips of your fingers to gently curl themselves around and touch the back edge of the handle with the thumb and index finger comfortably placed at the handle block. The fingertips provide added control and support of the bell, but should not wrap totally around the handle (as in *figure 4g*) because this will make table damping more difficult, less flexible, and will create tension in your hand.

figure 4f - **correct**

figure 4g - **incorrect**

You may need more grip support with mid-to-large range handbells. Squeeze the handle a bit more with the base of your thumb (the fleshy part of your palm, where your thumb connects with your hand). The increased curvature of larger bell handles also allows more clearance for the fingers; with these bells only, while retaining the essential alignment and position of the grip, you can extend your fingers further underneath the handle for support. In other words, you won't need to convert from the *basic grip* to the *matched grip* entirely. Simply ensure that this position does not create tension in your hand or wrist.

The *matched grip* is not used in the lower range of the fourth through sixth octave simply because it does not provide adequate support for these heavy bells. The basic handbell grip is still the grip of choice. In the center and upper ranges where the bells don't weigh as much, this adjusted grip proves to be the healthiest and most effective grip for most table techniques.

Grip tension

For any particular passage, there is a degree of strength that should be used when gripping the handbell in order to deliver a specific sound. Most ringers play handbells with tension throughout their hands and forearms, gripping the handbell much too tightly. If this is the regular state of your playing, you stand a good chance of developing tendinitis – otherwise known as lateral *epicondylitis* (tennis elbow), or medial *epicondylitis* (golfer's elbow).

There are times when gripping the handbell strongly is beneficial to your playing. You will find that even a light squeeze of the handle will produce a sharper, louder tone, which may be the perfect color for a quick staccato section. Conversely, if you release all strength on the handle and support the bell solely with the index finger and thumb, the handbell will tilt back slightly in your hand and your sound will become more mellow and round – perfect for a smooth, soft legato section. There are a million subtle degrees between these two dynamic opposites. So when ringing a handbell, a ringer should

Healthy Ringing

BASIC GRIP

always be considering the question: "For this passage, how firmly should I grip the handbell?" This is the ideal playing mind-set.

Constant grip strength awareness will not only help avoid muscle problems but also help strengthen the muscles of your hands and forearms. You should adjust your grip to emphasize certain notes in any passage and to focus your sound.

TRY THIS EXERCISE!

- Pick up a handbell and squeeze the handle, tightening your forearm and biceps.
- Next, relax your grip and the surrounding muscles (while maintaining your horizontal *circle of support*). Allow the handle to have some "play" in the palm of your hand.
- Now, ring your handbell using an array of different grip strengths – traveling from relaxed to firm hand positions. Listen to the sounds you create, and feel the subtle changes in the ringing of the bell. Think how you could apply these feelings to a melodic line or to an entrance in a composition you are presently ringing.
- Avoid tensing! Even when gripping the handbell strongly, your shoulder should be relaxed, your other hand should be relaxed, and the rest of your body should be relaxed. Learn to focus the strength into your hand, instead of allowing that valuable energy to be spent elsewhere in your body. This holds true especially if you are ringing with a loose grip; your hand certainly should not be rigid, but supple instead.

Grip strength

To master a proper grip, you must have adequate strength in your hand and forearm muscles. Without this grip strength, you may find it difficult to grip and ring handbells for any extended period of time without feeling some strain. You can develop a stronger grip at any age. By including regular hand grip exercises into your daily routine, you should feel a noticeable improvement within several weeks. (See *Grip Strength Exercises*, page 46.)

DEVELOPING GRIP STRENGTH

Start by exercising your hands and fingers using a grip aid product (see page 46). If you are interested in strengthening your hands, use anything that allows the hand to grip in a cylindrical or even conical fashion. Avoid using a spherical object, such as a tennis ball, because the spherical grip causes stress on the knuckles (*metacarpophalangeal* joints).

If grip strengthening is needed, it should be identified early and begun with the lightest exercise, progressing gradually. If your exercise routine is initially done too aggressively, as with any exercise, it may cause strain to your hands. If this strain does occur, it will be necessary to rest your hands.

For best results, use a grip aid once or twice a day. Use it as an effective warm-up tool prior to ringing.

After several weeks of gentle grip exercises, you may want to increase your grip strength (especially for bass ringers) by adding free weights to your exercise routine.

SECTION FOUR

Additional reading may be found in any library or book store. (For additional information in *Healthy Ringing*, see SECTION 20, RESISTANCE TRAINING.)

GRIP AID PRODUCTS

• Squeeze a rolled washcloth or a thick sponge over a sink filled with water. Start with gentle twisting. Squeeze more firmly the stronger your grip becomes.

• Try using a a *Bubble-Bell©*, an effective yet inexpensive start-up grip aid (see box at right).

• *Silly Putty®* or *Play-Doh®* are pliable and ready to use. You'll find both products in most toy stores.

• Action® hand exerciser. Highly recommended by physical therapists, this product is excellent for building hand and wrist strength for handbell ringing. Made with Akton® polymer (a soft synthetic rubber), this hand exerciser is highly pliable material that conforms to the hand and continually adapts to each grip. Three grip strengths are available, so anyone can use it to build up endurance regardless of age or ability. The Action® hand exerciser is available in some medical supply stores, special medical catalogs, and Handbell Services.

Avoid any spring device with two plastic handles (often used by weightlifters and boxers). This product is usually too demanding for the average person's hand and may cause unnecessary strain.

GRIP STRENGTH EXERCISES

• Hold onto a grip-strengthening device in a position similar to ringing a handbell. Flex your fingers and thumb to make a tight fist. Squeeze firmly and hold for a slow count of 10. Relax for a count of 10. Repeat. Breathe slowly as you work your grip!

This exercise may be done one hand at a time or both hands together. If at any time you feel strain, stop and rest.

Use the additional exercises found in SECTION 15, FINGERS, HAND AND WRIST. A daily, consistent routine is important!

Bubble Bell©

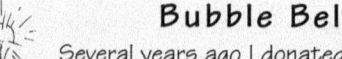

Several years ago I donated blood and was asked to squeeze a soft roll of bubble wrap. I saw an application for handbell ringing, so I created an inexpensive grip aid for handbell ringers, calling it a **Bubble-Bell!**

You can easily make one for your own use: for each bubble bell cut one 12" square piece of packaging bubble wrap in half. Take one of the half sections and cut it in halves  once again (you'll now have one 6" x 12" section and two 6" x 6" sections). Combine one large and one small section of bubble wrap: place the smaller in the middle of the larger and roll them up together into a tight cylinder (you'll have one 6" piece left over to use for another bubble bell). Next, take a single section of normal paper toweling and securely wrap it around the rolled bubble wrap. Finally, secure the edges of the bubble-bell with cellophane tape.

SECTION FIVE

BASIC RING

There is only one correct way to ring a handbell — the healthy way!

Ready-to-ring

BASIC POSITION

Here is a test to help find the correct ready to ring position:

STEP 1: Stand behind a handbell table. Select a handbell (any size above G3 will do). Hold this bell out in front but close to your body for 20-30 seconds. Again, the bell should be straight up and down, balanced on the circle of support (thumb and index finger). Don't let the bell rest on your body. Focus on the muscles being used to hold the bell in mid-air. *(figure 5a)*

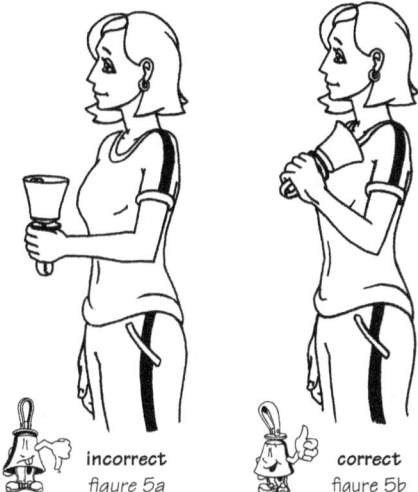

Do you feel your forearm and arm muscles working overtime? Do you feel any strain in your neck and upper back muscles?

STEP 2: Now, rest the backside of the casting against your pectoral muscle (about 2" directly below your collarbone). You should immediately feel less strain in the hand, forearm, and arm muscles. This is the proper ready-to-ring placement for handbell ringing! The weight of the casting is now equalized throughout your upper body and the strain is now gone. *(figure 5b)*

incorrect
figure 5a

correct
figure 5b

READY-TO-RING

For a correct (and healthy) *ready-to-ring* position, your elbows should be pulled in, close to the side of your body. Tilt the back edge (lip) of the casting *toward* your body, with the clapper mechanism in a state of rest. Resting the lip is important because it creates a safe starting point for the actual ringing of the handbell. It also creates a cohesive look for an ensemble, conveying alertness, precision, and readiness.

Don't hold a handbell out in front of your body! This position, when used with the initial stage of ringing, can cause unattractive punching motions – instead of the smooth lift-off that handbell playing requires. Unnecessary strain is also placed on the muscles and tendons of the forearm and hand – the heavier the handbell, the greater the stress to the body.

The handbell is **rarely** tilted away from the body. The weight of the casting causes extra strain on the hands and wrists (especially in the bass section), and the preparation for the movement toward the ringing of the bell is also affected.

Healthy Ringing

SECTION FIVE

READY-TO-RING FOR BASS RINGERS

To support the weight of large castings, initially think proper posture – feet shoulder-width apart, shoulders back and down, abdominal muscles tightened. Secondary support will also come from the large leg and pelvic muscles (the quadriceps and the gluteals). After your body is in position, lift the bell to its *ready-to-ring* position (*figure 5c*).

You may choose to leave a 4th and 5th octave handbell on the table instead of moving it to your body. This may help reduce muscle fatigue. (For further information on these as well as other important aspects of bass bell ringing, see SECTION 9, BASS BELL RINGING.)

figure 5c

Basic ring

Although there are a variety of styles being taught and used currently, only *one* allows the best performance and the least stress on joints and muscles! Every orchestral instrumentalist, every pianist, every percussionist is taught an optimal grip or fingering that produces balance and eliminates tension and danger while they play, and some of these grips have developed over hundreds of years. *Ringing handbells is no different!*

Production of the basic ring is the most important skill used in playing handbells! You can be shown how to correctly ring a handbell, but not until you can actually *feel* the working muscles being used and *energize* these muscles as you play does the real learning process occur. Once the proper muscle movement becomes a normal involuntary response, you can confidently acquire the playing skills necessary for advanced performance.

It is important to control the amount of energy exerted when ringing. The proper ringing technique always holds the kinetic energy of the handbell in check and produces matching and steady sounds that create little stress on the body.

A smooth, circular follow-through motion of the arm is needed to complete the correct ring. A ringer must be aware of the note value being played and must adjust the size of this circle to accommodate the notation. Any unnatural twisting of the arm, turning of the wrist, or overextending of the wrist and hand should be avoided. The rest of the body supports the arm much as a foundation supports a building.

The body is set up structurally through the skeletal and muscular systems from one joint to the next. Each joint is interconnected with the next joint by ligaments, tendons, and muscles. If we keep these in alignment, the area of the body will function smoothly as one unit. However, if improper alignment or an injury occurs, other areas of the body will compensate by supporting the overly stressed area.

BASIC RING

LET'S REVIEW

• Posture

Proper posture when ringing lets your larger lower muscles – the gluteals, abdominals, and quadriceps in particular – support your upper body and arms as they do the work. By keeping your feet shoulder-width apart, shoulders back and slightly pressed together, and head on straight, the energy of the entire body will be ready to ring.

• Breathing

Proper breathing warm ups activate the muscles for ringing. Anticipating an entrance or a tempo change with the conscious effort of a preparatory breath will make all the difference in performance accuracy and ensemble playing (see SECTION 3, BREATHING).

• Grip

The proper grip secures the movement, the dynamic levels, the tone quality, and the energy behind most techniques in ringing. It activates and creates the power behind the ring (see SECTION 4, BASIC GRIP). Think of a perfect grip as cuddling, cradling or gently surrounding the handle, just enough to control it without squeezing. A useful image is that of gripping an egg just enough to keep it firmly in your hand without letting it break.

Basic stroke (figure 5d)

The proper stroke controls the overall movement and beauty of the ring. It initiates all the styles, from ones with grace and fluidity to ones with rhythmic vitality.

The stroke always begins with a forward motion, *leading with the base of the handle*. Bend your elbow to help absorb impact and to reduce potential shock to that joint. Use the gentle word *flick* to describe the movement of your wrist instead of the harsh and perhaps harmful word *snap*.

The motion is more elliptical than circular. Think of the shape of a football: the stroke moves from the tip, down under, around the front, and up over the laces, returning the stroke back to the top.

figure 5d

OTHER HELPFUL IMAGES

There are several images that may also help your hand master a smooth and controlled motion:

The banana stroke

A banana is a great tool for understanding the basic ringing stroke. Grip the center of a banana with the stem facing you (as if you were going to eat it). Your thumb will naturally place itself in proper grip position. Now, *flick* your wrist; slowly and smoothly follow the banana's shape up toward your shoulder.

Healthy Ringing

SECTION FIVE

- Imagine toasting a crystal goblet of champagne with a friend. Gently "clink" the glasses together with a forward and upward motion and return them to your mouths to drink.
- Imagine a drop of water resting on the lip of this champagne glass, and that you are trying to gently *flick* it off.

- Think of the downward motion on a playground slide feet first, and floating upwards instead of hitting the sand pile.
- Think of the motion of the wheels while pedaling a bicycle backwards.

THE REBOUND

The rebound motion of the handbell – the movement after the clapper comes in contact with the casting – should be controlled and at the same speed that the handbell initially moves away from your body. It's an elliptical motion that flows around and back to the *Ready-to-Ring* position, relaxing immediately after the strike.

The size of the ringing circle and the distance away from your body are based on the tempo and on the note's value. You'll avoid a quick, jerky rebound if you think *resistance* in your body (see SECTION 20, RESISTANCE TRAINING). When perfecting this stroke, extend/flex your triceps and biceps, and let them help with the work (a necessary habit to develop for bass ringers).

Ringing Reminders

- Use all of your arm muscles (also traps, delts, and abs) to carry the weight of the handbell. If you do not feel in control of this part of your body, start strengthening these muscles today with the exercises in this book.
- Keep your hand, wrist, arm, and shoulder as flexible as possible – all parts must work together as a team. Learn to focus the energy of each ring.
- Feel the muscles in your fingers and hand at work. Learn to use your sense of touch to focus attention on these important little muscles. Practice contracting the specific muscles used; continue to study the relevant chapters found later in this book.

ADDITIONAL IMAGES TO HELP YOU VISUALIZE THE REBOUND

- Holding on to the energy inside a bell and not letting this energy be thrown over your shoulder.
- *Floating* the handbell back toward your body.
- Toasting your imaginary champagne glass (mentioned above), without spilling the contents.
- Bouncing a ball – the ball rebounds at the same speed in which it's tossed to the floor.

Healthy Ringing

RINGING QUICKLY

Finger flexibility is the key; locked wrists or a turned thumb will cause strain. With a gentle *flick* of the wrist, keep the casting parallel to your body and then immediately damp it against your pectoral muscle. This quick ring and damp will help create an accurate sixteenth or grace note. All notes regardless of note value require the circular motion to the rebound – it's the only way to ring!

Always anticipate the motion with a quick preparatory breath (see *Breathing for the handbell choir*, page 37).

PROPER CLAPPER ADJUSTMENTS

Becoming familiar with the clapper mechanism is important for general efficiency in ringing. You want the handbell to ring easily and fluidly. Avoid compensating for clapper tightness by snapping your wrist or by a thrusting motion of your arm.

When ringing a handbell, initial success comes from having a proper grip and ring. If you are still having trouble ringing with ease and comfort after you've mastered these two essential requirements, check the handbell clapper mechanism. It may be the cause of your discomfort.

Learn to adjust a clapper mechanism properly (or ask your director to help) so that every handbell you play responds easily without floppiness or tightness. A properly adjusted clapper should ring both quiet, soft passages and energetic passages that require extra exertion and should allow small bells to shake evenly.

Correct adjustment
The handbell should ring easily when slightly tipped. The clapper mechanism should make contact with the casting without any extra effort. Soft dynamic ranges should be executed easily.

Incorrect adjustment
When binding occurs, check the adjustment of the spring at the base of the mechanism. A tight spring can create too much tension (resistance) for proper clapper motion. If you are unsure how to adjust, remove, or replace a spring, check with the manufacturer's manual, ask the local representative, or contact the manufacturer directly.

SECTION FIVE

Common ringing concerns

LOCKING YOUR WRIST
Locking lacks flexibility, and actually creates tension in the muscles and joints. **Avoid completely locking your wrist under all circumstances!** A *controlled* movement using forearm and grip strength is necessary. (This is particularly important for bass bell ringers.)

OVER-EXTENDING YOUR WRIST
Over-extending is the general layman's word for the physiological terms of *lateral extension* (bending the wrist backwards, *figure 5d*), *radial deviation* (bending the wrist toward the thumb, *figure 5e*), or *ulnar deviation* (bending the wrist away from the thumb, *figure 5f*).

incorrect
figure 5d

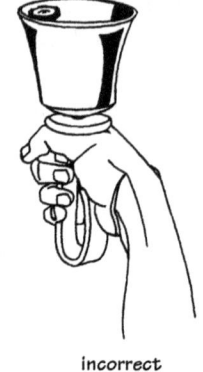

incorrect
figure 5e

incorrect
figure 5f

Over-extending, the opposite of locking your wrist, is often called *breaking the wrist* in the world of sports. If rung hard and fast, over-extending allows the handbell casting to drop toward the table below the level of the forearm, and greatly strains the hand, wrist and forearm. Forearm muscle strength must help support the casting's weight (*figure 5g*).

incorrect
figure 5g

Healthy Ringing

BASIC RING

REBOUNDING WITH A JERKY ACTION
Instead, adjust the return of the handbell to the body in a smooth and controlled manner. Use the imagery of *floating* the handbell through the air.

ALLOWING THE BELL'S WEIGHT TO CONTROL THE RING
If you can't easily lift and ring a bell, you may want to switch to a higher position until you've developed the strength to master a casting's weight. You should always be in full control of a bell's movement.

LEADING WITH THE CASTING AS YOU BEGIN YOUR STROKE
Depending on the weight of the bell and the physical strength of the ringer, leading with the casting may be harmful to the entire arm as it extends from the fingers to the shoulder and throws the weight of the casting out in front of the body. This scooping motion creates a lack of balance and places strain on the hand and forearm. From a musical standpoint, this motion will slow down the return of the casting to the ready-to-ring position, thus resulting in the slowing down of a tempo (especially when rapid eighth note and sixteenth note passages are rung).

"PAINTBRUSH" STROKE
The *paintbrush* stroke is occasionally used in order to create a more fluid motion and an extended sound in a musical passage which may include arpeggios and LVs. Instead of the proper leading of the handle, the wrist over-extends and thus allows the casting to tip over simultaneously as the bell is rung. Then using the motion of the entire arm, the casting is lifted vertically in an upward sweep. The teaching imagery used is often the upward motion of a painter's brush on a canvas.

The weight and outward position of the casting puts tremendous pressure on the muscles and ligaments of the wrist, hand, forearm, and even the back! In this stroke, with the wrist over-extended and the arm often stretched to its limit, the ringer is at the mercy of the casting's weight. This upward stroke may not be of concern to upper bell ringers, but center and bass bell ringers will be greatly affected. Caution has been indicated by all the medical advisors for this book – the *paintbrush* method is not a healthy choice and should be avoided!

Alternative ringing set-ups

BEGINNING RINGING USING EXTENDED OCTAVES
Learning to ring handbells in a two or three-octave range is hard enough: there's enough of a challenge in mastering just the basics in ringing without adding the extra effort involved with lifting heavier bass bells and reading notes above and below the musical

Healthy Ringing

staff. Careful thought must accompany any beginning ensemble learning to ring an extended range of bells!

Much depends on the physical makeup of the members within the handbell ensemble, because their ages, muscle strength, and physical stature all play a role in ringing large bells. The weight of these monster bells must be controlled; if not, they are dangerous to the individual! If a person is not in good physical shape and does not have adequate upper body muscle tone, then starting off at the first rehearsal playing heavy bells in the bottom of the fourth and fifth octave of handbells is asking for trouble.

A high school music teacher might be able to recruit a wrestler, a football player or a runner into the handbell ensemble. Physical fitness for an athlete is normal, so lifting and ringing a bass bell may be in a safe range of abilities for them. However, for the average adult handbell choir that meets only once a week, ringing *all* the handbells in a five-octave set may not be a healthy choice. Ringers should comfortably handle the balance and weight of the three-octave range (C4–C7) before moving down into the bass section of an extended set.

Initially, only ring handbells in the two or three-octave range. Add the outside octaves after mastering ringing basics!

ALTERNATIVE HANDBELL ASSIGNMENTS

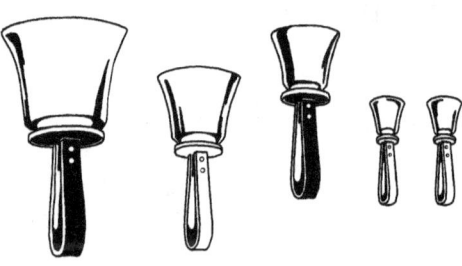

Over the past thirty years several handbell assignment theories have come and gone. One still in practice today uses a non-keyboard related handbell set-up. The bells are arranged out of keyboard order, and each ringer's position is regularly assigned bells of various sizes and weights.

Assigning three or four different sizes of handbells to one individual may help solve logistical concerns in the music but may cause problems to an individual body. Strain and uneven use of back, arm, and neck muscles is inevitable. The right side of the body will have to compensate for the extra stress placed on the left side (and vice versa), resulting in back or shoulder muscle strain. Think how difficult it would be to lift a barbell using two different weights attached at each end or for an adult to use a teeter-totter with a child. The uneven weight distribution will upset proper balance and equilibrium.

However, once in a while a handbell assignment necessitates a ringer playing a bass bell out of normal range. If this happens, ring with caution, and only if absolutely necessary! Maintain good posture, and ring with your dominant hand if possible. Always maintain controlled breathing as you lift differently sized bells.

Healthy Ringing

BASIC DAMP

Damping – stopping the casting from vibrating – is as important a concept to understand and master as ringing. Ringing allows the sound to begin; damping allows the sound to end. Sound and silence – it's that simple!

If basic damping isn't learned properly, sloppiness will occur that affects the overall quality of the music and its final performance. Sounds in the music become confused if the notes overlap, much as they do on a piano that is not properly pedaled.

Sense what your *own* body is doing when you damp a handbell. You must be able to *feel* the damp as it happens, from the bell's rebound to when it makes contact with your chest or the table. By concentrating on the movement, and with repetitive muscle memory, proper damping will become automatic.

A handbell, after its initial ring, should be constantly in motion until the damp. You must be able to sense when the handbell is in position to either damp or to prepare again for the ring. When the handbell is too far out in front, a jerky motion will occur that creates strain in the arm and hand.

Shoulder damp

Current terminology refers to standard body damping as *shoulder damping*; in fact, the name is a misnomer. The handbell casting is actually pressed against the *pectoralis major*, the chest muscle just below the collarbone (see *figure 1c*, page 26). The purpose of this muscle is to push objects away from your body; in the case of handbell ringing, however, we principally use this muscle as a cushion. Some of us have more fully developed chest muscles (pectorals), so only you can be the judge of the exact placement of your bell on this muscle.

PROPER HAND POSITION

At the end of a note, your hand should finish comfortably wrapped around the handle, with your thumb pointing directly away from you. Avoid twisting your wrist! Your hand and wrist must be in alignment with the entire arm, with your elbow pointing slightly downward (*figure 6a*). Avoid damping the entire lip of the bell (*figure 6b*).

correct
figure 6a

incorrect
figure 6b

DAMPING ACCURACY

Find the most comfortable spot on your chest muscle where the sound stops most cleanly. Practice damping several times. You do not need a lot of pressure to stop the sound of the bell. In the initial motion, you must *lead with the handle* (see *Basic Stroke*, page 49). If you lead with the casting, its weight and over-extended position will make quick and repeated damping awkward and difficult.

SECTION SIX

> ### A Healthy Exercise
> Here's an easy way to feel a shoulder damp. By counting out loud and emphasizing the word damp, the placement of the bell on your body will be more exact. Say the following words in a simple quarter note pattern:
> - For whole notes: **ring the hand bell, damp the hand bell**. Repeat.
> - For dotted half notes: **ring hand bell, damp hand bell**. Repeat.
> - For half notes: **ring bell, damp bell**. Repeat.
> - For quarter notes: **ring, damp**. Repeat.

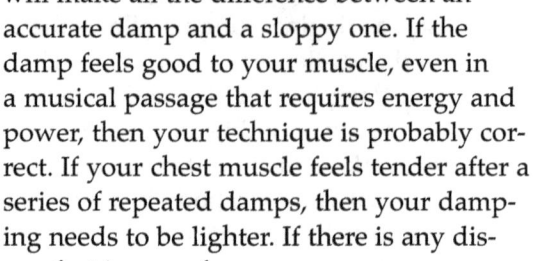

Pay attention to how the damp feels when touching your pectoral muscle. This will make all the difference between an accurate damp and a sloppy one. If the damp feels good to your muscle, even in a musical passage that requires energy and power, then your technique is probably correct. If your chest muscle feels tender after a series of repeated damps, then your damping needs to be lighter. If there is any discomfort in your forearm or near your elbow, then you know that your damping is incorrect and it needs an overhaul.

SHAPE AND SIZE AFFECTS THE DAMP

Each handbell manufacturer creates a handbell with an individual shape, profile and design. These differences – the casting's weight and overall size, the handle's shape and material, and the clapper mechanism's spring assembly – all contribute to the proper damping of your bell. Learn to feel your bell's overall characteristics; this sensitivity will help create exactness in damping.

Stay in the same ringing position until you are totally comfortable with the weight and size of your castings. Moving around from position to position is musically challenging, but may not be the best way to develop damping accuracy and may not be a healthy way to ring.

- Center and upper bells (approximately B4/C5 on up) – press the edge (lip) of the casting against your body (*figure 6c*).
- Bass bells – the amount damped will be adjusted based on the overall size of the bell. For bells ranging below B4, press the edge and *some* of the casting into your body. For bells below B3, press all of the casting – the lip, waist and shoulder – into your body (*figure 6d*).

(For additional information, see SECTION 9, BASS BELL RINGING.)

correct
upper bell damp
figure 6c

correct
bass bell damp
figure 6d

Healthy Ringing

BASIC DAMP

COMMON DAMPING CONCERNS

- The *slider*! Sometimes in a quick motion the bell doesn't damp exactly (the casting slides downward along the chest, with the sound lingering for a moment) (*figure 6e*). This is one of the hardest bad habits to correct. To correct the slider, feel the muscle and damp into it immediately!

- Rolling the casting as it's damped into the body (*figure 6f*). This will add strain to your wrist, force an incorrect alignment of your arm, and slow down your ringing as well.

incorrect
figure 6e

incorrect
figure 6f

incorrect
figure 6g

- Damping too far down your body (*figure 6g*). Although sometimes necessary for a bass bell or multiple bell ringer, damping low creates extra work for the center or upper ringer because of the added upward motion necessary to return the bell back to basic ringing position. Damping low also causes the arms to drop in toward the body, causing a slight delay and a slower reaction time. This incorrect position will strongly affect overall tempo and accuracy when executing fast moving eighth-note runs. Posture also becomes a problem, as this damping places extra work with the muscles of the upper back.

- Double damping. It makes no sense to damp a bell on your shoulder and then on the table! It's a waste of time and muscle. Double damping slows down ringing, affecting tempo and musical accuracy.

PHYSICAL AILMENTS

Sore wrist

- The wrist and forearm may be taking all the stress of the damp. Instead, create a more controlled and fluid motion.
- A twisted wrist (*figure 6h*). As your arm moves toward the body for the damp, the elbow incorrectly points outward and the wrist awkwardly rotates. Your thumb now points at 45° instead of aligning with the arm. The position is almost like a gentleman proudly standing holding his suspenders. Slowly work to correctly align the wrist for proper damping.
- Too tight a grip. Flexibility in your fingers and wrist is the key to proper damping. Don't lock your wrist! The thumb and index finger should do most of the work. Allow the base of the handle to have a bit of play in your fingers, especially in the upper bells.

incorrect
figure 6h

Healthy Ringing

SECTION SIX

Sore back muscles
- Too heavy a handbell! Switch to smaller handbells; start developing muscle strength, especially in your stomach and back regions.
- Poor posture. Think tall with head on straight. Press the shoulder blades back and down.
- Damp firmly into the pectoral muscle.
- Locked knees. Keep your knees bouncy and provide additional support with leg muscles.

Sore elbow
- Strain on the joint. Occasionally, a ringer incorrectly damps the entire circular lip of the bell casting.
- A rigid hand motion. Grip flexibility will help.
- A jerky or "plopped" damp. Instead, focus your energy and concentrate on the position of the damp.

Sore neck
- Bending over at the waist when table damping. Instead, lean or crouch into the damp and keep your knees unlocked.
- Slouching. Instead, think about keeping your body tall with your head on straight. Remember to position your shoulder blades back and down.

Sore chest
- Muscle soreness usually occurs by ringing fast notes too far out in front of the body causing a crashing return of the bell onto the pecs. Soreness also occurs from tightly-gripped ring touches or body-marts. Lighten the grip, watch the balance of the bell in your hand, and correctly feel the damp onto your chest muscle. This added sensitivity will save you unnecessary bruises.

For added protection, a soft, cloth pad can be worn inside clothing, and anything from a diaper to a custom-designed shoulder pad will work. While all these products may help, accurate body damping into the pectoral muscle is all that's necessary. If a ringer understands the distance that it takes to accurately damp a bell at the chest without attacking the body and learns to adjust the size of the ringing circle to the note's value, then wearing a shoulder pad is probably not necessary.

Finger damp

If you ring upper bells from C6 to C8 or if you have long fingers and can handle a larger bell, you can add a unique trick to your ringing. Instead of returning the bell back to the body for a *shoulder damp*, relax your grip and gently press your index finger (or thumb) onto the casting near the crown. You should be able to damp the casting immediately and move directly on to the next note being rung.

Finger damping is quite effective when ringing two upper bells in one hand. With a bit of practice, this technique will become an effortless and natural technique for an upper bell ringer.

Too tight a grip will cause strain, so think ease and flexibility. To avoid hand and finger strain, avoid finger damping on handbells lower than C6.

Table damp

Table damping requires you to modify your hand position from the *basic grip* to the *matched grip* (see BASIC GRIP, pages 43 and 44). Maintain a fluid transition between the two, which allows you to damp a handbell smoothly on the table without any tension in your grip.

"Place not plop"

DEVELOPING ACCURACY

- Use table damping only if you cannot effectively shoulder damp. It takes more muscle movement to position a table damp and return the bell to the normal off-the-shoulder ring.
- Control the bell – don't let the bell control you! Be careful that you distinctly place the bell on the table, even to the extent of pressing the bell into the padding (the larger the bell, the firmer the placement). Consider the analogy of damping the bell against your pectoral muscle; if you were to "drop" the bell against your muscle, then you'd probably bruise yourself. Think of the table padding as a sensitive muscle, just like your own, and control the bell as such.
- *"Place, not plop"* – don't drop a bell onto the table padding at any time! Know the exact moment the bell must be damped – at any tempo. A smooth transition from one bell to the other creates exactness and a musical presentation.
- Feel the "muscle" of the table as if it is the pectoral muscle of your body! To avoid strain when you ring a handbell and move your arm toward the table, you must position your arm and hand motion for an exact damp, without any jerky motion. Your bell should make a smooth landing!
- Every handbell has its own "home" on the table. Damping and placing a bell in the wrong position will cause confusion and may interfere with the flow of your ringing. A bit of recovery time will be necessary to unravel the incorrect placement.
- Always obey your body's signals! If you feel any muscle strain when table damping, stop and check your hand position. Is your thumb in correct alignment? Is your grip flexible enough for a comfortable release of the bell? Are you adjusting the grip?

important!

important!

The shape and size of the handbell will affect the damp

Center and upper range bells (B4 on up) can be damped by gently placing the bell into the table padding with little effort (*figure 6i*). Your grip may have to be adjusted from the *basic grip* to a *matched* grip to effectively release your handbell with ease and accuracy. (For a review, see SECTION 4, BASIC GRIP.)

figure 6i

SECTION SIX

Bass bells (A#4 – downward) can be damped by pressing the casting into the foam with a grip halfway between the basic and the matched grip (*figure 6j*). Because of the increased size of the castings, larger bells have handles with a natural curvature that allows extra space between the handle and the table. This extra space allows an easy grip release for table damping. Your arms, shoulders, abs, and quads will need to increase their workload, since adding this extra movement toward the table potentially places strain on the hand.

figure 6j

Sometimes an exact damp is required at the end of a musical section or at the end of a composition. To stop the sound of a large casting completely, additional muffling of the bell may be required. Use the opposite hand to grab the casting as the bell is being pressed into the foam. Or slide the ringing hand up over the casting just after the bell's release.

TABLE COVERS AND PADS

Proper table padding is essential to ensure quality damping. If the table padding and the cover are not correct, the damp's cleanness will be affected. With too dense a padding, the bell will continue to ring, and may even roll on the table.

The thicker the padding, the healthier it is for your body. Special techniques such as martellatos send shock waves throughout your hand and arm, and thick padding acts as a shock absorber to cushion the blow. A person's height is also a factor, since thick foam is comforting for the tall person's back muscles.

Table covers also affect damping. A synthetic fiber doesn't absorwb the sound as well as a natural fiber, such as cotton. If clean damping is difficult because of the wrong type of table covering, a ringer may compensate with extra exertion which, from a *Healthy Ringing* perspective, is incorrect.

SECTION SEVEN

WEAVING

Weaving "in a nutshell"

Mastering the weave is one of the most useful skills for a handbell ringer, falling within the essential arsenal of the advanced bell ringer. With adequate familiarity, a ringer becomes a more valuable player in the choir, since he or she can play more bells with ease. Ringers can also begin to play outside of their regular positions, in order to assist their neighbors. These benefits open doors to more advanced music and opportunities for small ensemble work (including solo ringing).

Weaving avoids the awkward hand cross-overs of the novice handbell ringer that too often lead to colliding handbells and uneven musical passages. It's not foolproof, however, and if done incorrectly, weaving can cause harm to the body just like any other technique. Weaving must be learned from the standpoint of *Healthy Ringing*.

Visualize the weave as a *total body workout*, with all of your muscles working as a team. Inexperienced weavers cannot make the connection between weaving and body movement, visualizing them as two separate things. Observing an advanced bell ringer weave is remarkably similar to watching someone dance – the whole body is coordinated, with fluid ringing as the result. Think in terms of muscle movement first, and ringing the bell second!

Weight shifting

The basic skill for weaving is learning to shift your weight from side to side, and from foot to foot. In basic ringing, your weight is normally centered directly between your feet. In weaving, you must continually shift your weight from foot to foot as you ring, moving your entire body's weight behind the new bell being rung.

Weaving requires a bit of concentration and anticipation, so that you always know what notes lie ahead and where to shift your weight next. If, instead of shifting your weight, you simply reach for a bell,

> ### Exercise for Weight Shifting
> **STEP 1:** With your feet shoulder-width apart, shift your entire weight onto your left foot, then onto your right foot. Remain light on your feet and keep your knees unlocked. Repeat this exercise several times until it feels comfortable.
>
> **STEP 2:** Next, shift your weight to your left foot, and without moving it, bring your right foot next to your left (the weight is still on your left foot). Reverse, shifting your weight to your right foot and bringing your left foot next to your right (the weight is on your right foot). Repeat this exercise several times. (This exercise is a basic dance step: Step touch, step touch.)

then your center of gravity must move away from your feet, causing strain to your elbow, lower back and legs as they overcompensate. Many ringers do not understand how to weave correctly, and simply twist their torsos to reach bells; this directly strains the spine, and forces a ringer to reach farther for bells. Just *shift* your weight – you'll find it easier if you do it correctly (see page 63).

Healthy Ringing

SECTION SEVEN

A "NEIGHBORHOOD" FOR BELLS
In basic ringing using two to four bells, each bell has its own space – a "home" on the table where it returns when a basic table damp occurs. When you have three or more bells rung in ascending or descending order, the normal method of table damping becomes complicated. If damped incorrectly, bells start finding substitute homes and they get all mixed up and out of order on the table until they are returned to their original spot. This is the main problem that basic weaving solves.

Consider the above illustration. Within each bell position, individual table spaces are indicated where each bell should be placed. Each bell has a home all to itself, one that it doesn't share with any another bell.

TABLE SET-UP
To start, take three or four bells and place them on the table in keyboard order (always place accidentals slightly above natural notes). Give yourself plenty of room, but don't place the handbells too far apart. Provide just enough space for each bell to table damp easily.

TIP: Tie a different colored ribbon through or around the handle of each bell. This simple but effective trick will aid you in your startup.

Weaving process
Follow the three-bell and four-bell charts, (see pages 64 and 66) first in slow motion; observe every damp, and continue this snails-pace until you fully connect each damp with each shift of weight. Keep in mind that each step happens all at once; the actions of the right hand, left hand, and weight shift happen simultaneously.

Rules for the road
- Think ahead. As you weave a bell you *must* have a plan of action for using the next bell.
- Always keep each movement even and smooth.
- *Place, not plop!* Damping must be carefully prepared. *Caressing* the damp (slightly pressing the casting into the foam) will help.
- Keep a flexible grip, knees unlocked, and keep light on your feet.
- Weaving larger bells will take more time to lift and ring, so allow extra space for each movement.

Healthy Ringing

WEAVING

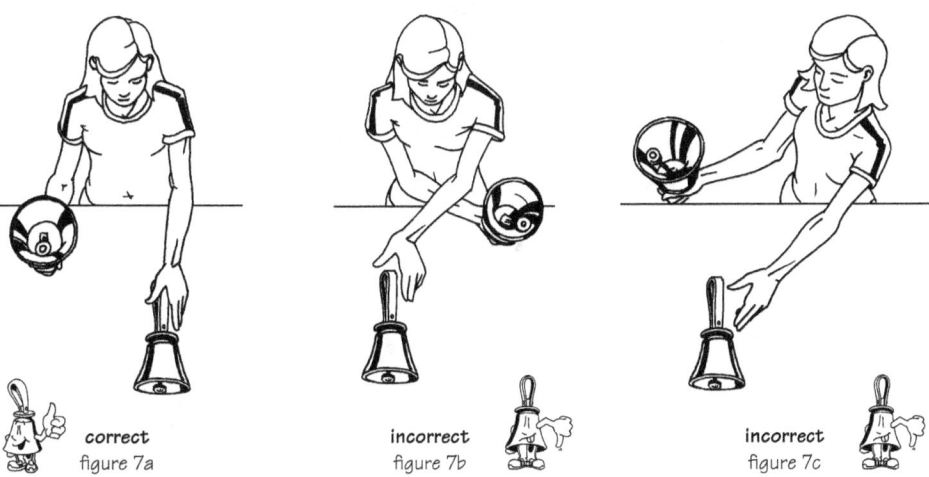

correct
figure 7a

incorrect
figure 7b

incorrect
figure 7c

- Except for the first bell you ring in a weave, you'll always take a bell along with you and ring it beyond the home of the next bell as you shift your weight (figure 7a).
- Don't cross your arms or ring a handbell at an angle in front of you (figure 7b).
- Avoid twisting or turning into position from the waist. Your body should always directly face the table, with your shoulders parallel to its edge (figure 7c).
- If you must reach a distance over the table for heavy bells, use your leg and abdominal muscles for support; avoid bending from your waist. The added weight of the handbells could strain your lower back.
- **REMEMBER! The weight shift, the ring and the damp occur simultaneously on the beat.**

SECTION SEVEN

Three-bell weave

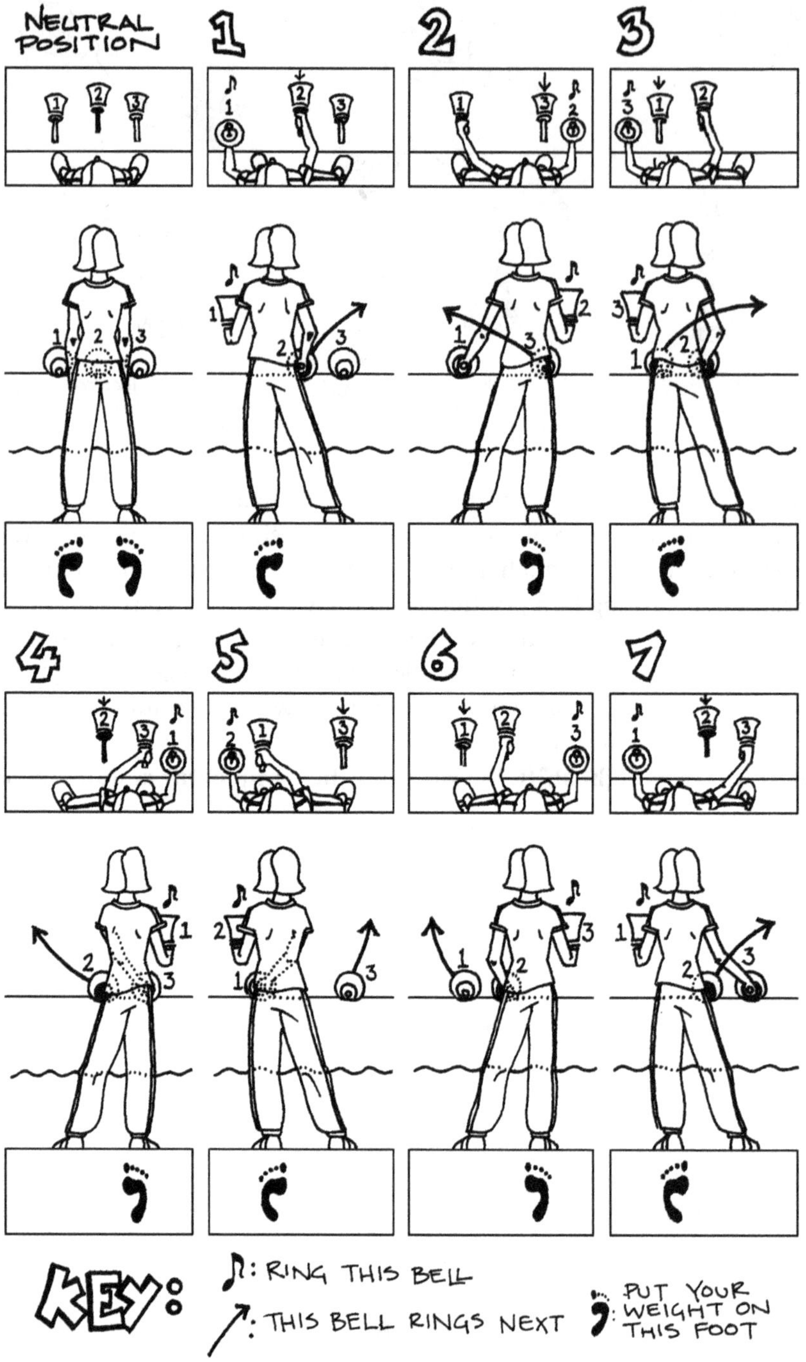

figure 7d

Healthy Ringing

Bell #1
- To begin this sequence, place your weight on your left foot.
- Pick up bell #1 and ring it with your left hand. Ring it directly over its home space.
- As you move bell #1 toward the table damp, pick up bell #2 with your right hand and begin to shift your weight to your right foot.

Bell #2
- As you ring bell #2 (r.h.), simultaneously shift your weight to your right foot and table damp bell #1 in its home space. (Important! This shifting motion allows you clearance to pick up the next bell and avoid an awkward reach.)

Bell #3
- Pick up bell #3 with your left hand.
- As you ring bell #3, simultaneously shift your weight to your left foot and table damp bell #2. (Again, this shifting motion allows you clearance to pick up the next bell and avoid an awkward reach.)

COMPLETING THE PROCESS
Now, you have the choice of either repeating the above sequence (1-2-3, 1-2-3) or switching the #3 bell from your left hand to your right for a normal shoulder or table damp (1-2-3, switch & damp).

SECTION SEVEN

Four-bell weave

Once you've mastered a three-bell weave, the four-bell weave will be a breeze.

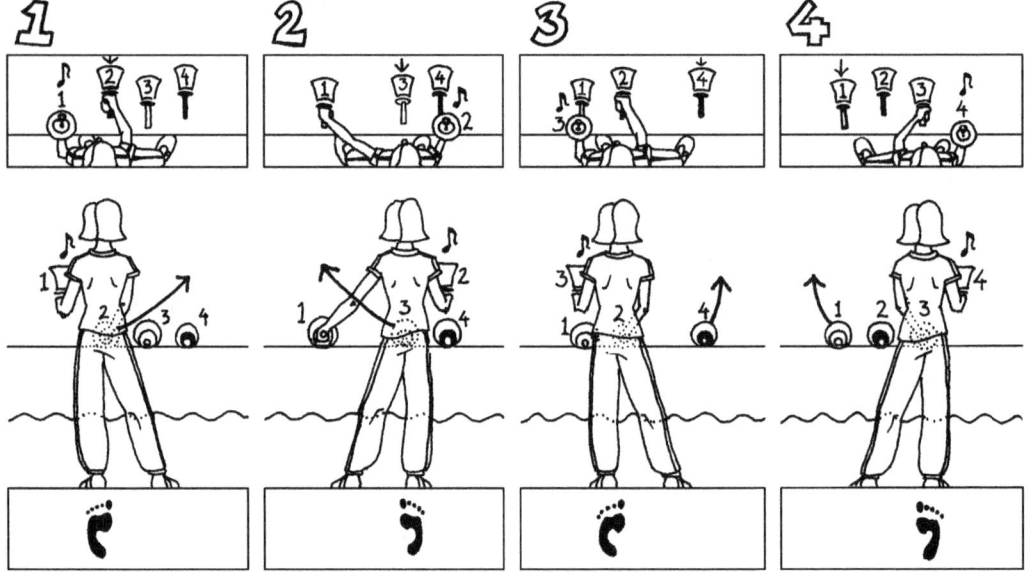

figure 7e

Bell #1
- To start this sequence, place your weight on your left foot.
- Pick up bell #1 and ring it with your left hand. Ring it directly over its home space.
- As you move bell #1 toward the table damp, pick up bell #2 with your right hand and begin to shift your weight to your right foot.

Bell #2
- As you ring bell #2 (r.h.), simultaneously shift your weight to your right foot and table damp bell #1 in its home space. (Important! This shifting motion allows you clearance to pick up the next bell and avoid an awkward reach.)

Bell #3
- Pick up bell #3 with your left hand.
- As you ring bell #3, simultaneously shift your weight to your left foot and table damp bell #2. (Again, this shifting motion allows you clearance to pick up the next bell and avoid an awkward reach.)

Bell #4
- Pick up bell #4 with your right hand.
- As you ring bell #4, simultaneously shift your weight to your right foot and table damp bell #3.

PRACTICE MAKES PERFECT!

Repeat both three and four-bell weaves until both patterns feel comfortable and natural. Slowly practice several of your own made-up sequences, throwing in a few normal rings and shoulder damps. Keep your grip as flexible as possible, table damp with exactness, and move each bell with total muscle control. Remember to keep your knees unlocked!

Once you've mastered both patterns, any section in music that once was a challenge can now be accomplished with little effort.

> **Healthy Hints**
>
> **With bells:**
> Tie different colored ribbons around the neck of each bell or place different colored dots on each handle. Mark each home position with the matching ribbon or dot. Remember! The bell will **always** return to its home on the table.
>
> **Without bells:**
> Use salad dressing bottles filled with rice. Or use three or four different utensils (e.g. knife, dinner fork, spoon, or salad fork).

BASS HANDBELL WEAVING

Weaving bass bells below C4 is a major weight lifting activity with additional dance steps thrown in, almost like dancing ballet while holding bowling balls. Ringing bass handbells is difficult enough; attempting to weave with bass handbells is asking for major problems. A ringer who attempts this requires an enormous amount of strength throughout the body. Also, since the steps are longer and since it is important to have the body straight, the weight shifts become stepping sideways and shifting.

Many handbell composers and arrangers are not active handbell ringers, and they often write music that appeals to their creative senses. An eighth-note run (for example) is easy to compose on paper and easy to play on a keyboard, but is quite difficult to master when applied to bass bells. A chromatic weave is even more challenging. Only skilled and prepared *handbell athletes* should attempt these feats! Most handbell ensembles that play this level of music are ones that have lots of strong and capable bass ringers that can share the load and, if necessary, "farm out" the extra bell. For the average choir, execution of a bass weave is not easy, and the space necessary to lift, ring and shift the body weight is too often minimal.

If you are a bass ringer, think *body first, bell second!* Don't get into the mindset of always having to use a weaving pattern. Analyze the speed in which the weave is rung and decide if it's physically possible without jeopardizing your health. If necessary, ask for help, pluck, use mallets, rearrange bells on the table (see *Healthy Hint* at left), or if musically appropriate, leave out a bell or two. Audience adulation (or even a personal challenge) does not justify a serious injury!

> **Healthy Hint**
>
>
> In order to limit movement in bass bell ringing, you could rearrange the normal position of bells on the table. For example, a standard set-up is C3, D3, E3, F3. For less strain and for easier ringing with less movement, rearrange in the following order — C3, E3, D3, F3.

SECTION EIGHT

SPECIAL EFFECTS
STOPPED TECHNIQUES

Plucking

When performed correctly, the plucking motion using the fingers and thumb is a normal and easy movement that shouldn't cause a problem. The movement is a natural turning of the thumb and wrist – a sensation much like shaking drops of water off your hands after washing them.

PREPARATION

The bell should rest on the table pad. In the technique of *plucking*, the fingers lift the clapper and the thumb *flicks* it downward in one smooth motion, without altering the bell's original position.

TECHNIQUE

Lift the clapper with the index and middle fingers, with the thumb positioned on top of the clapper (*figure 8a*). Flick the thumb downward as the fingers simultaneously *move out of the way*. The harder and more controlled the flick, the stronger the stroke. The

figure 8a

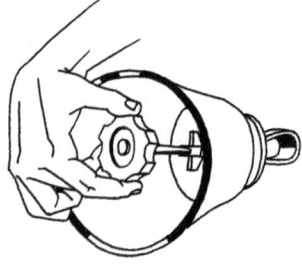
figure 8b

hand's position should allow you to pluck without strain; if necessary, slightly adjust the position of your arm (*figure 8b*). Larger bells may require you to lean over the table, so keep your knees unlocked, tighten your abdominal muscles, and slightly arch your back. Rearranging the table position of bass bells may be required when plucking consecutive eight-note runs; watch your posture and avoid torso twisting by shifting your weight instead.

Healthy Hints

A small handbell's casting makes it awkward to efficiently and quickly place your fingers and thumb on the clapper and throw it downward. If necessary, flick the clapper upward. You may need to use your other hand to stabilize the bell's position on the table. If it's still difficult to effectively pluck inside a small bell, substitute a *thumb damp* instead (page 69).

To avoid overreaching, bass handbells can be turned around with the casting facing you. However, be careful of a double ring.

Healthy Ringing

SPECIAL EFFECTS

Thumb damp

The thumb damp is an effective stopped sound that's easy to do. In most musical compositions thumb damps are used on handbells C5 and higher (*figure 8c*). When written for larger bells, the size of the casting can make this technique awkward unless the ringer has a large hand span and can adjust the grip accordingly (*figure 8d*). Substituting another stopped sound (e.g. pluck, mallet) may be a safer choice.

 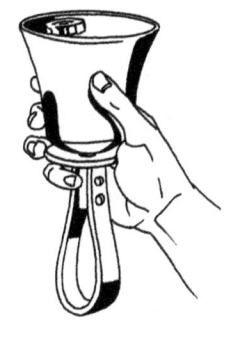

figure 8c   figure 8d

THE TECHNIQUE

Use a smooth, non-jerky arm motion. Create a gentle lift after each thumb damp. Avoid a short, punching motion – a flexible grip position will prevent wrist strain.

VARIATIONS ON THE BASIC GRIP

Hand flexibility is the key! In normal ringing the thumb and index finger provide the main support for holding the handbell. When playing a *thumb damp*, the entire hand is shifted upward, so that the thumb (and even the fingers for mid-range bells C5-B5 or so) move onto the casting. Support for the grip moves from the index finger and thumb to the middle, ring, and pinky fingers.

Support for the grip now lies in the bottom part of the hand. The middle, ring, and pinky fingers must carry the weight (and balance) of the casting. The thumb and index finger are now free to move in and out of normal position.

A small casting will only need a thumb to damp the sound; too much thumb will create a "clicking", muted sound. Listen carefully to your handbell, and if the sound continues, adjust the amount of thumb to stop the sound. A larger casting may require the additional use of the index finger (and sometimes even the middle finger). This is called *cupping* the handbell and is a variation of the basic thumb damp.

Martellato

There is only one correct way to ring a martellato – the healthy way!

When properly performed, a martellato is a clean and accurate percussive technique that is safe. When improperly performed, it can be bad news both for you and for your bell! It can be responsible for strained wrists and elbows as well as cracked castings.

The martellato technique is essentially a table damp, with added force to make a sound, instead of merely ending the sound. This added force could be dangerous when not controlled, prompting some directors to advise against using martellatos entirely. Indeed, martellatos cannot be recommended for any written note below C4. The strain placed on the hand, wrist and entire arm, as well as the possible expense of replacing a large casting, makes bass martellatos simply too risky. Substitute a pluck or use a mallet instead.

SECTION EIGHT

On the other hand, a martellato performed with treble or mid-range handbells can be done safely. And since it's appealing in so many compositions, it doesn't need to be avoided. It must be performed properly, however, for the safety of the handbell and the handbell ringer, and for a clean, controlled sound and appearance.

MARTELLATO GRIP AND EXECUTION (MART)

Before you execute a martellato, review the basic table damp (see SECTION 6, BASIC DAMP).

Don't slam or plop the handbell down onto the table padding, and raise the bell no higher than three inches above the table (approximately the width of your hand). (*figure 8e*)

It takes less effort than you might think. Beginning a martellato from chest or shoulder height is bad for your body (and for the bell!) and often sounds abrasive.

A phrase, previously mentioned, is: *"Place, not plop"* – a great statement for developing accurate martellatos that emphasizes the need for a controlled, deliberate martellato.

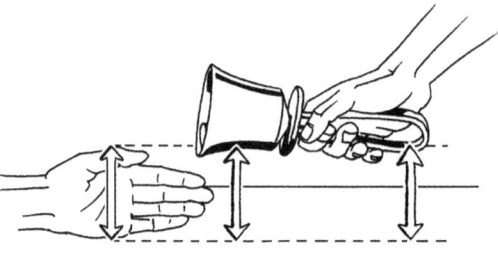

figure 8e

GRIP ADJUSTMENT

You will need to adjust your hand's position from the *basic grip* to a *matched grip* (review SECTION 4, BASIC GRIP). When a person marts using the basic grip, this standard technique sends shock through the knuckles and into the hand, producing immediate strain on the back of the hand and wrist. Instead, a slight unfolding of the fingers aligns the hand with the entire arm, takes the pressure off the back of your hand, and distributes the shock evenly throughout the arm, effectively minimizing any strain.

The amount of adjustment will depend on the size and weight of the handbell. To handle the heavier weight of larger handbells, you'll need a firmer grip. The natural space between the handle and the table places less strain on the knuckles.

For healthy ringing, martellatos below C4 should be avoided. Driving a large bass bell into the table padding sends stress to the elbow joint directly, not to mention the potential damage placed on the bell's casting. On occasion, a handbell composer will write a series of martellatos into a moving bass line; these composers probably don't ring bass bells, and aren't aware how the printed page transfers into reality! Use common sense when a problem passage appears, and have a set of mallets available to use instead.

Words of wisdom

- Keep a martellato simple. Avoid unnecessary, exaggerated, or theatrical movements. You should not feel any uncomfortable strain in your hand, wrist, forearm, or elbow! If you do, stop and examine the problem!
- *"No pain, no gain"* should not be a part of a bell ringer's vocabulary. Listen to your body's signs, and focus on the muscle or joint that feels strained. You might alleviate

SPECIAL EFFECTS

strain by simply adjusting your grip, by reducing the height of your mart, or by unlocking your elbow.
- For small bells, avoid slamming your knuckles into the padding. Tension is inevitably created in the joints of the wrist and elbow. However, the natural curvature of the larger handbells allows ample room for the knuckles to lead the way.
- Support a martellato with your entire body – make your muscles work! Flex the muscles and feel some resistance in your entire arm. Feel your larger back muscles at work and the shoulder blades pulling closer together. Feel your leg and lower back muscles lending support. If you envision your body working as a single unit, then a challenging technique like a martellato will become much easier.
- For accuracy, coordinate your breathing with the martellato. A preparatory breath prior to executing the technique and a simultaneous exhale when you mart will create exactness in your playing. Breathing helps coordinate a full body activity.
- You must use adequate table foam padding (at least 3 – 4") to absorb shock destined for your hand and the rest of your arm. Padding any less thick is simply inadequate.

Words of caution

- Avoid leading a handbell into the table padding with your knuckles directly underneath the handle (*figure 8f*). Although you may be trying to protect the bell's casting or to create a crisp sound, your hand must not be responsible for taking all the stress! Executing a martellato into foam padding (from any height) with your knuckles underneath sends immediate shock through your hand and arm; any hand position must always adjust to protect your body.

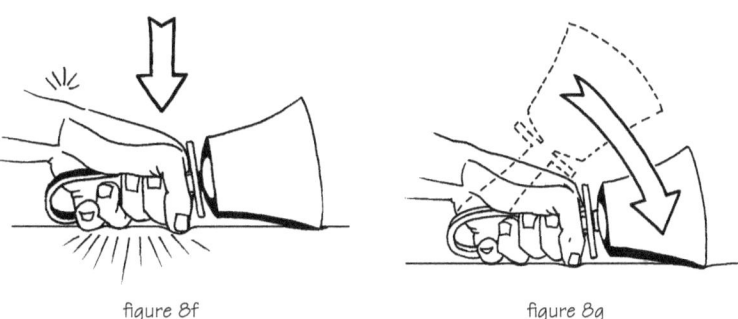

figure 8f   figure 8g

- Avoid any hand motion that resembles the movement of a hinge (figure 8g). The hinge *mart* places enormous stress on the back of the hand and creates a "whipping" motion with your wrist. Positioning the base of the handle on the padding prior to the martellato takes an extra motion.

VARIATIONS OF THE MARTELLATO
- *Mart, mart, mart:* avoid "slamming" the bell into the padding. This will only slow down your tempo. Instead control each repeated movement by using your flexible grip and focused forearm strength.

Healthy Ringing

SECTION EIGHT

- *Ring-mart-ring*: this is not an easy sequence to execute, but flexibility in hand position will allow you an immediate adjustment from the basic grip, thus enabling back and forth ringing from the mallet grip. Let the handle have some play in the palm of your hand.
- *Mart-mart-lift*: a slight angle adjustment of the casting and handle will help avoid a double ring of the clapper mechanism. However, pay careful attention to your wrist. If you feel any strain, ease up.
- *Ring, ring, ring, ring, mart*: ring repeated notes in a downward direction, so that the final note is rung just above the proper position for the mart. Flexibility is the key; your grip must gradually change from the basic grip to the mallet grip.

Ring touch

figure 8h

- Think of a quick sneeze – "ah-choo". With a flick of the wrist, ring the handbell (on "ah") and then immediately damp the casting into your pectoral muscle (on the word "choo"). (*figure 8h*)
- *Flexibility is the key*. Avoid a tight grip.
- To avoid bruising your body, *place, not plop* the damp. Keep the casting in an upright position. A tiny, circular arm motion (always lead with the handle) will help prevent the dropping of the casting.
- Avoid twisting or rolling your wrist. The weight of the casting and the quick reflex necessary for damping will cause muscle strain.
- Proper posture is essential – keep your shoulder muscles pressed back and down.
- Avoid this technique with the large 5th octave bass bells. The weight of the casting,plus balance, when you combine this technique with lifting, ringing, and damping, happens too quickly and you can't get your body into proper position.

Mallets

Using mallets does not raise **Healthy Ringing** concerns – except for your handbell! It's important not to hold mallets in a tight grip, or to "whack" the bells with too much energy, but the general lack of strain makes malleting an excellent alternative to more harmful techniques. For the elimination of potential strain, a handbell ringer should learn the

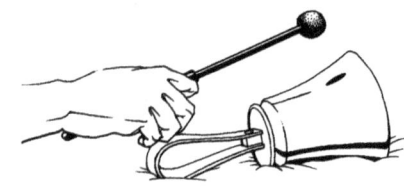

figure 8i

right way to hold a mallet (*figure 8i*). Learning the correct mallet grip is vital for handbell performance anyway, since many handbell compositions require their usage (see BASIC GRIP; *Grip adjustment*, page 43).

TIP FOR DIRECTORS: Consider bringing in a *trained* percussionist as a guest instructor to teach correct mallet techniques.

Healthy Ringing

SPECIAL EFFECTS

A Review of the Basics

(*Matched grip*, page 43-44):
- Hold the mallet horizontally. Unwrap your middle, ring and little fingers from around the mallet handle, relying on your thumb and index finger for support. The weight of the mallet should rest directly between your index finger and your thumb pressed lightly alongside (your thumb must also adjust to this new position). Your wrist should be rotated so that your palm faces the table's surface. Gradually wrap the other fingers lightly around the handle to control the mallet's natural rebound.
- Tap the table with your mallet a few times for practice (the motion is in your wrist, not your elbow). The mallet must still be in alignment with your wrist and arm. This should always be the case and is essential to avoid wrist and forearm strain. The hand, wrist, and arm must work as a single unit in all handbell ringing if strain is to be avoided!

NON-STOPPED TECHNIQUES

Shake

Ringers too often perform a shake with excessive wrist tension and a rigid hand position, causing unnecessary muscle strain. Below are a few suggestions that will make this technique safe:

Grip
- *Flexibility is the key* – don't *lock* your wrist! Allow the handle to have some play in the palm of your hand. (see *Proper balance*, page 40)
- The grip's firmness needs to be adjusted to accommodate the size and weight of the handbell. Smaller bells may only require a light hold. Larger bells may need the grip of two hands.
- Keep your thumb in proper alignment. Twisting causes muscle strain.

Motion
- Basic rule: Don't lock your wrist! Always shake forward and backward with a flexible grip. (*figure 8j*)
- Shake easily, allowing the clapper to set up its own motion.
- Flex and use all arm muscles (forearm, biceps, triceps) while keeping the wrist as relaxed as possible. Larger handbells will also need to rely on the use of the upper back and shoulder muscles.
- If a continuous shake is required for several beats, avoid "planting" the position. Rather, move the handbell in an upward, circular motion toward the body. Use successive circles for each measure or two. These suggestions will help prevent the arm muscles from tightening.

figure 8j

Healthy Ringing

SECTION EIGHT

A HEALTHY STRETCH
Following rigorous shaking, do a gentle stretch to prevent muscle cramping. You can quickly and discreetly stretch before the next musical selection (see *Cool down stretches*, page 124).

CLAPPER ADJUSTMENT
If shaking is difficult to execute, check the clapper mechanism. The spring may be adjusted too tightly or misaligned, hindering the ease of clapper movement. Simply using the appropriate tool and relaxing the spring (or loosening the washers) should help. If tightness still occurs, binding in the yoke assembly may be the problem, and additional maintenance will be necessary.

> **Healthy Hint**
> A healthy alternative in rehearsals, after learning a musical section that requires a series of continuous shakes, reduce muscle strain by ringing softly and lightly or by leaving the shake out. Give your body a temporary rest. Return the shake to the music during the dress rehearsal, and then, of course, to the concert or performance.

SHAKE INTO A MARTELLATO
When shaking, remember to adjust the hand's position from the basic grip into the mallet grip while moving the handbell into the proper placement of the martellato. This is not an easy transition to master, so keep your hand relaxed and as flexible as possible. Control is the key to accuracy.

To avoid slamming the handbell on the table, shake the handbell in a downward direction toward the padding in preparation for the stopped technique.

Toll *(Swing)*
This technique requires a full arm motion, and, if not controlled by proper muscle use, will cause strain near your elbow. Swinging the handbell in a synchronized sequence of up, down and up (especially bass bells) requires stamina and control (*figure 8k*).

TIP: To minimize strain, try thinking in terms of a dance step and try tolling this way:

The foot on the side of the body that is tolling the bell moves back one small step. This movement rotates the hip toward the back. As the arm tolls the bell, the bell goes in the area once occupied by the hip. This puts the energy flow in accordance with the body's position. As the bell returns to the front, the foot follows through and with the hip, returns to the normal standing position.

figure 8k

This technique is easy to do with upper bells. However, when tolling bass bells, use caution! To avoid strain, press your shoulders back and down, flex your arm muscles, and keep your elbow unlocked throughout the entire motion. Consciously use good posture, and remember to tighten your abdominal and gluteal muscles as well.

LV *(Let Vibrate, "Laissez Vibrer")*

Ringing a handbell beyond the actual note value is quite effective if done correctly. LV requires forearm muscle control – holding a bell out in front of you for an extended length of time requires the continuous flexing of your arm muscles. Bass bells will also require the extra support of the quads, glutes, and abdominal muscles.

Avoid the *paint-brush* technique (see page 53). Although often taught as a variation of an LV, it places unnecessary strain on the hand, arm (elbow) and back.

Gyro and Shimmer

Gyro – rotation of a handbell in a slow circular motion must be smooth and controlled. Hand flexibility is important – but let the handle move easily inside of the closed palm of your hand, keeping your ring and pinky finger around the handle relaxed. Use forearm strength to keep the handbell vertical, and control your arm motion closer to your body (*figure 8L*).

Shimmer – the *shimmer* technique is performed similarly to the *gyro* except that a sideways "wobble" is substituted instead of a rotating motion (*figure 8m*).

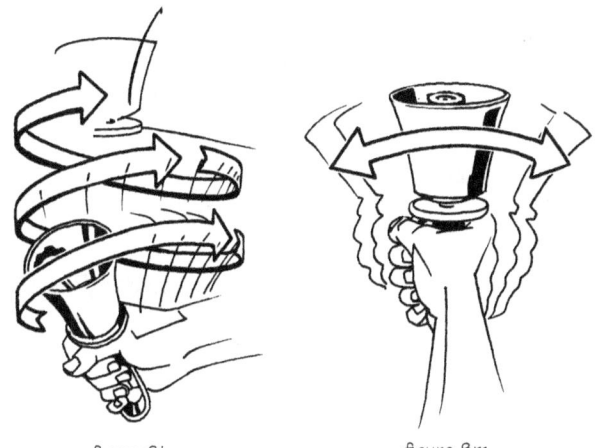

figure 8L   figure 8m

Bass bells: for both techniques, support the weight of a larger casting by avoiding overuse of your wrist. Contracting the muscles throughout your entire arm and pressing your shoulder blades together will help with balance and weight distribution.

Bell Tree

In the early Christian church, the use of bells in a procession was quite common, often suspended from a metal bar, a rope, or attached to the cross bars of a T-shaped wooden beam. Most processional bells were light in weight, so they could be comfortably carried. One person could vigorously shake all the bells simultaneously or strike each bell with a mallet while walking.

Although this tradition has evolved into the world of English handbell ringing, a *handbell* bell tree isn't nearly as light! A handbell ringer generally uses the method of interlocking the handles of several bells – (*figure 8n*), then strikes them with a mallet. By adding this sparkling dimension to worship and concert settings, we have also added to our chances for trouble.

figure 8n

SECTION EIGHT

PREPARATION
- Warm-ups and proper stretches are essential.
  (See PART III for warm-ups and stretches.)
- In general, your dominant hand will use the mallet; your weaker hand will carry the bell tree. Until you become used to the weight of a large group of bells, initially lift only a small or light bell tree.
- Breathe regularly and deeply.
- Proper posture is important.

LIFTING
- Use proper posture – head on straight, shoulders back. Take in a deep breath, flex your muscles and lift.
- To lift a bell tree from the table to the playing position, use both hands and firmly grasp the handle of the highest bell as well as the casting and handle of the lowest bell. Lift with both arms at the same time.

Grip
- Securely wrap fingers through the handle of the highest bell.

Carrying
Position the bell cluster no higher than shoulder height, approximately twelve inches from your body; avoid extending your arm too far in front of you or over your head. This position will distribute the overall weight of the bells as much as possible and allow your body's larger muscles to help carry the weight.

Developing strength
Lifting and carrying a bell tree is no task for the weak and weary! It takes increased muscle strength and endurance to accomplish this ringing for any extended period of time. If the bell tree is held incorrectly, it will wear out the ringer holding it in no time (especially since bell trees are usually held with the weaker hand). If they're frequently used, strengthening the hands and arms with free weights is necessary (see SECTION 20, RESISTANCE TRAINING).

BELLTREE STANDS
A floor-based stationary stand is useful for a heavy bell tree, ringers with physical limitations, or a lengthy piece of music. The top handle of the interlocked bells is hooked onto an arm of the stand, or the stand's arm is looped through each individual handle. Several manufactured bell tree stands are now available. A less expensive, alternative stand is a birdcage holder or a stationary dress rack. However, check for sturdiness before and after the bells are suspended.

BASS BELL RINGING

Many articles have been written on how to set-up, lift, ring, mallet, and mark scores for bass bells, but few seem to consider bass ringing's effect upon the human body! Bass bells are heavy, weighing as much as nineteen pounds.

Not everyone ringing these lower bells is a body-builder with developed strength that can handle an entire rehearsal or performance without fatigue. Without proper preparation, a bass bell ringer's body may eventually rebel!

A UNIQUE BREED – THE BASS RINGER

Bass bell ringers are a unique breed! They take joy in complicated passages, difficult runs, the deep sound of their bells, and the attention given them by the audience. Many bass bell ringers like to surround themselves in bells and enjoy ringing all of them, all the time. Bass ringers often don't realize the potential physical price that might be paid later on. Bass bell ringers, in particular, must pay attention to *Healthy Ringing* because of the extra demands placed upon their bodies.

Men are naturally able to handle bass bells easier than women, simply because they have more muscle mass in general and can build up larger torso and upper arm muscles for coping with large bells. Many women who are physically fit through active sports or resistance training have developed adequate muscle strength for bass bell ringing and should also ring them.

For a child, a C4 handbell (or handchime) may be impossible to pick up, let alone ring. The same idea applies to an adult who attempts to ring a C3. The size of the hand, length of fingers, height, and muscle strength all are factors in any ringer's comfort zone. If you aren't large enough, strong enough, or have large enough hands to feel comfortable, then you probably should avoid ringing bass bells.

Preparation

WEIGHT TRAINING

How many bass ringers work out three or four times a week? They should. How many bass ringers lift weights (over 10 pounds) to build up muscle strength before and during a busy ringing schedule? Again, they should. Unless bass ringers have had sports training, they may not have been taught to use muscles correctly.

Pre- (and post-) rehearsal stretches are important preventive measures in preparation for bass ringing. Think of bass bell ringing as a *musical sport*. Would a tennis player go out on the court without warming up first? Of course not, and neither should musical athletes, **especially bass ringers**. If you are serious about ringing bass bells and concerned about your physical health, take action and prepare like an athlete.

SECTION NINE

In an ideal world, all bell ringers would be well acquainted with the stretches and exercises they need in order to ring. Since this isn't yet the case, **Healthy Ringing** provides many such basic exercises in PART III. Contacting a personal trainer or trained athlete (like a high school gym coach) would allow creation of a more customized program suited for the individual ringer. For a bass bell ringer, this suggestion carries more importance, because without resistance training on a regular basis, strain and injury can occur. Tell the trainer about ringing handbells and what is involved with playing the instrument. Show the bells, or better yet have this trainer attend a rehearsal – observing is the best way to understand what's involved. Then get started on a weight training program to develop sufficient muscle strength for playing bass bells.

If a club or health center is not available in your community, other options might be available. Check out your local high school's athletic department; some high schools have a weight training facility – perhaps it would be available for use during off-school hours. Many corporations are now adding health centers in their facilities – add a workout to your daily schedule, perhaps in the early morning or during your lunch break. If none of these options is available, then you can find sufficient sets of weights at sports stores so you can begin a program at home.

REHEARSAL WARM-UPS

Bass bell ringing is not always a series of smooth and effortless motions; movements are often quick, with little preparation time. Sight-reading music is particularly testing for the bass ringer. Bass ringers should anticipate all notes and movements and prepare for them. Without sufficient time to prepare muscles for ringing and without knowing the location of difficult spots in the music, strain to the body can easily occur.

When sight-reading music, it's best to *airbell*. Pretend to ring the bells without having them actually in your hands (or use *Bubble Bells*©; page 46). This will allow the bass ringer to warm-up and at the same time locate any tricky spots in the music, including complicated weaves, chromatic runs, special techniques, etc. After a few additional run-throughs, automatic muscle mechanics and muscle memory will take over, and ringing the music will be a lot easier to master.

BREATH SUPPORT

Proper controlled breathing is more essential in lifting and ringing bass bells than with any other position in the ensemble. Inhaling helps focus and prepare while lifting the bell; exhaling helps control and "energize" the handbell when ringing.

Don't hold your breath when lifting and ringing bass bells! For added muscle control, you should simultaneously exhale when exerting the force necessary to lift the heavy bell. Imagine that your breath is actually *lifting* the bell for you. Breathing as you lift bells will make your ringing a lot easier.

In addition, a bass bell takes longer to sound than other bells in the ensemble, requiring the bass ringer to anticipate beats even more than other ringers in the ensemble. A controlled preparatory breath will assist with this anticipation. (For additional information, see SECTION 3, BREATHING.)

POSTURE

Stand up and think tall! Positioning your feet shoulder-width apart provides better balance and helps support the entire body for ringing. Knees must stay unlocked! Don't lean over or bend at the waist when reaching for a bell. Use the support of your legs and core muscles and *lift*. Keeping your gluteal muscles tucked in and your core muscles rock solid will help avoid lower back strain. (Review SECTION 2, POSTURE.)

Regular consistent exercise will help maintain good posture. Start to develop a consistent routine of exercise today!

Proper ringing

GRIP

When holding a bass bell, use your entire hand. You must be able to wrap your hand securely around the entire handle. For proper alignment and safety, the thumb *must* be pointing directly away from your body. Engage all of the muscles in your arm – flexing the forearm and biceps muscles will take some pressure off your hand.

Regular hand strengthening exercises are important for any bass bell ringer. Grip strengthening devices are available at most sport shops or medical supply centers. (See *Grip Strength*, pages 45-46.)

LIFT

Don't lift a bass bell parallel to the surface of the table; this causes too much strain to your entire body. Instead, immediately raise the casting to an upright position with one of the following methods. Be sure to bend knees and lift your legs (see next page).

- One-hand lift (*figure 9a*) while gripping the handbell, push the handle into the table pad with the fleshy part of the palm. This will cause the heavy casting to lift slightly. Use this as a head start to raise the handbell into a normal upright position. Now use all your muscle strength to get the bell into its ringing position.

figure 9a

- Two-hand lift (*figure 9b*) if you have time, pull the lip of the casting upward (or pull the clapper toward the casting) with two or three fingers of the opposite hand as you grip, press, and lift the handbell with the support hand. The pivoting motion helps to equalize the weight of the bell; it's by far the easiest and healthiest method to use.

figure 9b

SECTION NINE

Do not lock your elbow (this could be very dangerous), and flex both the forearm and biceps muscles *before* executing any bass bell lift from the table (and also from in and out of their cases). Always use good posture, feel your leg muscles at work and to avoid back strain keep your knees unlocked. For the heaviest bells, bend your knees, sqaut down a bit and lean back to "get under" the bell.

Use more than just your arm muscles when lifting – rolling your shoulders back when lifting will help distribute the weight of the bell throughout the upper body.

Healthy Hint
Handling bass handbells only when necessary alleviates a lot of muscle fatigue. A bass ringer is wise to leave the 4th and 5th octave bells on the table instead of moving them to the ready-to-ring position with the rest of the ensemble. Anticipate a ring by preparing your grip ahead of time, placing yourself directly behind the handbell and supporting the lift with your leg and abdominal muscles. If you then grab the bass bell handle and press it into the foam just as you lift, you can avoid some wrist strain while the casting rises. Feel a sense of balance when you raise the bell; the weight should feel evenly distributed throughout your body (use all those supporting muscles!), and place your center of gravity directly between your feet. Keep your spine erect and your shoulders back!

READY-TO-RING POSITION
(Review page 48, *Ready to Ring for Bass Ringers*.)

RING
Handbells in the range below C4 should be approached with caution. Attempting to ring bass handbells without built-up endurance and muscle strength is *asking* for injury! Bells that are too heavy for their ringer can be a recipe for disaster, so use common sense. If bells feel too heavy, they probably are!

Look for your body's warning signs. Ringing through pain is not safe! If anything hurts, don't play these large bells!

Caution! The general elliptical motion of ringing higher bells is not recommended for bass bells because of the strain placed on your wrists (*figure 9c*). If you have adequate muscle strength to lift a bell, you'll have success ringing it if you keep the bell in a vertical position as the clapper comes in contact with the casting. Instead of leading with the handle and then flicking your wrist, raise the bell upward with the strength of you forearm muscles (*figure 9d*). As you return the bell back toward your chest or table, let the bell ring naturally from the momentum of the clapper coming in contact with the casting on the downward motion. This technique will reduce the amount of shock to the elbow and upper arm.

figure 9c

correct
figure 9d

Healthy Ringing

BASS BELL RINGING

RINGING A BELL UPWARD – AN IMPORTANT CAUTION
Maintain balance and control if you ring a bass bell above your head! Because of the weight of the bell, this jerky, snapping action may cause arm joints and tendons (especially around the elbow) to go into shock! Be warned of the dangers that range from sore muscles all the way to dislocated shoulders and damaged rotator cuffs! Every medical advisor consulted for this book agrees that throwing a bass bell over the top of a ringer's head is courting nothing but trouble (*figure 9e*).

WEAVING
Correct weight shifting is paramount in bass bell weaving. Planting your feet, pivoting or twisting your body, or crossing your arms are potentially injurious (review SECTION 7, WEAVING). Learn to weave large bells by using smaller handbells first. After you've mastered them, move into the bass with the same footwork and weight transfer. Use good posture and always engage your core muscles. As a substitute for a difficult weave, try sharing a bell with a neighboring ringer.

caution
figure 9e

Proper damping
GENERAL INFORMATION
Damping bass bells requires extra carrying power – the leg, lower back, and abdominal muscles must be well developed. Without this muscular support, your arm and chest muscles cannot manage the moving force of the bell.

When damping and lifting a bass bell, you want it to be as close to your body as possible. Lifting a bell at arm's length is far more difficult than lifting a bell that is right in front of you. Before starting a piece of music, check and see which bells are rung most frequently and which bells are rung less frequently. Reserve the table space closest to you for these handbells and leave the remaining space for those rung less often. If a bell is not being used at all, put it away temporarily.

Keep your posture erect as you place a heavy bass bell on a table to avoid immense strain on your lower back. Bend at your knees instead, and use the support of your core and leg muscles, especially your quadriceps, as the bell descends.

Body damping
The damp on your chest (pectoral) muscles must be adjusted to the overall size of the bell. In general damping, pressing the entire casting into your chest will be sufficient (*figure 9f*).
Use of the opposite hand touching the side of the casting will sometimes create a cleaner and more precise damp.

correct
figure 9f

Healthy Ringing

Many bass bell ringers have found an alternative for special damping situations: damping the bass bell into the muscles at the waist (*external oblique*, see *figure 1b*, page 25). This is acceptable if approached with the same care that other bass bell techniques require. Sufficient muscle strength throughout the body is necessary, since without enough body strength and firm leg support, your arm will bear all the stress. A sudden pulling or twisting movement may injure an arm muscle, causing pain and inhibiting the ability to lift the bell.

Table damping

Damping a large handbell on your body can be difficult because of the weight of the bell or because it is simply too large for your body to stop the sound. In these situations, use table damping with the assistance of your free hand or arm.

Table damping is often the technique of choice for the big bells, simply because of the space a table provides, with plenty of cushioned area for damping even large sixth or seventh octave aluminum bass bells. Table damping is covered in detail in SECTION 6, BASIC DAMP, but some concerns are unique to bass bell ringing.

> **Healthy Hint**
>
> For added leverage and control of table damps and for a slight reduction of stress to your forearm and wrist, create a custom-made foam piece – often called a "cradle" – for each individual bell you use. Starting with a four-inch thick piece of foam, carve an indentation of each large bell with an electric knife.
>
> The bottom of this cradle-like piece of foam is flat, and lies directly on top of the table. This cradle needs to only be one inch or so high at the top of the curvature to hold most bass bells. Each piece of foam is custom-cut to the actual size of each bass bell; each needs to be sightly wider than the width of the bell to allow some flexibility when damping.

caution...

Pay careful attention to your wrist and elbow as you table damp! You are suspending a large weight in front of your body, and this extra strain is absorbed initially by your arms, placing great strain on these lower arm joints. If you feel any continuing discomfort, stop ringing!

Whenever possible, use two hands to table damp a large bell.

Option 1:
Support the weight at the casting with two hands on the handle (similar to a two-handed backhand in tennis).

Option 2:
Lower the bell with one hand while lightly supporting the lip of the casting with the other, and place the bell on the table.

Special techniques

THUMB DAMP

This is not a technique for bass bells! Use a mallet instead. If this technique is written in the music, cup your entire hand around the bell ("hand damp"), and adjust the hand's position to create a clean, crisp sound.

BASS BELL RINGING

MARTELLATO
It is recommended by all bell manufacturers that bass bell martellatos below C4 be avoided. Driving a large bass bell into the table padding sends stress to the elbow joint directly, not to mention the potential damage placed on the bell casting. On occasion, a handbell composer will write a series of martellatos into a moving bass line. Use common sense when a problem passage appears; many composers give the bass bells other options, such as malleting or plucking.

MART-LIFT
Avoid mart-lifts *entirely* when playing bass bells. A bass ringer is already placing high stress on the elbow and shoulder when executing a martellato; now the addition of a lift abruptly reverses this damaging movement into an opposite and equally damaging movement. No way can a bass ringer prepare muscles for this type of abuse!

TOLL
In bass bell ringing, tolling places enormous strain on the elbow, neck and back muscles and should be avoided below C4 unless you've developed sufficient upper body strength. Always support this movement with firm footwork and the use of your leg and abdominal muscles.

LV
This technique is usable if the bell doesn't have to be played for any extended length of time. Creating a controlled, slow moving motion is not easy and can create strain at the elbow and back. If you are able, use both hands and center the bell in front of you to more evenly distribute the weight.

SHAKE
This is not a good technique to use. Large bass bells generate a lot of ringing momentum, which is difficult for a ringer's muscles to control. Rapidly shaking a large bell back and forth, with necessary arm tension, will surely injure your arm after repeated use, and will probably strain your back and neck as well. Don't do it, even if the music calls for it, unless both hands are available for support. Substitute a two-mallet roll.

RING-TOUCH
When a handbell is rung and then immediately damped into the body, your upper torso takes all the shock! If you do not press your shoulder blades together and use the strength of your quads and abs you may be prone to sore muscles. Ring-touch also risks bruising your chest if the casting hits your body too quickly or too hard. This technique should be used with caution. If necessary, special padding should be worn to protect pectoral muscles. Another pluck and hand-damp solution: damp with the other hand.

Healthy Ringing

SECTION NINE

RING-HOOK

DEFINITION:

Hooking one bell onto one finger (or two or three) while holding another bell in the same hand

caution...

figure 9g

Although quite a useful and convenient little trick for sustaining the sound of one bell and simultaneously damping another in the same hand, with big bass bells, this is not a healthy way to ring (*figure 9g*). It may cause joint and ligament damage to your hands. You could dislocate a finger! While a ring-hook may be used quite effectively for treble bells as a subtle damping variation, this is dangerous when the weight of the bell exceeds the strength of the ligaments and muscles of the players. Only ringers with big strong hands and fingers should use this method, and only with caution. Most importantly, if you try it and it hurts, even just a little, *don't do it again!*

Alternative ringing setups

Standard height of 33 – 34" tables (including the standard 4" foam padding) is not always enough height for bass ringing (especially since many bass players are tall). An adjustment of one inch can make a difference in ringing comfort. Adding adjustable table legs to bass tables will help. A bass ringer should be able to lift and return a bell to the table without overreaching or overstraining.

Treat the bass section like a separate percussion ensemble with individual set-up requirements. Don't worry if the height of the tables doesn't match the rest of the bell choir. Instead, consider the special needs of your bass bell section.

CUSTOM-BUILT TABLE

A custom-designed table will allow a ringer to play several bass bells without lifting them off the table. Bells are positioned upright with the handle pushed down through holes that have been drilled through the top of the table and the padding. Each bell handle is securely fastened underneath by special locking devices (metal bolts or wooden pegs). Bells cannot be easily removed from this table.

FLOOR RACK

A wooden rack is an excellent, healthy way to house bass bells. Custom-engineered and designed, a special rack hangs each bell on a wooden or metal rack with the use of special pegs that hold each handle in place. The bells are rung in this stationary position by hand-throwing the clapper mechanism against the casting and damped by grasping the lip or edge of the casting with the opposite hand. Mallets can also be used.

If necessary, bells can be taken off the rack by easy removal of the pin and returned to a table for standard ringing.

BASS BELL RINGING

**A BASIC DESCRIPTION OF
A BASS BELL RACK PLAN:**

A sturdy wooden bell rack, capable of supporting the lower 7 bells in a 5-octave set (C3 through F#3), is convenient for positioning bells to be played with appropriate mallets. Bass bells are suspended by their handles and attached to a solid oak floor stand. These bells are locked in place by a metal pin so they cannot be dislodged accidentally. For added stability, this stand needs a sturdy, broad base.

The plan should be drawn so that parts can be easily duplicated by any competent woodworker. Solid oak, ¾" thick, is the recommended material. The assembled product would be moderately heavy in weight. This stand may be disassembled for portability.

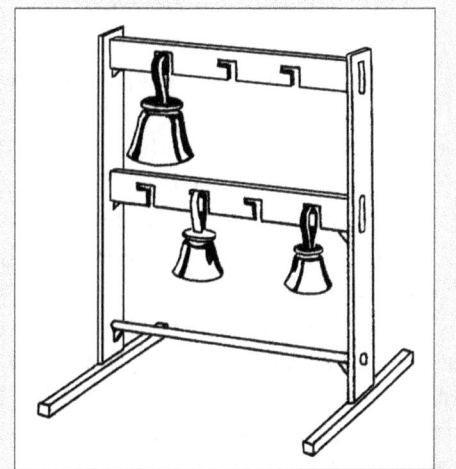

Protecting the body

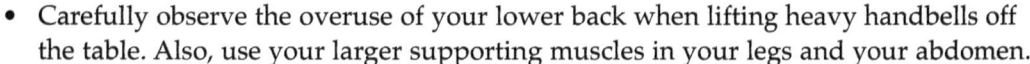

BACK CARE

- Carefully observe the overuse of your lower back when lifting heavy handbells off the table. Also, use your larger supporting muscles in your legs and your abdomen.
- Consciously feel these muscles contract and tighten as you lift.
- When reaching for a bass handbell, avoid bending from the waist. Use the strength of all your legs and core muscles. Use proper posture, lean toward the table, and then lift with the entire strength of muscles in your legs, torso, and upper body.
- Pay attention to your body and study your limitations! Take time off from playing bass bells if back strain recurs. Even with proper exercise and strength training, you may not have the height, upper body strength, or overall muscle mass necessary to handle the size and weight of bass handbells. Move to bells that will be kinder to your back.
- Always position yourself directly in front of the handbell you are lifting. Prepare before you pick up the bell. (For additional information, see SECTION 16, page 130.)

PREVENTING CHAFING AND BLISTERS

For extra protection while ringing bass bells, you can wrap contact areas on the palm and some of the fingers with one of the following products:

- Sport tape – this helps pad the hand and reduces friction while ringing. An assortment of sport tape is available from sporting goods stores that can be applied to your hand or fingers prior to ringing. Note where rubbing is occurring and apply where needed.

Healthy Ringing

- Adhesive bandage – the padding on the center of an adhesive bandage (like a Band-Aid®) will give extra comfort to a specific contact spot on your finger or your palm. The drawback: an adhesive bandage tends to wear off easily or to clump uncomfortably when rubbed by a pair of gloves or the edge of the bell handle (this may cause blisters).
- Molefoam® – this product helps reduce the amount of soreness caused by the handle rubbing against the body. It can be found at most drug stores. Cut the Molefoam® to fit your hand's pressure-points, and peel off the backing.

With all the above products, the outside packaging should say, "easily removable". If you are allergic to adhesives, avoid them.

Double gloves may be the answer to chafing and potential blisters in the bass section of your ensemble. However, you want to avoid the feeling that the gloves will pull off easily! Losing your grip when ringing bass bells could be a disaster for you and for the bell. Perhaps wearing bicycle gloves could be your answer. (For additional information, see SECTION 27, GLOVES.)

SUPPORT BANDS
(For detailed information, see SECTION 28, SUPPORT DEVICES.)

Director's responsibility
Protect your bass ringers!
You are the shepherd of the flock! You must see that all your bass ringers are carefully attending to the health of their bodies. Avoid selecting heavy-duty bass parts, with lots of fast-moving runs, simply because it sounds good and looks fun to perform. Instead, select music based on what your ringers can handle! If a part is too difficult to ring safely, consider substituting techniques like malleting that avoid potential injury. If there are not enough ringers to play all the bass bells, adjust the part and leave out a few notes. Don't risk anyone's health striving for musical perfection.

Caution your bass ringers when you see castings tipped forward or improper lifting and ringing! Bending over a table or torso twisting when reaching for or lifting a heavy bass handbell – thereby twisting your spine – is the worst type of body abuse! If any ringer mentions soreness during or following rehearsal, a concert, or a festival, don't delay finding the cause of the problem. It's your responsibility to protect your ringers!

—— SECTION TEN

MULTIPLE BELL TECHNIQUES
There's only one way to ring two bells in one hand – the healthy way!

Ringing two bells in each hand can become second nature if learned correctly and practiced with patience. It cannot be an "on again, off again" process. Ringing must always be consistent with total control; the ringer must know what the body is doing at all times.

Multiple handbell ringing is merely an extension beyond the foundation of basic ringing. You can be shown how to correctly ring two handbells, but not until you can actually *feel* the working muscles being used – and *energize* these muscles as you play – does real learning occur. Only when the proper muscle movement becomes a normal, involuntary response, can you acquire these advanced playing skills.

The phrase *"no pain, no gain"* must never enter your vocabulary! If you feel strain, stop and evaluate your ringing. Something must change – your hands and wrists must not hurt! Avoid twisting your wrist. "Swatting flies", flipping your wrist, pushing or snapping your hand are all multiple bell "no-nos"! Placing a bell between your middle and ring, or ring and little finger is asking for trouble! Any stroke that does not move the two handbells in proper alignment with your natural arm motion is incorrect!

The correct way to ring multiple bells is based on proper alignment of the entire hand, wrist and arm! Any method that rotates the forearm with a bell ringing inward toward the center of the body reduces the effective full muscle use that is available and should be avoided.

EXERCISE AND STRETCHING
Prepare for multiple techniques through warm-ups. Developing adequate grip strength is essential to control the movement of both handbells. Stretching prior to ringing any multiple bell combinations is essential. Select several hand and finger stretches from SECTION 15, FINGERS, HAND AND WRIST, and develop a standard routine for use prior to and following every rehearsal.

RANGE OF RINGING
Ringing bells using multiple techniques is recommended only in a range that is totally comfortable with the size of your hand. Normally, multiple bell ringing begins from C6 on up; however there are always exceptions to the rule. Persons with very wide hand spans may be able to grasp two larger bells (e.g. C5/D5) and ring them without strain, but this should not be done on a regular basis and generally not with bass bells.

Some individuals may have trouble ringing multiple bells due to small hands or lack of sufficient hand strength. If ringing multiple bells is uncomfortable, then this technique shouldn't be used.

H e a l t h y   R i n g i n g

SECTION TEN

NAMES OF HANDBELLS

- *Primary* – the handbell held between the thumb and the index finger. The primary bell is closest to the palm when the pair is picked up, and is usually the heaviest bell.
- *Secondary* – the handbell held in the same hand between the index and middle fingers.

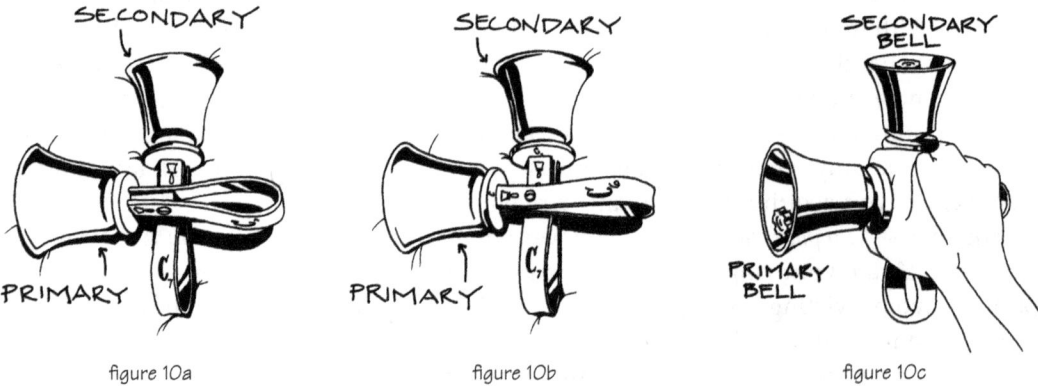

figure 10a   figure 10b   figure 10c

Basic grip

The basic grip remains identical for all three multiple bell techniques

The only changes between the different techniques involve rotating the primary bell along its axis (see *figures 10a* and *10b*). The secondary handbell always remains in the same position, but the primary bell is adjusted to ring either simultaneously with the secondary bell, or turned 90° to ring by itself.

Generally, the two bells should not be reversed. There is less space and muscle support between the index and middle fingers than between the thumb and index finger. This is especially the case when the two bells are of highly different sizes; the webbing between the thumb and palm, as well as the hand's muscular and skeletal structure, provide the larger bell with much more support.

Multiple bells must be comfortable

Our hands aren't designed for playing multiple bells, and the bells aren't necessarily designed for them either. The width as well as the density of a handle can make it inherently difficult for some people to play two bells at one time. Stretching exercises

Healthy Hint

If irritation occurs, a simple adhesive bandage or a small, thin piece of Moleskin® applied near the knuckle may help. Removing rings from your fingers may also aid in flexibility and comfort.

will help, but you can't change your natural skeletal structure – the stretch between the index and middle fingers must be the deciding factor in your ability to ring multiple handbells. With proper grip and occasional stretching breaks, there shouldn't be any strain. However, if playing multiple bells hurts, leave them for someone else and find a range of handbells that is more comfortable to ring.

Healthy Ringing

Keep a flexible grip

A tight grip will prevent easy bell changes, limit dynamic ranges, and hinder fluid motions.

Both the primary and secondary handbells should not be held together through an entire composition!–

You have much more control over one bell than two! Put down the secondary handbell when it's not in use! Prolonged use of the multiple handbell grip will cause strain and cramping, especially to the thumb and to the base of the fingers. A momentary rest enables the hand to relax and allows the fingers and thumb to take a break.

Picking up and gripping the secondary bell is easy. The index and middle fingers do all the work! After placing the primary bell into the correct position for the technique being used, spread the index and middle fingers, pick up the secondary bell, and gently squeeze the fingers together to hold this additional bell in place (*figure 10c, page 88*). Don't use a "death grip" – you need the finger flexibility to be able to easily grip, then release the secondary bell in and out of its position.

To return the secondary bell to the table, just reverse the process. Gently spread the index and middle fingers, then return the bell to its home position on the table. Avoid dropping it; control the return as smoothly and effortlessly as possible. Remember, *place not plop!*

Proper Alignment

A grip used for multiple techniques should be one that creates the least amount of body strain, because it conforms to the body's natural alignment. A balanced, correct grip positions the handbells so that they always ring in the same forward motion. Learn to adjust your hand position with subtle thumb and fingertip control so that you feel no discomfort anywhere.

Hand strength is important

If you have strong hands through exercise and practice, then multiple bell techniques will be significantly easier for you. Hand strength allows freedom for adjusting from individual to multiple bell grips smoothly and helps you to endure longer periods of demanding multiple bell ringing. (See SECTION 4, BASIC GRIP for additional information on how to develop grip strength.)

Basic ring

The ringing of multiple bells should feel even, controlled, fluid, and natural. Ring with the hand and arm moving upward slightly, creating a feeling of lifting each bell as it rings.

Initially, ring in slow motion and observe every movement you make. The thumb, index and middle fingers should guide the technique, with the ring and little fingers providing extra balance and control. These auxiliary fingers wrap lightly around the handle.

Always ring with a smooth and circular motion.

Basic rule! Don't lock your wrist

A relaxed wrist is important! Any sign of strain in the fingers, on the back of the hand, or near the wrist are warning signs that something is being done incorrectly. Pay attention to your muscles, and if something hurts, stop ringing.

Always ring both handbells with a forward motion
The ring must be a natural extension of your arm's motion. With a flexible hand position, rotating the primary bell into position and ringing it separately or together with the secondary bell is an easy task.

Always ring both handbells with an upward motion
Think of *lifting* as you ring. The casting must not drop below the natural alignment of the wrist and forearm. Over-extending the hand and wrist will lead to strain.

Avoid the imagery of knocking on a door, or cracking a whip

Knocking may give a visual direction, but it also implies a snap and quick rebound of only the wrist and hand. It can also imply using the elbow as the fulcrum instead of equalizing the movement throughout the arm. You must also use the forearm muscles to help keep your motion steady and in control. Avoid the idea of a *wrist snap*. Instead, think of the word *flick*, implying a gentler, safer action.

Keep your grip flexible
Flexibility is the key. You want a bit of play in your hand's position to enable you to ring each bell separate or together. Avoid a "death grip".

Ring at a comfortable distance from your body
You want to feel the body's symmetry and balance. By keeping the multiple technique closer into your body, you'll find you have more control and extra stamina as well.

Basic damp
Damping one bell is safe and easy to master, especially in the treble bells. Damping the secondary bell adds a multitude of muscle concerns.

BODY
The setup of your handbells as well as your individual body structure will affect the position of a multiple handbell damp. Select the one that creates the cleanest damp without obvious strain. When ringing, you may need all three of the following damping options at different times, so be prepared to keep a flexible grip!

Damping against your chest
Option 1 – *damping in alignment with the arm:* As you move the handbells toward your chest, bring your elbow slightly forward and out, and let the two bells damp into the natural curvature between your shoulder, chest and arm muscles. The primary bell will damp against your pectoral muscle, and the secondary bell will damp against your deltoid (*figure 10c*).

figure 10c
recommended

MULTIPLE HANDBELL TECHNIQUES

Option 2 – *turning your arm in toward your chest:* As you move the handbells toward your chest, move your wrist inward toward your body with your fingers securely positioned on the handle (without creating a "death grip"). Slightly move your elbow out to your side to avoid bending the wrist too much (*figure 10d*). Avoid "rolling" your wrist!

Damping at your waist
This is the least recommended way to damp multiple bells because of the distance to travel and the potentially awkward arm position. Adequate flexing of the wrist must be used to avoid strain (*figure 10e*).

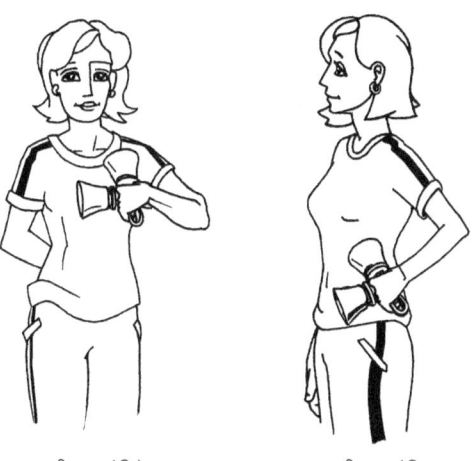

figure 10d   figure 10e

Damping with your thumb and fingers
In the range of upper bells, finger damping (stopping the sound with the thumb or finger) is generally acceptable, as long as you have the necessary and additional finger support for comfortable ringing. With multiple bells below C6, finger and thumb damping should be avoided altogether because of the extra strain placed on the back of your hand.

Correct damping changes with personal preference; no single method is gospel for everyone. Each person will find a damping technique most comfortable – no one will know how the damp feels except the person ringing! There should never be soreness or strain when damping two bells in hand; it should feel comfortable and natural.

Give yourself some elbow room
Relax. Allow your elbows to extend away from your sides; don't strain to pull them in close to your body. You may think you look obvious with your elbows sticking out from your sides, but nobody else will notice.

Avoid the "death grip" when damping two bells simultaneously
Flexibility is the key! If necessary, adjust the firmness of your grip! Keep the ring and little fingers slightly unwrapped around the handle, and secure the grip by gently squeezing the thumb, index and middle finger. This will allow the wrist to move easily while damping.

TABLE
Table damping is useful when making changes between Shelley pairs or when a Four-in-hand secondary bell is removed. Avoid squeezing the bell in a "death-grip" – your wrist must maintain a flexible position without over-extending the wrist. As a bonus, with a controlled and flexible grip, you can easily table damp the secondary bell while simultaneously ringing the primary bell.

For passages of rapid-fire multiple ringing, the table damp is a great tool for quick and accurate damping and saves potential strain of the wrist.

SECTION TEN ─────────────────────────────

Shelley

DEFINITION:

Ringing two handbells held in one hand simultaneously; clappers move in the same direction

Preparation

- Hold the primary bell in the basic grip. Now rotate your hand, so that the primary bell turns inward 90°. Lay the primary bell on top of the secondary bell **with both logos visible.**

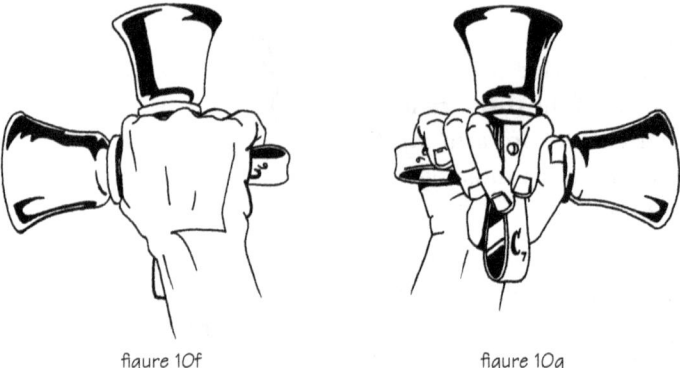

figure 10f   figure 10g

- Pick up both bells – the primary bell is held between the thumb and index finger; the secondary bell between the index and middle finger. Your thumb acts as the main support for the primary bell so that the index finger is also able to help grasp and support the weight of the secondary bell (*figure 10f*).
- Curve your fingers so that your fingertips support and touch the backside of the secondary bell's handle. The little finger is also there for extra support as it rests on back of the primary handle (*figure 10g*).
- Now, hold the bells upright in a vertical, ready-to-ring position.

THE RING

important!

Focus your energy, gently squeeze the bells together, and *flick* your wrist – both bells should ring simultaneously. If not, check your grip – is it flexible enough? Are you lifting rather than knocking?

After ringing several times, return both bells to the table and start over. Grip and ring the primary alone, then pick up the secondary bell off the table, and ring both handbells together. Feel the grip as you add and remove the secondary bell. The grip of the primary bell should remain the same throughout. Repeat over and over again until you're comfortable with the technique.

Healthy Ringing

Four-in-hand

DEFINITION:

Ringing two bells in one hand independently in opposite directions

PREPARATION

- Hold the primary bell in the basic grip. Rotate your hand so that the primary bell turns inward 90°. Lay the primary bell on top of the secondary bell but **with the primary bell's handle block facing upwards**. The secondary bell still remains in the normal position with the logo visible.
- Pick up both bells – the primary bell is held between the thumb and index fingers, the secondary bell between the index and middle finger. Your thumb acts as the main support for the primary bell so that the index finger is also able to help grasp and support the weight of the secondary bell (*figure 10h*).
- Curve your fingers so that your fingertips support and touch the backside of the secondary bell's handle. The little finger is also there for extra support as it rests on back of the primary handle (*figure 10i*).
- Now, hold the bells upright in a vertical, ready-to-ring position.

figure 10h

figure 10i

THE RING

Pay attention to your wrist and forearm as you ring from one bell to the other, and move smoothly from the primary to the secondary bell. No sideways snap or twist should occur – the thumb should always move in alignment with the arm movement. Relax the grip and allow the bells to ring easily in your hand. Feel the different muscles in your wrist as you move from the primary to the secondary bell. Notice how the thumb helps control the ring of the primary bell. Are you using a lifting motion?

After you are comfortable ringing Four-in-hand, set the bells down on the table and start all over. Grip and ring the primary bell alone, then pick up the secondary bell off the table and ring both one after the other. Feel the grip as you add and remove the secondary bell. The grip of the primary bell should remain the same throughout. Repeat over and over again until you're comfortable with the technique.

ARRANGEMENT

A standard Four-in-hand bell assignment is four handbells in diatonic order (e.g. G6, A6, B6, and C7). To reduce wrist strain set up these bells in thirds (e.g. lh – G6 & B6; rh – A6 & C7). From a musical standpoint, this configuration will make damping more accurate.

If two bells are rung separately at the beginning of a measure and then rung simultaneously at the end, you'll want to use the *Combo-ring*.

SECTION TEN

Combo-ring® *(formerly called Four-in-hand lift)*
DEFINITION:
Ringing two bells in one hand independently and also simultaneously without having to reposition the primary bell; clappers move in perpendicular and also parallel planes

This is an underused technique allowing marvelous flexibility in the upper octaves. With practice, this multiple technique can completely replace switching between *Shelley* and *Four-in-hand* positions. A *Combo-ring* allows a smoother, quicker transition between simultaneous ringing (usually with notes in octaves) followed immediately by separate ringing.

PREPARATION
- A Combo-ring takes practice to master. The position of the two handbells in your hand is exactly the same as the standard Four-in-hand technique (review *figures 10h, 10i*). Practice ringing both bells independently a few times.
- Now hold both bells upright in a vertical, ready-to-ring position.
- Using the same Four-in-hand position, look at the space between the two castings, and visualize the *sweet spot* between these bells. In tennis the term sweet spot is used to describe where the racket makes the best contact with the ball – the place where the stroke will feel most solid and deliver the most powerful shot. The Combo-ring's *sweet spot* is located directly between the two castings.
- The bells will ring simultaneously when you aim for dead center, flick your wrist, and follow through with a smooth and controlled action. Squeeze the handles lightly as you ring, and keep your wrist relaxed and flexible. With a bit of practice and concentration you'll get it!

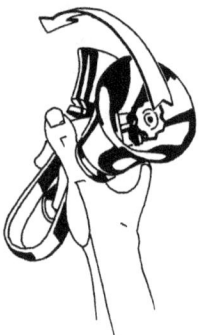
figure 10k – primary

figure 10L – together

figure 10m – secondary

THE RING
- Ring the primary bell alone (*figure 10k*).
- Now ring both bells together (*figure 10l*).
- Ring the secondary bell alone (*figure 10m*).

MULTIPLE HANDBELL TECHNIQUES

Prevent wrist and forearm strain by avoiding a twisting or snapping action. Eliminate downward knocking or sweeping motions by always lifting the bells immediately following ringing. Always ring in a forward motion in proper alignment with your arm. Avoid "swiping" the bells sideways.

TIP: When a ringer experiences the correct way of ringing the Combo-ring for the first time, it simply feels right; an imaginary light bulb goes on, and the technique immediately makes sense. Hang in there! Mastering this technique is like learning to ride a bicycle – once you figure out the balance and position, you'll never forget. *Practice makes perfect*; you'll know when you've done it correctly.

SIX-IN-HAND

Six-in-hand is not recommended for healthy ringing!

DEFINITION:

Ringing three handbells held in the same hand independently

Despite its allure and popularity among solo ringers, anyone who advocates healthy ringing should avoid *Six-in-hand*. It may be exciting to watch, challenging, and inventive, but it can really hurt your hands. Holding three bells in one hand stretches the fingers beyond anything they are accustomed to, placing much strain on the joints and muscles. Damping becomes awkward and risky (and inaccurate), increasing the chance for major hand and forearm strain.

In order to support and ring a Shelley, a Four-in-hand, or a Combo-ring technique correctly, you need to provide support for both bells, using the combined strength of all your available fingers. In addition, the Shelley technique consists of one ringing motion, and the Four-in-hand position only requires a simple forearm adjustment to ring from one bell to the other. In each of these techniques, your thumb, index and middle fingers function as the primary support for the bells, and the other two fingers wrap around the handles for additional help. This is a proper, solid foundation for ringing, with just enough necessary finger support.

Six-in-hand taxes your fingers beyond capacity! First, you have only five fingers for supporting three bells, which adds up to less than two fingers for each bell. Second, you are forced to tighten all of your hand and forearm muscles just to hold the bells, much less to ring them. Sooner or later, this technique will strain one of these muscles (most likely one of your flexor muscles, which must constantly squeeze just to hold on to three bells). Third, your hand no longer works as a single cooperative unit but as a conflicting jumble of muscles and bones. The fingers that supply necessary additional support for ringing bells (the ring and little fingers) become occupied with a third bell. This isn't their usual task, as these fingers are poorly equipped for ringing a bell by themselves. They aren't handy to assist the thumb, index, and middle fingers as they should. Last, the muscles between your hand's metacarpal bones must stretch unnaturally to handle this many bells, leading to strain within your hand itself.

SECTION TEN

Variations on the Six-in-hand seem to be just as dangerous. Interlocking the handbells (a Six-in-hand alternative endorsed by some bell ringers) does not change the situation; the same problems exist, with the same potential for hand strain. Ringing sequentially within a Six-in-hand position can cause even more discomfort to your hand than ringing together, owing to the many different hand motions that must happen simultaneously.

Consultations with physical therapists (including a specialist in hand therapy) and doctors always come to the same conclusion: the Six-in-hand technique is a dangerous method of ringing and should be avoided. An alarming number of ringers have mentioned hand discomfort resulting from Six-in-hand. Why create unnecessary discomfort (with potentially damaging effects) if it can be easily avoided? Six-in-hand is difficult to learn and takes more time to execute than more conventional ringing. It serves little purpose other than for show.

PORTABLE RINGING

Ringing multiple bells without tables is not recommended for healthy ringing

It is true that playing handbells without tables can be challenging and exciting to watch. The portability of not using tables is attractive to many choirs who would like to play on church steps or play a quick song at a senior center or nursing home. As a rule, ringing portable bells requires a ringer to hold onto two (or more) bells in each hand continually without the relief of a nearby table. With small handled, lightweight treble bells, this may not be a problem. However, often a group of ringers (usually a quartet) decides to put on a real show and play an entire two-octave piece without tables by using multiple bell techniques. This means that one or two of the quartet members are obliged to ring bells from the lower range (approximately between G4 and C5).

Unless a ringer has a large hand span and high level of hand strength, ringing two bells in each hand in this lower range encourages major hand strain. Holding two of these lower bells in one hand is heavy for any average ringer. Without conditioned hand and arm strength plus a large hand span, ringing these bells for entire pieces of music becomes exceedingly difficult and could be downright dangerous.

There will always be a quartet willing to take on the challenge of *table-less* ringing, regardless of risk. If this describes you, then condition your upper body – especially your hand and arm muscles – with increased resistance training. Build up your endurance; do not start a period of table-less ringing without a thorough warm-up or without resting often as your muscles recover. As with all *Healthy Ringing* – but especially for table-less ringing – warm-ups and stretches prior to and following rehearsal must become a normal routine. And to reiterate – if you feel pain, your body is in trouble right now. Stop!

Healthy Ringing

SECTION ELEVEN

HANDCHIMES

Since its introduction in 1982, the handchime's popularity has created a need for expanding its range beyond the basic two-octave set, which is often used in the classroom and with beginning ensembles. Advanced choirs currently perform on four and five-octave sets to complement their handbells, creating a fuller "orchestral" sound.

Much larger and lower pitched handchimes have been recently manufactured which enhance the deep bass sound of the ensemble.

This increase in size (and weight) of handchimes, as well as a handchime's unique design, inevitably raises some concerns regarding proper grip, ring, and damping. The increased torque and momentum of long handchimes does threaten to strain wrists. In general, since they're rarely as heavy as their handbell cousins, chimes tend to be easier on your body, and (in the middle to high ranges) require less strength to play.

This doesn't mean you shouldn't learn how to use handchimes correctly. In ringing handchimes, you are participating in a physical activity. Always ring handchimes the *Healthy Ringing* way, with proper technique, warm-ups, and regular exercise.

Basic grip

A handchime grip is almost identical to that of a handbell – the hand wraps around the tube with the thumb pointing directly away from the ringer (*figure 11a*). The difficulties in ringing handchimes are not always the same as with handbells. Most problems with

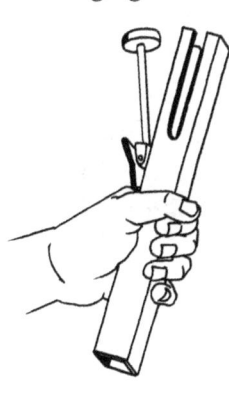

figure 11a

ringing handbells concern the weight of bass castings, but chimes weigh much less than their handbell counterparts. Instead, most difficulty with gripping handchimes concerns their inherently awkward design. Handchimes tend to be long and cumbersome, with the lowest octaves (fifth and sixth) possessing remarkably large circumferences, making them difficult to hold with small hands.

When picking up a handchime, the nameplate should face you, and your hand, wrist and elbow should align with your shoulder. Hold the tube just below the clapper mechanism (you'll find the comfortable place that feels balanced) with your thumb pointed directly away from you; with a larger chime, you may find better balance near its middle. If the chime is too large for you, you may experience some discomfort in your hands or you may not be able to wrap your

fingers entirely around the tube. If this is the case, find a position using smaller chimes. If no other chimes are available, ease up on the grip with your fingers, cradling the backside of the chime – avoid grasping the handchime too tightly.

For a fourth- through sixth-octave bass handchime, it's best to use two hands for added security. Position one hand a few inches below the clapper mechanism; the other one near the end of the tube. This will provide extra leverage for ringing the large chime. Adjust the position to fit your comfort zone – control without strain is what's important. If the bass chime is still too large for your hand, balance the end of the chime on the table (or your thigh) and strike the chime with an appropriate mallet.

With handchimes, flexibility in the fingers and wrist is even more important than with handbells. A metal handchime is a little more unforgiving than a pliable handbell handle. **It's important that you avoid locking your wrist.** Keep your grip loose, but controlled; in the upper chimes especially, allow the lower section of the tube to have some play between your fingers and palm. The thumb, index and middle fingers should do most of the work. Unlike a handbell with a curved, flexible handle that fits neatly in the palm of your hand, the handchime is more awkward. Depending on the ringer's size and grip strength, small chimes are easily rung; but the giant bass chimes may take two hands to control and hold steady.

Gloves are not necessary; in fact, gloves decrease your grip traction, owing to the chime's slick surface and straight tube. (Manufacturers now coat the metal with a textured powder that provides a more secure grip.)

Ready-to-ring position

Generally, the handchime's *ready-to-ring* position is located a few inches away from your body – the external clapper mechanism makes it difficult to lean the chime directly against your pectoral muscle. When the chime is too heavy to hold for any extended time, leaving the chime on the table is an adequate alternative. This is often the case with bass handchimes in the fourth through sixth octaves.

Ringing

The motions of ringing a handchime are similar to those of ringing a handbell. However, the design of this instrument limits the special techniques easily performed by handbells. Handchimes are basically rung and damped, period.

figure 11b

Always lead with the base of the handchime, and like a handbell, ring with a smooth, controlled circular movement. Handchimes should stay in a perpendicular position. The tempo and note value will affect the size of this movement. After ringing, return the handchime to the beginning position by *floating* the chime upward toward your body (*figure 11b*).

Avoid flipping the handchime over the top. This awkward motion would be similar to fly-casting or cracking a whip; it makes handchime ringing quite awkward and, in the case of a bass chime, quite cumbersome. Your hand and wrist will also take most of the chime's weight, causing unnecessary strain.

Healthy Ringing

HANDCHIMES

Think of positive ringing images – "clinking" champagne glasses, a "J" stroke, or the motion of pedaling a bicycle backwards. (See SECTION 5, BASIC RING for a review.)

Always feel the motion of your body "in sync" with the handchime. Without a fluid and precise ring, placement and damping will be more difficult. The handchime should remain in motion until the damp, which happens either against your body or on the table.

Bass handchimes often are rung using two hands; large chimes in the lower fifth and sixth octaves may require the use of a floor stand and mallets. Trial and error will help find the best way to ring without adding strain to your body.

Damping

The pitch of a chime is determined by its weight and length. As manufacturers expand the note range of chime sets, the lowest chimes become increasingly heavier and longer. The length of the lowest chimes now available makes lifting them difficult, let alone ringing and damping them. A custom-built rack may be necessary, and some innovative damping techniques will need to be used. Table damping is also a common substitute.

Because of its external clapper mechanism and slow response time, ringers often find damping a handchime more awkward than a handbell. Stay with the same ringing position until you are familiar with the weight and size of your chimes; it takes time to adjust to different ringing positions. This familiarity will pay off in damping accuracy.

BODY DAMPING

The damp is as important as the ring – it must be precise and accurate. Find the most comfortable spot on your chest muscle, where the sound stops most cleanly. Practice damping several times. You do not need a lot of pressure to stop the sound of the chime completely.

Pay attention to how the damp feels when touching your pectoral muscle. This will make all the difference between an accurate damp and a sloppy one. If the damp feels good to your muscle – if you don't hear a "clunking" sound – then you are probably damping correctly. If your chest muscle feels tender after a series of repeated damps, then your damping needs to be lighter. If there is any discomfort in your forearm or near your elbow, then you know that your damping is incorrect and that it needs an overhaul.

To shoulder damp a handchime, several options present themselves, but none of them are as basic as shoulder damping a handbell – the handchime's external clapper gets in the way. Several obvious damping options require an awkward wrist or body twist, and all have their disadvantages. Therefore, you must find an accurate and easy way to damp which doesn't place **too much** stress on your body.

Flexibility is the key! Strain in the hand and wrist (and elbow, perhaps) can occur unless the ringer's grip eases up, allowing the chime some play in the hand.

Five options are given on page 100. The wrist is *always* in a natural position without any strain! Individual comfort is the deciding factor!

Healthy Ringing

SECTION ELEVEN

Option 1: Standard damp (figure 11c)
With the elbow and arm positioned in front of the ringer's body (still in alignment, of course), the wrist bends to complete the damp, with the top of both tines touching the chest.

For this damp, you may need to adjust the location of your grip on the chime, depending on the length of the chime and your arm.
- Advantage: similar motion to a handbell body damp.
- Disadvantage: a longer bass chime is difficult and awkward to damp.

Option 2: Damp against the center of your pec (figure 11d)
With your arm out to the side of your body, rotate your elbow and bring the chime in close to your chest. Then comfortably turn your wrist to damp both tines.

By lifting your chest and shoulder muscles and by pulling your elbow slightly back, more of the metal will come in contact with your chest.

figure 11c

figure 11d

Option 3: Damp against side of your pec (toward your armpit) (figure 11e)
For comfort, your elbow will be pulled back.

Option 4: Damp against your abdominals (figure 11f)

figure 11e

figure 11f

Option 5: Cross-over and damp against your entire torso (figure 11g)
Hold the chime normally, but damp it on an angle on the opposite side of your chest.
- Advantages: less twisting of hand. Allows easier damping of the larger chimes. Good application for persons with special needs.
- Disadvantage: will not work if two chimes are rung and damped simultaneously unless one chime is damped high on your pectoral muscle and the other one is damped low on your chest.

figure 11g

Healthy Ringing

Other options:
Other damping styles not illustrated but quite effective with handchimes are table and hand damping. Use the style which enable you to ring musically without any muscle strain or discomfort.

The size of the handchime affects the damp
Upper chimes can be damped with little effort. Stopping the sound of the tube is all that is necessary. Avoid over-extending your wrist beyond its comfort zone. The chimes are light enough in this range that you can hold them with only the thumb and index finger, so keep your grip relaxed. The larger the handchime, the more fingers are required for support.

Bass chimes (approximately A#4 downward) are more difficult to damp because of the increased length of the chime. Touching both tines simultaneously on the chest may feel awkward. In addition, your stature may make bass damping difficult. In these cases, table damping may be the only viable option.

The chime is a slow-speaking instrument. Repeated note passages are difficult; none of the damps mentioned are designed for rapid ringing. If the damp feels good and effectively stops the sound, then it's probably correct. Avoid damping on your clavicle (collarbone), but instead press the handchime below, against your pectoral muscle.

TABLE DAMPING

Do not use table damping if you can effectively shoulder damp. Table damping chimes is more difficult than handbells because the larger surface area must come in contact with the table. Unless the chimes are correctly damped, you'll receive an unattractive "thud" for your troubles. But if you do need to table damp, either because your body or the music requires it, table damp correctly.

An image that I often mention for general damping is to consider the table as a muscle, much like the ones found on your body. You wouldn't damp hard on your pectorals because you'd bruise yourself and strain your arm. Likewise, avoid damping hard on the table's surface – your chime should make a *smooth landing!*

Place, not plop. Don't drop any chime at any time! It takes little table contact to damp a chime, so anticipate the exact moment that the sound must cease.

Weaving

There's little difference between handbell and handchime weaving, except that handchimes require more exactness when placed on the padding. If the damp is sloppy, you'll hear a metallic out-of-place sound.

Picking up a handchime in a weave is somewhat awkward because it sits flat on the table with no curvature of a handle to put your hand around. Pick up a chime initially by using just your fingers, then reposition it to the entire hand; in the case of a fast passage (especially with smaller chimes), just ring chimes with your fingertips.

SECTION ELEVEN

 Multiple chimes

A handchime's design makes multiple ringing difficult. Unlike a handbell, with its symmetrical casting and internal clapper mechanism, picking up two handchimes at once is awkward, especially with large chimes. Shelley ringing will be easier to execute than the Four-in-hand or Combo-ring.

Whichever technique you decide to use, avoiding strain means keeping your hand and wrist position as flexible as possible. Ring multiple handchimes sparingly and only with the smaller chimes.

To avoid the clunky metal-against-metal sound, wrap a small piece of thin moleskin or athletic tape (used to wrap a tennis racket or bike handle) around each handchime, just where this contact occurs. A thick gauge rubber band, wrapped a couple of times around the handchime, may also do the trick.

Special techniques

Most handbell techniques (pluck, martellato, and ring touch, for example) do not cleanly transfer over to handchimes. When reading a musical part that uses one of these techniques, leave it out.

PART THREE

Excercises for Ringing

- **Introduction to Healthy Exercise**

- **Warm-Ups for Ringing**

- **Shoulder and Neck**

- **Arm**

- **Fingers, Hand and Wrist**

- **Back**

- **Abdomen**

- **Legs**

- **Ankles and Feet**

- **Resistance Training**

EXERCISES FOR RINGING

Introduction to Healthy Exercise

Exercise is important for everyone who plays handbells. You can start today! Picking up and ringing a handbell, plus performing other demanding techniques, is a physical challenge. If the overall technique were relaxed and controlled, used only one hand position, and remained the same from treble bells to bass bells, there wouldn't be cause for much concern. Handbell ringing, however, often seems anything but relaxed, requiring ringers to move and alter their positions constantly. No other musical instrument makes so many physical changes – ringing and shoulder damping, table damping, switching bells from one hand to another, picking up a mallet, passing an extra bell to a neighbor, shifting weight from side to side, turning a page, lifting cases, etc. Handbell ringing is a very physical activity!

In all such physical activities, participants must follow certain guidelines to ensure that they remain healthy and will be able to continue into the future. Handbell ringers tend not to follow specific healthy ringing rules and could end up hurting themselves. This doesn't have to be the case! Ringing once a week doesn't condition your body adequately for the demanding physical requirements of handbell ringing. Rehearsals generally occur immediately following a workday and often last only an hour or two. In addition, unlike any other sport, these rehearsals probably commence without proper warm-ups by the ensemble.

Results cannot be achieved overnight! A handbell ringer must develop good habits of regular exercise. When a ringer follows a good program, he/she will experience long-term benefits of better balance, increased muscle and joint flexibility, and the ability to easily survive a handbell rehearsal (or festival) without discomfort.

Occupational therapists, physical therapists, doctors, and sports physiologists agree that handbell ringing causes strain on your body. Building muscular endurance prior to ringing is important for resisting this strain as well as for overall fitness. Exercises used by athletes are designed for this endurance – they increase muscular strength, the very thing that handbell ringing requires.

The exercises throughout PART III are effective and safe for general use. They were researched from many sources, including direct consultations with active professionals in music, sports, and medical fields, and are retold in a user-friendly way for the handbell ringing community. These warm-ups have been successfully used in group rehearsals, workshops and seminars.

These exercises have helped me as I teach and ring handbells, and carry over into my daily life. On an airplane with cramped quarters, I've learned to breathe deeply and keep more relaxed, and have learned a few exercises that work well in such a situation. During a long period of sitting at the computer, I've learned to periodically take a break to stretch and work the muscles. I've adapted the stretching patterns included in this publication

into a morning warm-up/stretching routine. My husband has used the basic warm-ups and the hand/arm stretches with his bands and orchestras.

I know rehearsal time is the essence of good performance. However, the five to ten minutes spent before (and after) a rehearsal doing warm-ups will pay off greatly in the long run. The results will not happen overnight! Make a conscious effort to stretch – not just as part of one weekly rehearsal but as part of your daily routine for several weeks. Soon you'll notice the difference in your endurance and in your attitude.

These exercises can be done by anyone, but always consider your normal activity level, your weight, and your age! Should you have any questions or concerns, *consult your physician*. In fact, unless you are already well acquainted with exercise programs, you should talk to a professional trained in the fitness industry first.

These exercises must be practiced slowly and carefully! We often push our bodies beyond limits that we think we have, driving ourselves to new levels of achievement. However, while pushing our bodies physically, *pain is not acceptable*. When discomfort occurs in a joint or muscle, rest is absolutely necessary! Physical exercise exposes your body to carefully controlled stress in order to encourage development. Stress, when uncontrolled, can stretch a joint incorrectly, pull a muscle, or strain a tendon. If you feel pain, stop! It means you are doing something incorrectly, or an exercise is too advanced for you. Solve and correct the problem before you continue.

SECTION TWELVE

WARM UPS FOR RINGING
(and cooling down afterwards)

Why are warm-ups important?
They...
- Prepare an inactive body for activity.
- Prepare the cardiovascular system for active duty.
- Increase the blood flow through the active muscles.
- Increase your endurance for work to come.
- Increase the flexibility of all joints.
- Decrease physical and mental tension.
- Decrease the chance of physical strain and injury.

Ringing handbells (or directing an ensemble) is *exercise*. Warm-up prior to a rehearsal as you would for any strenuous activity!

Warm-ups can be done in many gentle ways, such as:
- Moving the arms in gentle circles.
- Pretending to swim a freestyle in the air.
- Rolling the shoulders.
- Opening and closing the hands.
- Moving the wrists in light circles.

Anything that gets circulation going in your shoulders, neck, arms and torso can be an adequate warm-up.

GENTLE STRETCHING – THE MAIN PART OF WARMING UP
Think of a cat taking its time with a good ol' stretch after a pleasant nap, or standing up from its resting position. The cat's natural instinct to stretch makes the cat feel good, waking up its body so it can move and function easily.

Benefits of stretching
When stretching is done correctly, it's safe for your body. Anyone can stretch, regardless of age or flexibility; your body will tell you how far you can go. You can stretch at home, in the office, in a car, as well as before, after or during a rehearsal. As you stretch on a regular basis, your flexibility and mobility will increase. This can help deter possible injuries as well as shorten recovery time if injuries do occur. Stretches can be done before and after a workout; they help decrease your muscle soreness and improve the capacity for added activity. Stretching prevents tightness in your muscles and develops muscle awareness. Regular stretches tend to relax the mind and put you in a better mood!

Healthy Ringing

How do you stretch?
- Slowly stretch a muscle.
- Hold the position.
- Focus on the stretch and deepen it if possible.
- Relax.

Stretching the same muscle a second time is called *repetition*, which can further stretch a muscle. This works best after you've stretched a neighboring muscle (stretching one muscle will affect other muscles nearby).

If you stretch a muscle a bit further than the time before, you are doing a *developmental stretch*. Your muscles elongate as you stretch, relaxing them and increasing their mobility and flexibility as well as the mobility and flexibility of attached joints. After several days of stretching, your stretch will deepen and you will need to stretch further for the same effect; this means that you are becoming more flexible.

Pay attention to your body's signals. You should feel no pain! A stretch should feel good! Any discomfort is counterproductive.

Basic stretching guidelines:
- Breathe normally and easily as you do stretches; holding your breath deprives your muscles of necessary oxygen.
- All movements should be slow and controlled.
- Be patient, and settle slowly into a stretch. This will create a comfortable tightness in a specific muscle. Focus attention on the muscle and slowly deepen the stretch.
- Feel some resistance in each stretch Push yourself, but...
- Avoid over-stretching. Absolutely *NO PAIN* should be felt. Ideally, you should feel a strong pulling sensation without anything hurting; if any discomfort occurs, ease up.
- *Don't bounce a stretch*: this will create too much tension and muscle contraction; bouncing shocks your system and can easily strain a muscle. Always move smoothly, slowly, and evenly.
- *Static Stretch* – hold every stretching position for at least 10 seconds, preferably, double that.
- All the stretches included in this manual can easily be done individually. Don't allow someone to help you stretch (unless they are qualified to do so). Nobody but you knows how far you can go.
- Always keep your knees and elbows slightly bent. Don't *lock* your joints, since this causes stress.

SECTION TWELVE

A stretching routine

Develop a consistent stretching routine – recommended is an eight to ten-minute warm-up of muscles throughout your body prior to any ringing. During the rehearsal, occasionally stretch a muscle or two – it will revive your energy level energy level as a side benefit. Following ringing, remember your cool-down stretches, especially for the muscles of the hands, arms, neck, and shoulders.

Group warm-ups led by the director are a great way to establish cohesiveness at the beginning of rehearsal. If someone is late for this important preparation to ringing, then it is up to the individual to do a few independent warm-ups prior to ringing.

BEFORE RINGING

- Take in several deep breaths before and during stretching.
- Create a pre-ringing stretching routine. Select a variety of stretches from SECTIONS 12-19 that will warm up all the general areas of your body.
- Stretch in this order: start with the shoulders, neck muscles, then arms, hands, fingers, followed by back, legs, and finally feet.
- Steady yourself against the top of a table or the edge of a doorframe when stretching calves, ankles, and feet.
- Allow adequate room for stretches. Back away from the table for exercises of the arms and torso.

DURING RINGING

When your body (or your mind) feels tense during a ringing session, you can easily stretch several of the muscles of your body from behind the table to alleviate discomfort. A perfect time for a simple stretch is between pieces or during a rehearsal break.

- Focus on a problem muscle (one that feels tight).
- Find a static stretch that works this muscle. This doesn't have to be a dramatic stretch – just a slight shift of weight may help to stretch a side muscle, or a gentle press of a hand into the foam can help stretch your forearm.
- If you are a director, it might be a good idea during a long rehearsal, to coordinate short stretch breaks for your ensemble. This will help keep the group's energy going late into a rehearsal.

FOLLOWING RINGING

Cool down your muscles with a few slow, gentle stretches. This will return the muscles gradually to their normal activity level as well as help minimize swelling and stiffness in the used joints and muscles. You need not do an entire routine of stretches; just a basic, general few are sufficient.

Post-rehearsal stretching helps the body recover from the stress of bell ringing and helps decrease next-day muscle soreness. This cool-down will help avoid muscle cramping and leave you limber. The following areas should be emphasized: neck and shoulder; hands and arms; torso and legs.

Healthy Ringing

WARM-UPS FOR RINGING

 ## Understanding Resistance

Learn to feel resistance within your muscles as you exercise. This is called *biofeedback*, a sense of the muscles being used. As you become more comfortable with this muscle awareness, you will be able to focus your energy on a particular muscle. This focus has its advantages. You can focus on: relieving a sore muscle; lifting heavy objects like a large bell, cleanly; lifting a bell or chime case without strain; ringing bells with less fatigue.

GENTLE DISCOVERIES:

- Close your eyes. Without wiggling your nose, can you feel it? Can you sense your big toe? Can you sense your right foot? In exercise programs, your brain processes these sensations automatically – and you *can* focus on the muscles or groups of muscles that you wish to control! With discipline and self-motivation, any ringer can learn exercises that will aid in controlling the handbell or handchime with less strain and more endurance and energy.

- Slowly close your hand as if squeezing a soft rubber ball. Now relax and open your fist. The tension you feel as you tighten is *resistance*. Repeat the motion with slightly more tension in your grip and feel the increased resistance. You can easily see that if you go to an extreme, the grip will become uncomfortable. This is *too much* resistance!

- Gently and slowly bring your arms up over your head and down again, as if you were making an angel in the snow or signaling to a friend down the road. Now repeat this motion, and this time pretend you are doing it under water – feel the increased resistance.

- Pretend you are ringing a handbell or handchime. Grip the imaginary handle, bring the bell up to your *ready-to-ring* (casting resting on body) position, prepare the ring and ring the bell. You should feel the resistance out in front, so bring the bell smoothly, and with control, back toward your body. Repeat slowly and then quickly. Feel your muscles working; focus your mind on these individual muscles. Repeat using a *Bubble Bell*© (see page 46).

SECTION THIRTEEN

SHOULDER AND NECK

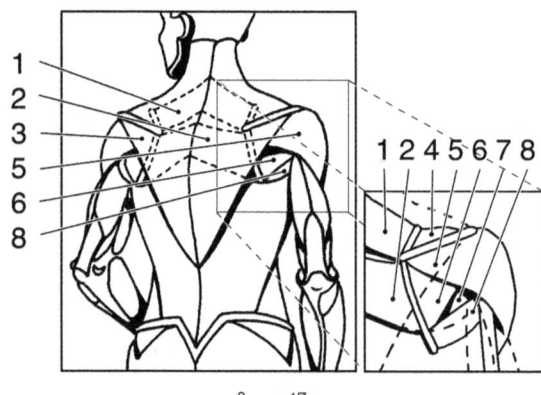

figure 13a

Major muscles used

1. Rhomboideus minor
2. Rhomboideus major
3. Trapezius
4. Supraspinatus
5. Deltoid
6. Infraspinatus
7. Teres minor
8. Teres major
9. Subscapularis (lies under - behind - the shoulder blade, not visible in this diagram)

(For a review, see SECTION 1, MUSCLES)

THE BASICS

Shoulder and neck muscles take a lot of abuse. Poor posture, emotional stress, awkward lifting of a heavy object (like a bass bell), or incorrect movement can all contribute to neck and shoulder strain. By sitting and standing up straight, by warming-up and stretching, and by combining other muscles with them when lifting, you'll reduce neck and shoulder muscle strain and avoid potential discomfort.

Your body is an interconnected system; sometime the discomfort in your hand is attributable to a neck or back muscle strain! Therefore, it's important to keep all these muscles as flexible and relaxed as possible. Know the signs of neck and shoulder strain, and learn how to gently "work" your muscles to alleviate some of the potential discomfort in the rest of your arm.

important!

Care of your neck when ringing

The following preventive measures are important:

- Make neck stretches a part of your pre-ringing (and daily) warm-up routine. They will only take a small amount of time and will do wonders for your incoming stress level.
- Keep an eye on your posture, even when not ringing.
- Keep your head straight over your shoulders, without raising or tucking your chin down.
- *Avoid rolling your neck!* Any movement where you roll your head around from front to back and return it to the front position is *not* a good stretch, and rolling your neck backward places great strain on the spine.
- Small stretch breaks during rehearsal relieve tight necks and shoulder muscles and prevent tension headaches.
- A few minutes of gentle neck and shoulder stretching helps avoid stiffness, especially when returning to a sedentary position, like driving your car home from rehearsal. Include neck stretches in your post-rehearsal cool down session.

SHOULDER AND NECK

Stretching Reminders

- Breathe slowly and steadily throughout all exercises.
- Isolate the muscle you are working to stretch – create resistance.
- Conserve your energy, working each exercise slowly.
- Back off the stretch if you feel any discomfort.
- Relax following each stretch.
- If the stretch feels good, repeat.
- Hold each position for at least 10 seconds.

Shoulder & neck warm ups

The following exercises can be done in a standing or sitting position.

ARM ROTATIONS (figure 13b)
Ball your hands gently into fists and extend them out to your sides with your arms parallel to the floor. Slowly rotate your arms and shoulders forward 10 times, then in reverse 10 times. Relax.

figure 13b

Shoulder & neck stretches

SHOULDER ROLL (figure 13c)
With your arms in a comfortable position, gently and slowly roll your shoulders forward 5 times. Then reverse 5 times. Relax. Repeat.

SHOULDER SHRUG (figure 13d)
Let your arms hang down comfortably, with your shoulder blades gently pressed back and down. Inhale as you raise your shoulder up toward your ears. Hold. Slowly exhale and make a slow controlled return to your initial position. Pause. Repeat. Relax.

TIP: This exercise is a good exercise for relaxation, since it works your trapezius muscle, an area where people tend to incur a lot of stress.

figure 13c

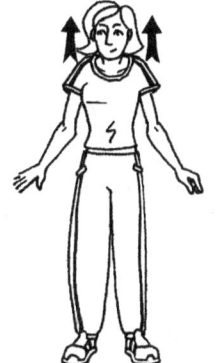

figure 13d

Healthy Ringing

SECTION THIRTEEN

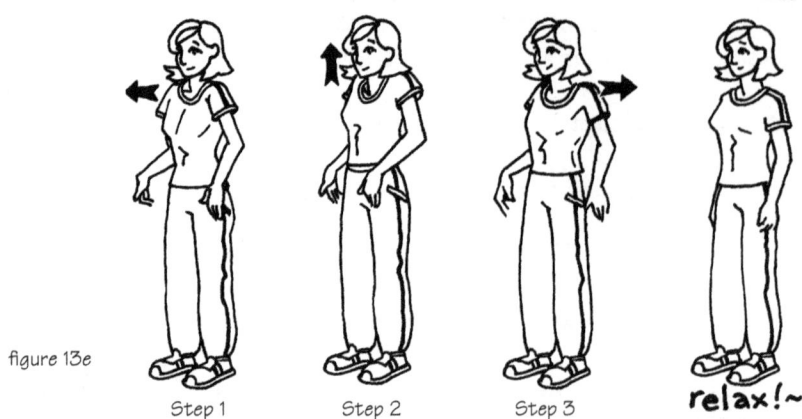

figure 13e

Step 1   Step 2   Step 3   relax!~

SHOULDER SQUEEZE (figure 13e)
This is a combined version of the *Shoulder shrug* and *Shoulder roll* (previous page) Slowly move and squeeze both your shoulders into the following three positions:
- **STEP 1:** Forward. Hold.
- **STEP 2:** Upward toward your ears. Hold.
- **STEP 3:** Down toward your back as you press your shoulder blades together. Hold. Relax. Repeat.

HUG (figure 13f)
Give yourself a hug! Gently grab each shoulder with the opposite hand. Stretch gently without pulling. Hold. Relax.

TIP: This stretches the middle part of your trapezius muscle, across the upper part of your back and your shoulders.

BELL HUG (figure 13g)
(An excellent warm-up for the arms and back, SECTION 14 and 16.)

Reach out in front of you as if hugging a large G2 bell. With your arms in this wide circle, gently touch your fingertips together. Hold. Relax. For a greater stretch, widen the circle of your arms.

figure 13f

figure 13g

TIP: Feel your muscles – from your back to your shoulders to your fingers – at work. This exercise can also be done in a seated position.

Bell Hug Variation: After touching your fingertips together, slowly collapse the circle toward your body. Your entire torso will feel involved!

Healthy Ringing

SHOULDER AND NECK

Step 1   Step 2   Step 3

figure 13h

 NECK STRETCH (figure 13h)
With shoulders pressed back and down, *slowly* move into the following three positions:
- **STEP 1:** Drop chin toward chest. Hold. Pause.
- **STEP 2:** Drop left ear to left shoulder. Hold. Pause.
- **STEP 3:** Drop right ear to right shoulder. Hold. Pause.

Important! *Slowly* and with control, move your head to each position. Avoid rolling your head to each position, and do not drop your head backward. (This places too much strain on your spine and can pinch nerves at the base of your skull and in your neck.)

TIP: To create an even deeper neck stretch, turn your face 45° to the right, then gently bend your left ear 45° toward your chest. Reverse for the other side (no illustrations shown).

 SHOULDER STRETCH (figure 13i)
Touch your fingertips together behind your head. Gently squeeze your shoulder blades together. Hold. Keeping your fingertips together, raise your arms up and out as far as the stretch will allow without lifting your shoulders. Hold. Relax.

figure 13i

Healthy Ringing

SECTION THIRTEEN ─────────────────────────────

Step 1

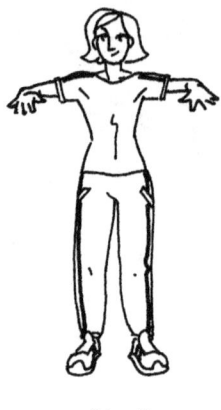
Step 2
figure 13j

Step 3

FULL SHOULDER ROTATION (figure 13j)

Without changing the height of your arms or resting between each position, do the following: position your arms out to your sides, parallel to the floor, elbows bent so that your arms point directly forward with your palms down. Keep your shoulders back, and progress slowly throughout the steps below; hold each position for at least 10 seconds.

- **STEP 1:** Rotate your arms pointing your fingers toward the ceiling, as if surrendering.
- **STEP 2:** Rotate your hands back to the original position, palms still down.
- **STEP 3:** Rotate your arms pointing your fingertips toward the floor. Relax.

TIP: For even a greater muscle flexion, repeat the above steps with both hands balled into fists.

SECTION FOURTEEN

ARM

THE BASICS

Handbell ringing requires strength in all your hand and arm muscles. Within a simple ringing motion, every arm muscle is used and each must be sufficiently developed. When ringing a heavy handbell, your hand and arm muscles are your first line of defense against strain; without strength in these muscles, you will lack the control and support necessary for healthy, precise ringing.

It's easy to see ringers with weak arm muscles: they play with jerky, uncontrolled arm motions, sloppy special techniques, inaccurate damping, and wobbly bells that wiggle from side to side. They forget to *sense* the movement of the handbells because they have no control over them and can not feel their muscles at work. They ring without ease and confidence, making their music timid as well.

The following warm-ups and exercises will help strengthen your arm muscles. Do each warm-up slowly and smoothly. When your arms are in correct position, focus on the muscles being used and feel them working for you! For maximum benefit, use good posture and breathe deeply during each exercise. These exercises can be done standing or sitting.

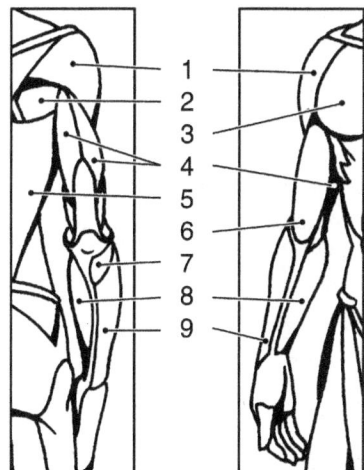

figure 14a

Major muscles used

1. Deltoid
2. Rotator cuff
3. Pectoral
4. Triceps
5. Trapezius
6. Biceps
7. Anconeus
8. Flexors
9. Extensors

(For a review, see SECTION 1, MUSCLES)

Arm warm ups

ARM ROTATION (figure 14b)
Extend arms straight out to the side. Rotate arms forward 10 times. Reverse the circle backwards 10 times. Relax and repeat.

Variations:
Repeat the entire exercise with...
- smaller circles.
- circles that gradually expand, then contract.

figure 14b

 Healthy Hint
Feel your own body's resistance! To increase the benefit of this rotation, create more tension in your arms by making a tight fist. This contracts your triceps and biceps muscles and gives them an additional workout.

EXERCISES FOR RINGING

Healthy Ringing

SECTION FOURTEEN

"AIR-BELL" WARM-UP (figure 14c)
Let your arms get ready by practicing a series of bell-related ringing motions without using any handbells. Make circular gestures of various sizes. You may warm-up on an actual piece of music, using this effective *air-bell* technique.

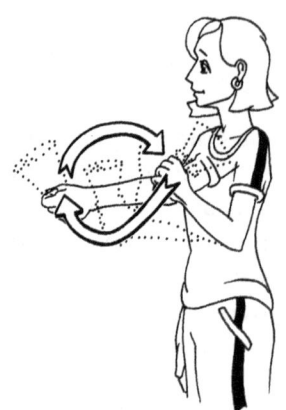

figure 14c

Arm stretches

FOREARM STRETCH (figure 14d)
- With both arms out in front of you, elbows unlocked and palms down, point fingers away from you. Hold.
- Repeat stretch with fingers pointing toward the ceiling. Hold.
- Repeat stretch with your fingers pointing toward the floor. Hold.

Stretching Reminders

- Breathe slowly and steadily throughout all exercises.
- Isolate the muscle you are working to stretch – create resistance.
- Conserve your energy by working each exercise slowly.
- Keep your elbows unlocked.
- Back off the stretch if you feel any discomfort.
- If the stretch feels good, repeat.
- Relax following each stretch.
- Hold each position for at least 10 seconds.

figure 14d

Healthy Ringing

ARM

UPPER ARM STRETCH (figure 14e)
Position your right arm straight out, level with your shoulder, with elbow and wrist relaxed. Gently move your arm across your body and pull your right elbow from underneath with your left hand. Hold.

Reverse the above exercise. Gently move your left arm across your body and pull your left elbow with your right hand. Hold.

Variation: For a deeper stretch, lower each elbow closer to your body.

figure 14e

PRAYING (figure 14f)
With arms in front of your chest, firmly press the palms of your hands together as if praying, with fingers pointing toward the ceiling. Hold. (You should feel the stretch in the flexor muscles of your forearm.)

Variation: For a deeper stretch, pull your hands closer to the floor while keeping your elbows in approximately the same position.

figure 14f

BELL HUG (figure 14g)
(This exercise is also an excellent warm-up for the shoulders and back, see SECTIONS 13 and 16).

Reach out in front of you as if hugging a large G2 bell. With arms in this wide circle, gently touch fingertips together. Hold. Relax. For a greater stretch, widen the circle of your arms.

TIP: Feel your muscles – from your back to your shoulders to your fingers – at work. This exercise can also be done in a seated position.

Variation: After touching fingertips together, slowly collapse the circle toward your body. Your entire torso will feel involved!

figure 14g

Healthy Ringing

SECTION FIFTEEN

FINGERS, HAND AND WRIST

THE BASICS

Although there are other important muscles, these primary muscles work together as a team to help fingers, hands, wrist, and arm work together as a unit. They are all interconnected giving you the flexibility and agility required for daily living. All need a balance of stretch and strength to accomplish their tasks.

Your hand is the most complicated, agile part of your body and is also the most involved part in handbell and handchime ringing. This is why *preventive* measures that protect the hand must be important daily routines. Most problems with soreness can be improved through the steady, accurate application of stretches, warm-ups, and strengthening of hands and wrists.

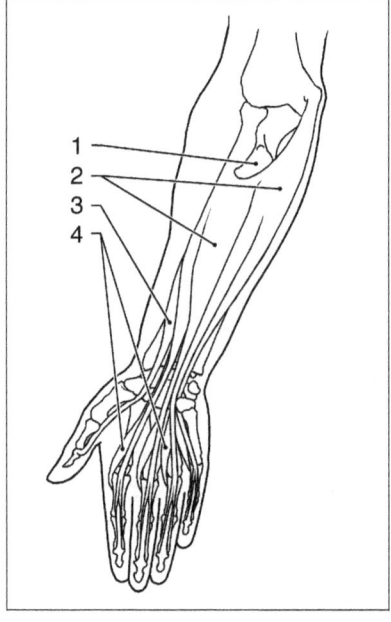

figure 15a

How can you avoid muscle strain?

- Warm-up and stretch prior to a rehearsal or concert.
- Warm-up and stretch your hands, arms and shoulders prior to conducting.
- Cool down with stretches following a rehearsal or concert.
- Use a correct grip.
- Keep wrists flexible, not locked.
- Damp in alignment with the entire arm; avoid twisting.
- Avoid over-extending the hand in any direction.
- Develop adequate grip strength.

Major muscles used

Extrinsic hand muscles
1. Flexor digitorum profundis (extends under superficialis)
2. Flexor digitorum superficialis
3. Flexor pollicis longus

Intrinsic hand muscles
4. Lumbricales

(For a review, see SECTION 1, MUSCLES)

Stretching Reminders

- Breathe slowly and steadily throughout all exercises.
- Isolate the muscle you are working to stretch — create resistance.
- Conserve your energy by working each exercise slowly.
- Back off the stretch if you feel any discomfort.
- If the stretch feels good, repeat.
- Relax following each stretch.
- Hold each position for at least 10 seconds.

Healthy Ringing

FINGERS, HAND AND WRIST

Basic warm-up

THE FLEXIBLE SNAKE (figure 15b)
Without closing the hands or locking the wrists, interlock fingers of both hands and move them in an imaginary wave, like a snake wiggling along the ground.
Keep this motion as fluid and flexible as possible.

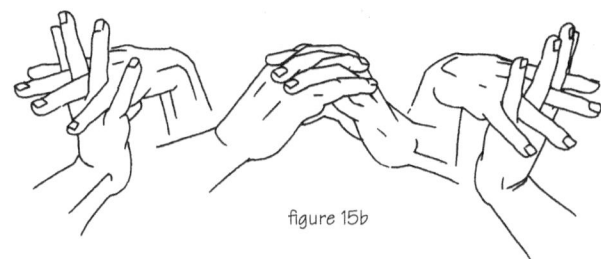
figure 15b

Finger stretches

The following stretches can be done with both hands simultaneously or one at a time. If you feel any strain, stop and do a flexible snake to relax the muscles.

PUTTY PLAY (no illustration)
Hold in your hand a large piece of putty or other type of soft, grip-strengthening device (a *Bubble-Bell*© works well). Hold a gripped position as if ringing a handbell. Flex your fingers and thumb to make a tight fist. Squeeze firmly and hold for a count of 10. Then relax for a count of 10. Repeat several times.

PUTTY PRESS (figure 15c)
Spread both hands out in front of you, *palms up*. Using both hands simultaneously, curve your thumbs and fingers one at a time, pretending that they are pressing into one or two inches of putty held in each hand. Reverse starting with the little finger, slowly and independently curve each finger and thumb. Make each part work with some effort.

figure 15c

KEYBOARD PRESS (no illustration)
Curve your fingers (palms down) as if playing a piano. Using both hands simultaneously, play the piano by pressing thumbs and fingers down, one after the other.

THE FAN (figure 15d)
Slowly spread apart your fingers and thumb into the shape of a fan. Stretch until you feel the tension of the pull. Hold. Relax. Repeat. Relax.

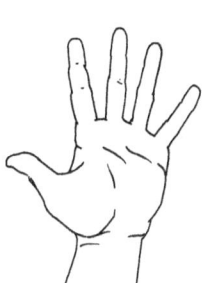
figure 15d

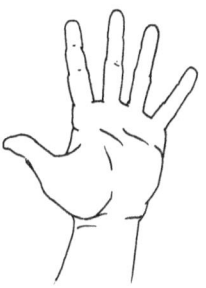

Healthy Ringing

SECTION FIFTEEN

FINGER SPREAD (figure 15e)
Wrap an office-style rubber band (one that offers some resistance) around all four fingers and thumb. Slowly spread your fingers and thumb outward against the resistance of this rubber band. Open and close hand slowly. Repeat.

TIP: Experiment with different gauges and thicknesses of rubber bands to see which gives the best resistance to your fingers. Wider bands tend to be stronger. Start off with rubber bands that give you less resistance, and move on to more difficult ones.

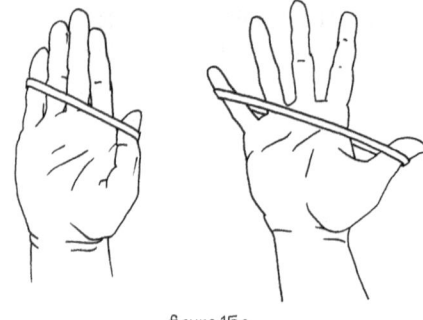

figure 15e

FINGER PLAY (figure 15f)
Spread apart your fingers and thumb into the shape of a fan. Slowly close the space between your thumb and index finger; between your thumb and middle finger; thumb and ring finger; and thumb and pinky finger. Feel the stretch in each position.

 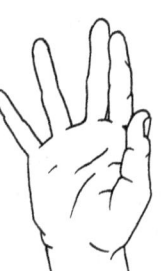  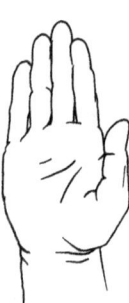

figure 15f

Now, slowly bend your thumb into the palm of your hand. Repeat, using each individual finger (figure 15g).

TIP: Keep fingers and thumb always curved. Stretch only to the position that you can handle comfortably.

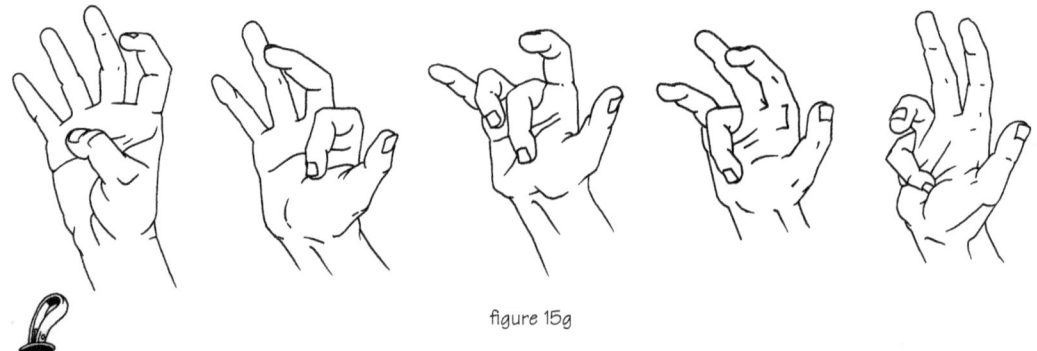

figure 15g

Healthy Ringing

FINGERS, HAND AND WRIST

OK KNUCKLE BEND (figure 15h)
Using both hands simultaneously, bend your index finger and thumb, then slowly move them together as if making an *OK* sign. Gently press and hold for 5 seconds. Repeat with remaining fingers, holding each position for an additional 5 seconds. Reverse the sequence.

TIP: To create resistance, keep each finger and thumb curled as you move into position.

figure 15h

THE CLAW (figure 15i)
Using both hands, slowly bend your fingers and thumb into the shape of a claw. Don't close your fist. Hold. Relax. Repeat 5-10 times.

Repeat *The claw*, but this time open your fingers wide and then close them into a fist. Hold. Relax. Repeat 5-10 times.

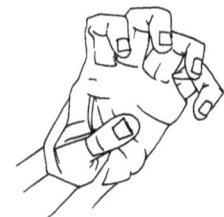
figure 15i

PRAYING (figure 15j)
Press the palms of hands and fingers together, as if praying; hold hands at neck level. Press shoulder muscles toward your back, squeezing the shoulder blades together. Firmly press and hold. Keep your breathing pattern slow and controlled.

Variation: For a deeper stretch, repeat everything, lowering the praying hands' position (still touching palms and fingertips together) to chest level; elbows are outward with both forearms in a horizontal line. Hands are positioned approximately chest high.

TIP: This is a great stretch that can be done anywhere and at almost any time.

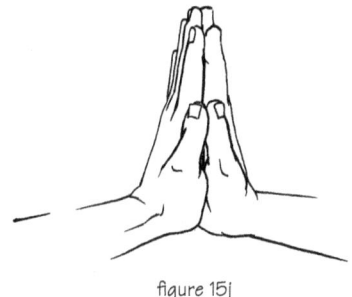
figure 15j

Healthy Ringing

SECTION FIFTEEN

HEALTHY HANDS (figure 15k)
(This is an effective pre-rehearsal warm-up!)

- Position both hands out in front of you, chest high. Create your own resistance by tightening both hand and arm muscles. The muscles must work hard to make this exercise effective – you should feel as if some force is pushing upward as you are pushing downward.
- Position your hands out in front of you. Start this warm-up with your palms down. Hold each position for 4 slow counts.

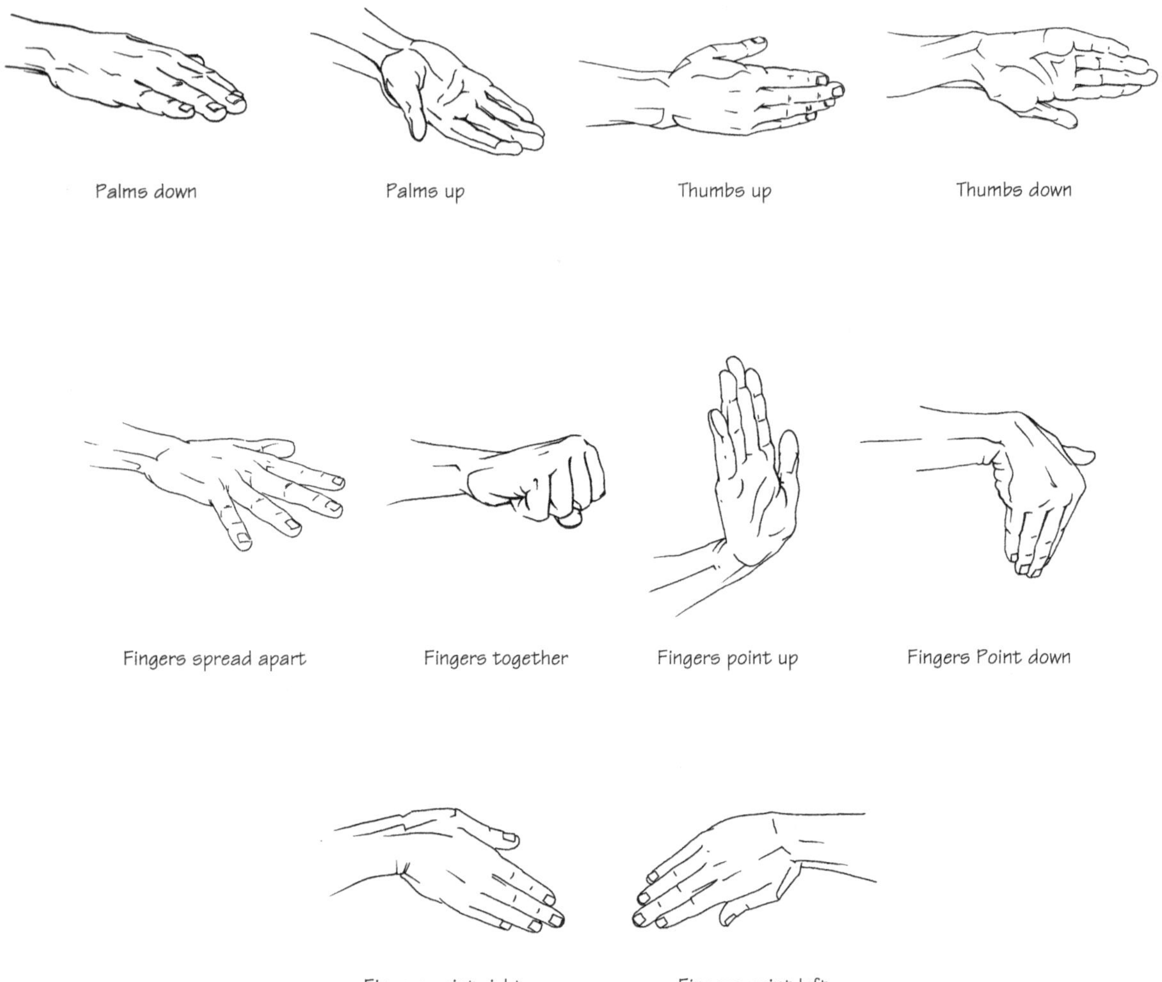

| Palms down | Palms up | Thumbs up | Thumbs down |

| Fingers spread apart | Fingers together | Fingers point up | Fingers Point down |

| Fingers point right | Fingers point left |

figure 15k

Healthy Ringing

Hand and wrist stretches

The following stretches can be done with both hands simultaneously or one hand at a time. If at any time you feel strain, stop and do a *flexible snake* (see *figure 15b*) to relax the muscles.

- Control your breathing.
- Exhale on the flexion (curling wrist).
- Inhale on the extension (returning wrist to its neutral position).

HAND AND WRIST

WRIST CURL (figure 15L)
(*flexing* – palms up)

Without moving your forearm, *slowly* lift your wrist **toward** you, and then return it slowly to its starting position. Repeat 10 times. Pause. Repeat this exercise using your opposite hand. Relax.

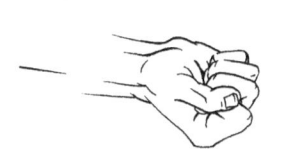

figure 15L

WRIST CURL (figure 15m)
(*extending* – palm down)

Without moving your forearm, *slowly* lift your wrist toward you and then return it slowly to its starting position. Repeat 10 times. Pause. Repeat this exercise using your opposite hand. Relax.

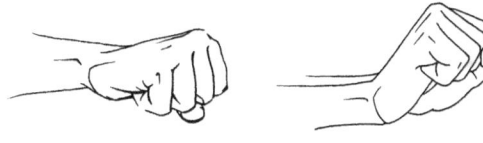

figure 15m

WRIST ROTATION (figure 15n)
(*pronating and supinating* – wrist rotated sideways)

Without moving your **elbow** position, *slowly* **rotate** your wrist from palm up to palm down, using your full range of motion. Always return your wrist to the starting position. Repeat 10 times. Pause. Repeat this exercise using your opposite hand. Relax.

figure 15n

After mastering both wrist curls and the wrist rotation with only the resistance created by your body, they may be done with hand-held weights, called *free weights* (see SECTION 20, RESISTANCE TRAINING).

SECTION FIFTEEN

Cool down stretches

After ringing, cool down your muscles with the following set of stretches. Take each one to the point of a stretch that "feels good", and back off if you feel an "ouch". If you have any hand or wrist injuries, you may want to avoid these stretches entirely.

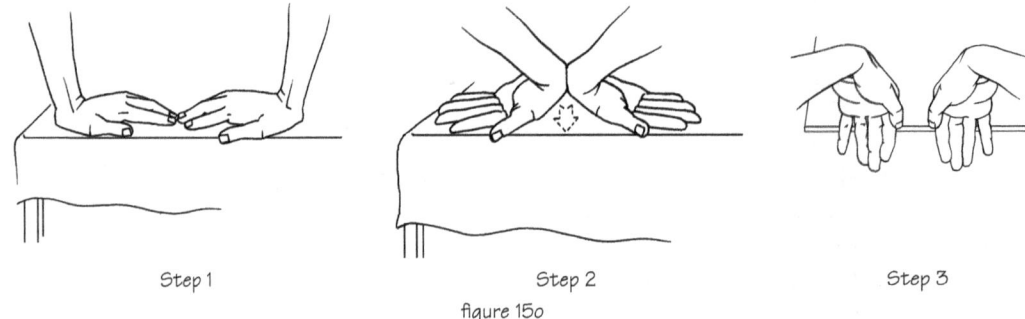

Step 1   Step 2   Step 3

figure 15o

TABLE PRESS (figure 15o)
- **STEP 1:** Place your hands flat on the table, palms down, hands *parallel* to the table's edge, with fingers pointing *toward* each other. Gently press. Hold. Relax.
- **STEP 2:** Place your hands flat on the table, palms facing up, parallel to the edge, with your knuckles pressed into the padding (left hand pointing to the left and right hand pointing to the right). Gently press. Hold. Relax..
- **STEP 3:** Place your hands flat on the table, palms down, wrists facing away from you with fingertips pointing toward you. Gently press. Hold. Relax.

TIP: Do the above three stretches slowly and work into each stretch at your own pace. At first your hands may not comfortably meet; your height (standing on your tiptoes sometimes help), the height of the table, and the initial stretch of your muscles will be factors. Initially, do them with your hands apart. Over days and weeks, as your stretch develops, your hands will come together. Remember, no pain should be felt. If you feel an "ouch", back off the stretch until you reach your comfort zone.

End your cool-down stretches with this last exercise!

THE FLEXIBLE SNAKE (figure 15p)
Interlock fingers of both hands without closing the hands or locking the wrists, and move them in an imaginary wave like a snake wiggling along the ground.

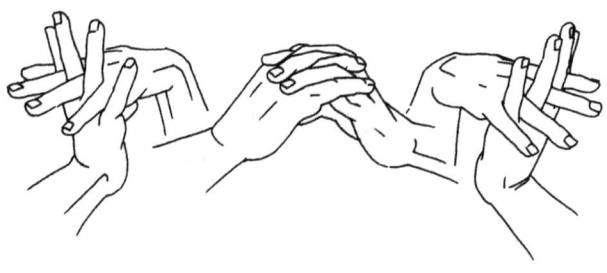

figure 15p

Healthy Ringing

SECTION SIXTEEN

BACK

THE BASICS

The back and lower shoulder area seems to give bell ringers the most physical trouble, but ringing alone does not always cause these aches and pains. Some backaches may be caused by bad posture or obesity or triggered by simply carrying a package or opening a door incorrectly. Slouching in a chair, spending too much time at the computer, or standing in one spot for a prolonged period of time can all contribute to back problems.

Lower back pain is extremely common. We abuse our lower backs by the way we walk, by how we stand and by what we lift, and by improperly using our muscles. A pain on one side of your lower body that hurts when you turn is usually due to a muscle strain. After an injury, the muscle may contract into a spasm, causing a firm and tight feeling. Breathing may even seem difficult.

Unless handbell ringers develop a *Healthy Ringing* posture with proper exercises and warm-ups prior to playing and with understanding of proper ringing techniques, we will continue to invite back and shoulder discomfort. If our muscles are strong, we can normally handle the instrument; if they are weak, then strain and injury will occur much too easily.

Handbell rehearsals often start without a proper warm-up to help our muscles survive for an hour or two. We rush into the rehearsal, grab, lift, and empty a case (which can weigh over forty pounds!), and commence ringing without any concern for our body's readiness, and then we wonder why our backs ache at the end of rehearsal. There's no mystery here!

We need to use body energy carefully and properly to lift a bass bell, weave three or four bells in succession, or execute a martellato. As any athlete, we can maximize our overall effort with advanced planning that includes stretches.

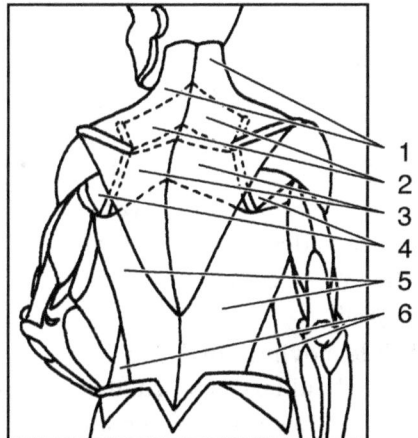

figure 16a

Major muscles used
1. Trapezius
2. Rhomboideus minor
3. Rhomboideus major
4. Rotator cuff
5. Latissimus dorsi
6. External oblique

(For a review, see SECTION 1, MUSCLES)

SECTION SIXTEEN

Back stretches

SHOULDER ROLL (figure 16b)
(Also a combined upper back and shoulder stretch.)

With arms in a comfortable position, gently and slowly roll shoulders forward 5 times. Then reverse 5 times. Relax. Repeat.

While moving slowly, roll your shoulders forward, then upward toward your ear, and then toward your back as you press your shoulder blades together. Hold. Relax.

figure 16b

> **Stretching Reminders**
> - Breathe slowly and steadily throughout all exercises.
> - Isolate the muscle you are working to stretch – create resistance.
> - Conserve energy by working each exercise slowly.
> - Keep knees unlocked.
> - Back off the stretch if you feel any discomfort.
> - If the stretch feels good, repeat.
> - Relax following each stretch.
> - Hold each position for at least 10 seconds.

Step 1   Step 2   Step 3   relax!~

figure 16c

SHOULDER SQUEEZE (figure 16c)
(Also a combined upper back and shoulder stretch.)

Slowly move and squeeze both your shoulders into the following three positions:
- **STEP 1:** Forward. Hold.
- **STEP 2:** Upward toward your ears. Hold.
- **STEP 3:** Down toward your back as you press your shoulder blades together. Hold.
- Relax. Repeat.

Healthy Ringing

BACK

SUNSHINE STRETCH (figure 16d)
With feet shoulder-width apart, clasp your hands together and reach toward the ceiling. Hold. Now, slowly bend to one side. Hold. Repeat on the other side. Hold. Relax.

SWAYING BRANCH (no illustration)
With feet shoulder-width apart, place your hands over your head. Pretend you are holding a dowel rod. Bend to the left from your waist. Feel the stretch. Hold. Return to the neutral position. Now bend to the right from your waist. Hold. Relax.

SHOULDER PULL (figure 16e)
- Make a fist with each hand and place hands on hips.
- Gently pull elbows and shoulders back. Press shoulder blades together. Hold. Relax.

SHOULDER RAISE (figure 16f)
- Press shoulder blades together.
- Clasp hands together behind your back- (keep your elbows unlocked). Raise arms out and up as far as the stretch will allow. Don't lift your shoulders. Hold. Relax.

Variation: For more resistance, use an exercise rubber band or a hand towel, one hand holding each end.

BELL HUG (figure 16g)
(Also an excellent warm-up for the shoulders, neck and arms.)

- Reach out in front of you as if hugging a large G2 bell. With arms in this wide circle, gently touch fingertips together. Hold. Relax.
- Feel your muscles – from back to shoulders to fingers – at work. This exercise can also be done in a seated position.

Variation: After touching fingertips together, slowly collapse the circle toward your body. Your entire torso will feel involved!

figure 16d

figure 16e   figure 16f

figure 16g

Healthy Ringing

SECTION SIXTEEN

PRAYING (figure 16h)
Press the palms of your hands and fingers together at neck level, as if praying. Press shoulder muscles toward your back, squeezing the shoulder blades together. Firmly press and hold. Relax.

- Keep slow control of your breathing as you stretch.
- For a deeper stretch, repeat the above – but this time, lower your hand position (still touching palms and fingertips together) toward your waist.
- Keep elbows outward with both forearms creating a horizontal line.
- Keep forearms approximately level with your chest.
- Firmly press and hold this stretch for at least 10 seconds.
- Keep breathing as you stretch.

figure 16h

GENTLE FORWARD BEND (figure 16i)
Start in a standing position. Keeping knees unlocked, back straight, palms placed on the front of thighs, slowly and smoothly slide hands down your legs as far you can go without strain. Your head will naturally move downward as if taking a slow and gracious bow. Hold this position.

Slowly return upright to the standing position. Relax.

figure 16i

RAG DOLL BEND (figure 16j)
While seated, knees spread apart, fold your body forward between your legs. Keep back rounded and let arms dangle, releasing your head and neck. Hold.

Roll up slowly and rest for a few seconds before standing.

figure 16j

Healthy Ringing

BACK

DOOR PUSHUPS (figure 16k)
- Stand facing an open doorway at arm's length, and place your hands on the doorframe. Avoid locking elbows or knees.
- Slowly bend your elbows and lean into the door, as if doing a floor pushup.
- Keep head upright and neck tucked in to avoid straining your neck. Hold. Relax.

TORSO TWIST (figure 16L)
- Place hands on hips. Without changing foot position, gently twist your torso to the *right*. Hold. Breathe deeply as you feel the stretch.
- Repeat, extending the stretch as far as you can without discomfort. Hold. Pause.
- Gently twist your torso to the *left*. Hold. Breathe deeply as you feel the stretch.
- Repeat, extending the stretch as far as you can without discomfort. Hold. Relax.

TIP: Always keep your knees unlocked! Move slowly with this stretch, and do not attempt this if you have any back problems!

figure 16k

figure 16L

> ### Healthy Hints
>  It's important to make back stretches part of a five to ten-minute pre-rehearsal warm-up, *especially* if you are a bass handbell ringer.
>
> Small stretch breaks during rehearsal relieve a tired back, and stretching will often help reduce discomfort from an existing backache.
>
> A few minutes of gentle stretching following rehearsal is necessary to avoid back stiffness.
>
> For all the exercises in a standing position, place your feet shoulder-width apart. Point your toes straight ahead and keep your knees unlocked. Tighten your abdominal muscles as you do each stretch. Breathe deeply throughout each stretch.

Healthy Ringing

SECTION SIXTEEN

Back care

To avoid back strain, a few preventive measures are important:
- Always make back stretches a part of your pre-ringing warm-ups!
- Stay mobile, movable and active while ringing!
- Align your feet, placing them apart and positioned under your shoulders. Avoid "planting" your feet – be able to move comfortably from the heels of your feet to your toes.
- When standing, always keep your knees unlocked – locking places unnecessary strain on your lower back. Unlocking knees will also keep a balance throughout your entire body.
- Maintain a *pelvic tilt*! Tighten gluteals and abdomen, then push your pelvis slightly forward. The leg muscles now correctly support your body's weight. This simple movement changes your center of gravity, and takes the pressure off your lower back. (For a review, see SECTION 2, POSTURE.)
- Shift your body's weight from one foot to another, often – move smoothly with small steps. If possible, occasionally sit down.
- When rising from a sitting position, avoid bending over from the waist. Sit forward on your chair, tighten your stomach muscles and push from your thigh muscles (quadriceps). If necessary, place hands on thighs (or the sides of the chair) and use your body for leverage.

- Keep your head straight, directly over shoulders, with shoulders positioned directly over your hips. Think tall, with head centered directly on top of your body as if on a skewer. Keep your chin tucked in, not up. If looking at music is difficult from this position, consider a sight-line riser or floor-style adjustable music stand.
- When weaving, avoid twisting at the waist! *Reposition your body* by shifting your weight from one foot to the other. Keep your body and shoulder movement parallel to the table. Proper footwork is essential (see SECTION 7, page 61, Weight shifting).
- Ring only as many handbells as you can comfortably reach with controlled and supported movements.
- Take brief stretch breaks. A gentle back stretch can be done discreetly without anyone noticing.
- Prolonged standing produces back fatigue. To help alleviate long periods of standing, raise one foot up periodically onto a low stool.
- The height of the table (and the thickness of the foam padding!) may initiate back and shoulder strain; this is not often considered by ringers or directors. The bells should be comfortably in reach of your arms as they hang loosely at your side. A low table encourages frequent bending at the waist, and a high table causes strained shoulders. Consider raising your table with leg casters or raising your body by standing on a wide bench or low riser at your position.

H e a l t h y   R i n g i n g

— BACK

- Female ringers should not ring bells in high heels! This throws the body's center of gravity forward, straining back muscles.

- Take care of your back when lifting or carrying bell cases (see SECTION 26, MOVING HANDBELL CASES AND TABLES).
- Sense what your body is telling you. If you feel the beginnings of back muscle strain, learn to reduce it by moving *into* the muscle with a static stretch.

Back strain

- If you sense a back muscle being overused, chances are you didn't warm-up and stretch enough prior to ringing. You may also be ringing too many bells, or heavier bells than normal. If possible, temporarily ease up on the ringing; the muscle ache may subside.
- If your back doesn't return to normal after a couple of days – and if it becomes increasingly difficult to move through a daily routine – seek medical advice. Your doctor can evaluate the problem, adjust your back if necessary, perhaps prescribe a stronger anti-inflammatory drug, or suggest rest from handbell ringing, with limited activities (such as slow walking) until your back returns to normal.

SECTION SEVENTEEN
ABDOMEN

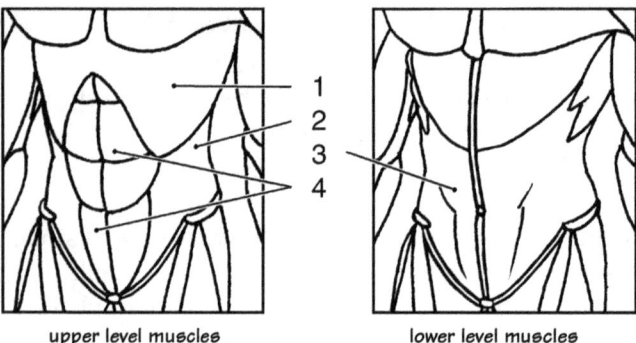

Major muscles used
1. Intercostals – lie between ribs (see figure 1e)
2. Internal oblique
3. External oblique
4. Rectus abdominis

(For a review, see SECTION 1, MUSCLES)

upper level muscles   lower level muscles

figure 17a

THE BASICS

Working your abdominals gives you the added strength to support your upper body, improve posture, and relieve pressure on your back. The abdominal muscles are the counter for your spine muscles. They help you bend forward and rotate the trunk of your body.

The obliques run diagonally down the side above your hips. For a visual direction, imagine the obliques as sliding your hands into your pockets, using outstretched fingers.

Abdominal stretches

OBLIQUE STRETCH (figure 17b)
- Spread the fingers of your right hand and place it on your right quadriceps (thigh). Take in a deep breath.
- Slowly run your hand down the side of our leg and exhale simultaneously. Work into the stretch.
- Repeat on the opposite side of your body, using your left hand.

Stretching Reminders
- Isolate the muscle you are working to stretch – create resistance.
- Conserve your energy by working each exercise slowly.
- Back off the stretch if you feel any discomfort.
- If the stretch feels good, repeat.
- Relax following each stretch.
- Breathe slowly and steadily throughout all exercises.

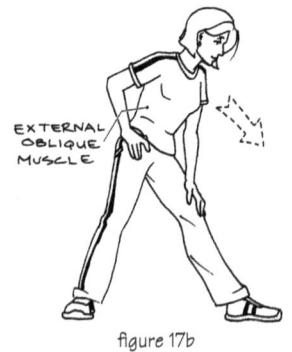

figure 17b

Healthy Ringing

— ABDOMEN

Although most exercises for abdominal muscles are positioned on the floor, the following two exercises can easily be done in a standing position, directly behind the ringing table. Pay special attention to your breathing: *exhale as you contract your abdominal muscles; inhale as you release the contraction!*

ABDOMINAL PRESS (no illustration)
Finger press onto a tabletop and inhale. In a holding position, tighten your abdominal muscles and exhale for 5 seconds. Relax. Repeat several times.

TIP: If you are doing this exercise correctly, your abs should feel firm.

PELVIC TILT (no illustration)
Tighten your gluteus muscles and, at the same time, tighten your abdominal muscles. This will flatten your lower back. Hold this position for 5 seconds. Relax. Repeat 2 times. Concentrate on the abdominal contraction.

TIP: This gentle exercise will help you maintain good posture and will relieve lower back tension as well.

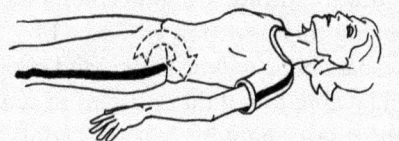

Healthy Hint
Try this at home!
- Lay down on a carpet or mat.
- Push pelvis down flat on floor to allow hips to rotate externally — press your back against the floor.
- Hold this position 5 to 10 seconds. Relax.
- Keep breathing.

AN ADDED BONUS!
When you tighten your abdominal muscles as you perform exercises in this book, you are supporting your back and stabilizing other muscles in your body. As a bonus, your abs are receiving extra workout time!

Healthy Ringing

SECTION EIGHTEEN

LEGS

THE BASICS

Strong legs hold up our body, give us balance, keep us mobile and provide overall endurance. If we lose leg strength, we tire easily; we cannot stand for a full handbell rehearsal or move with agility and control.

Leg muscles support your knees, and their strength guides the movement of your ankles and feet. All parts are interconnected – when you warm-up your legs, you are tending to your ankles and feet as well.

When leg and foot muscles have been exercised and strengthened, you'll be able to ring handbells or handchimes more easily. Movement from one bell to another will be more fluid. Shifting weight when weaving or moving to a new bell will be a breeze. Lifting bass bells will be supported properly. You'll be able to *feel* the muscles at work and therefore ring with ease and confidence.

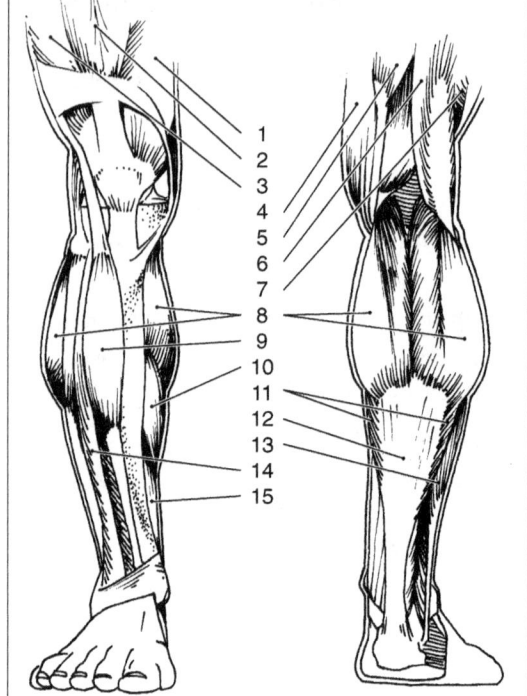

figure 18a

Stretching Reminders

- Breathe slowly and steadily throughout all exercises.
- Isolate the muscle you are working to stretch – create resistance.
- Conserve energy by working each exercise slowly.
- Keep knees unlocked.
- Back off the stretch if you feel any discomfort.
- If the stretch feels good, repeat.
- Relax following each stretch.
- Hold each position for at least 10 seconds.

Major muscles used

1. Vastus medialis
2. Rectus femoris
3. Vastus lateralis
4. Semimembranosus
5. Semitendinosus
6. Biceps femoris
7. Iliotibial tract
8. Gastrocnemius
9. Tibialis anterior
10. Soleus
11. Soleus
12. Achilles tendon
13. Peroneus longus
14. Extensor digitorum longus
15. Flexor digitorum longus

Muscle diagram may include more muscles than are referred to in the text.

(For a review, see SECTION 1, MUSCLES)

Healthy Ringing

Calf stretches

Maintain a straight upper body posture, tighten your abdominal muscles and keep your knees unlocked as you do the following exercises:

AT THE TABLE

TIP-TOE STRETCH (figure 18b)
- For balance, gently touch the table in front of you with your fingertips.
- Slowly lift onto the balls of your feet. Hold.
- Slowly return to a comfortable standing position. Hold. Relax. Repeat.

TIP: This exercise can be done anywhere that's appropriate, even behind a handbell table in the middle of a concert! Just remember – for best results – tighten your calves, using a static stretch only – avoid bouncing! (You should also feel your glutes and quads at work.)

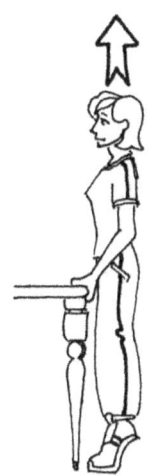

figure 18b

AWAY FROM TABLE

STAIRCASE STRETCH (figure 18c)
(Basic position: stand on the first step of a staircase. For balance, hold onto the railing.)
- Place the balls of your feet near the edge of the step (feet are parallel to ground). Hold.
- Slowly rise up onto your toes, and tighten your calf muscles. Hold. Slowly return to the basic position.
- Slowly lower heels toward the floor. Hold. Slowly return to basic position. Relax.

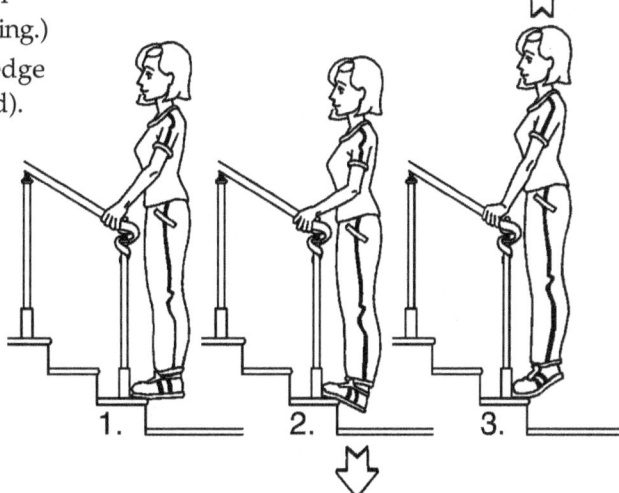

figure 18c

Hamstring stretch

The hamstring muscles are the big muscles in the back of your leg, above your knee, and opposite your quadriceps muscles. The quads are generally stronger than the hamstrings, so stretching the hamstrings regularly will prevent excessive tightness in the thigh. Tight hamstrings can also be a cause for low back pain, a common complaint of bell ringers standing for hours behind a table.

SITTING LEG RAISES (no illustration)
While seated on a chair with both feet flat on the floor, straighten one leg out in front, keeping toes pointing up as you go. Lean over without lifting your head. When you feel the stretch, hold. Reverse legs and repeat the stretch. Hold. Relax.

TIP: This exercise also creates resistance in your quadriceps.

Quadricep stretches

The quads are your largest group of leg muscles. They are important for standing, walking and running. Regular stretching here will improve your endurance and your mobile techniques such as weaving.

LEG LEAN (figure 18d)
(Your feet are pointing in the same direction.)
Settle your weight consciously lower, with your feet a little wider than shoulder width, and with your knees bent. Step forward and place your weight onto your left foot. Lean into the quadriceps and hold. Relax.

Shift your weight onto your right foot. Lean into your quadriceps and hold. Relax.

figure 18d

STEP TO THE SIDE (figure 18e)
(Your feet are perpendicular to one another.)
Repeat the previous stretch, but turn your right foot to the right at a 90° angle. Hold and relax.

Repeat using the left foot. Hold and relax.

For balance, place a hand on your thigh.

figure 18e

LEGS

LEG RAISES (figure 18f)

Gently touch the table surface in front of you. Stand with right foot slightly behind the left. Without flexing your foot, lift right leg up toward your bottom, flexing the back of your hamstrings as your leg rises. Hold. Return to start. Reverse and repeat the stretch with your left leg. Hold. Relax.

Variation: For an additional stretch hold right leg with right hand just below the ankle. Slowly lift right leg with knee pointing towards floor. Repeat with left side.

figure 18f

QUADRICEPS LIFT (figure 18h)

Stand beside a chair. For balance hold the back of the chair with one hand. Place your right foot on the chair seat. Bend your left leg and lower your body. Hold.

Repeat with your left foot. Hold. Relax.

TIP: This exercise also creates resistance in your hamstrings.

figure 18g

Healthy Ringing

SECTION NINETEEN

FOOT

THE BASICS

The following stretches will help strengthen your feet, ankles and legs, and prevent leg fatigue. Do each one slowly and smoothly. For maximum benefit, breathe deeply during each exercise and sit or stand, using good posture. Keep your knees unlocked at all times!

Standing for prolonged periods is not easy on your feet. Handbell festivals or long rehearsals often make them tired and achy. When this occurs, you *must* take a brief stretch break to relieve the problem!

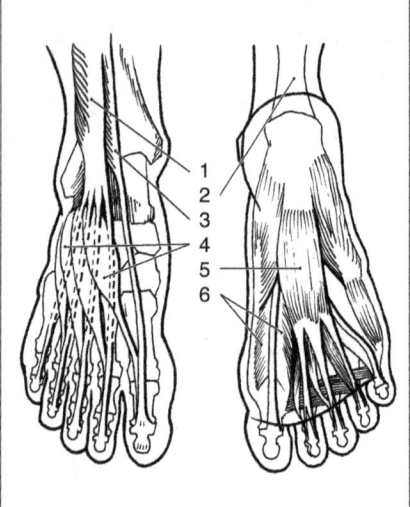

figure 19a

Stretching Reminders

- Breathe slowly and steadily throughout all exercises.
- Isolate the muscle you are working to stretch — create resistance.
- Conserve energy by working each exercise slowly.
- Keep knees unlocked.
- Back off the stretch if you feel any discomfort.
- If the stretch feels good, repeat.
- Relax following each stretch.
- Hold each position for at least 10 seconds.

Major muscles used

1. Extensor digitorum longus
2. Achilles tendon
3. Extensor hallucis longus
4. Extensor digitorium brevis
5. Flexor digitorum brevis
6. Flexor hallucis brevis

(For a review, see SECTION 1, MUSCLES)

Foot stretches

TIRED TOES (figure 19b)

Sit down with both the heels and soles of your feet gently pressing into the floor.

- **STEP 1:** Spread your toes in each foot as far apart as possible. Hold for 5-10 seconds. Relax.
- **STEP 2:** Scrunch your toes together. Hold for 5-10 seconds. Relax.
- **STEP 3:** Point your toes upward. Hold for 5-10 seconds. Relax.

Repeat the sequence.

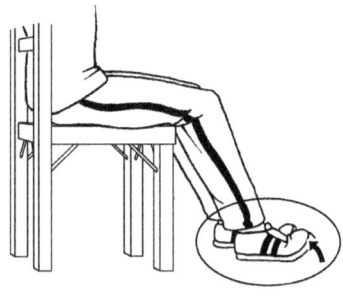

toes only!
figure 19b

Healthy Ringing

FOOT

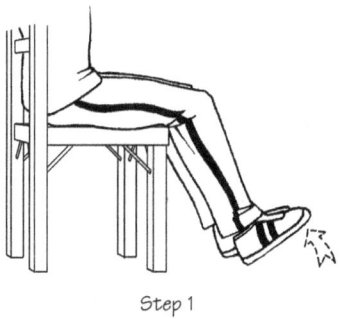

Step 1

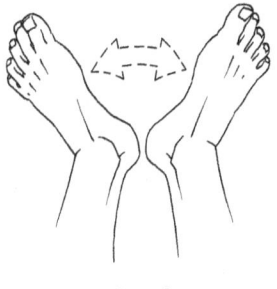

Step 2
figure 19c

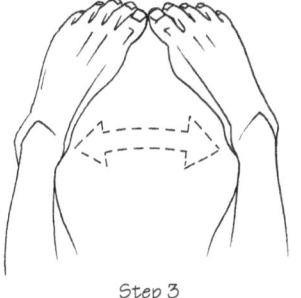

Step 3

TIRED ANKLES (figure 19c)

(adapts *Tired Toes* exercise to your ankles).

In a sitting position, keep your heels pressing gently into the floor, as in the previous stretch. This time, however, lift your toes and the soles of your feet off the floor

- **STEP 1:** Point your toes up toward the ceiling. Stretch as far as possible. Hold for 5-10 seconds.
- **STEP 2:** With your heels still down, spread and fan your feet apart. Feel the stretch in your calves and ankles. Hold for 5-10 seconds.
- **STEP 3:** Point your feet inward and stretch. Hold for 5-10 seconds. Relax.

ANKLE SPINS (figure 19d)

- Work each ankle separately!
- Lift your left foot off the floor and rotate it slowly clockwise 10 times. Then rotate it slowly 10 times counter-clockwise. Use a full range of motion. Relax.
- Repeat with right foot. Rotate it slowly clockwise 10 times, then rotate slowly counter-clockwise. Use a full range of motion. Relax.

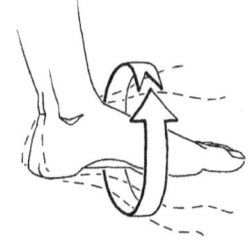

figure 19d

Foot protection

PROPER SHOES

Thanks to the modern array of athletic shoes, our feet and legs, at bell rehearsals and concerts, have been helped. During concerts, however, sometimes women wear their fanciest shoes – the ones with the heels or pointed toes that can cause discomfort and pain.

Avoid high heels! They throw the body's gravity forward, upsetting your balance and placing too much strain on your lower back. Also, avoid low arched, thin-heeled shoes without laces. They offer no support and may cause foot injury when lifting a heavy bell or case of bells.

Healthy Ringing

Athletic shoes or well-fitted shoes with good arch support and flexibility are recommended when playing handbells. Rubber or composition soles do have a drawback – they can stick to some floor surfaces, causing movement restriction when shifting body weight or moving alongside the table. Shoes with laces will give better ankle support while lifting and moving heavy bass bells and cases.

Like any athletic endeavor, we must think comfort *before* style and wear what is appropriate for conditions. The choice is personal!

PROPER SUPPORT

Strained feet can result when muscles that support the arch of your foot are weak, forcing the foot ligaments to support your weight; your feet and ankles can easily become sore after prolonged standing. As you age, your feet change and enlarge, and may require better shoes and even perhaps orthotic inserts (prescription devices that realign the foot to the ground).

Prevent foot stiffness and create foot flexibility by continued daily stretching and strengthening exercises for your feet and legs. If your feet are regularly uncomfortable, seek the aid of a podiatrist who can evaluate your problem and prescribe proper relief.

PROPER FLOOR SURFACE

Adequate padding is important! Hard cement and linoleum and wooden surfaces are difficult to stand on for any length of time. If possible, place a carpet square or foam pad under your feet for rehearsals. Additionally, to keep the blood circulating throughout your legs and feet, continually shift your weight and move around in your place.

WALKING

Building body endurance is a key for developing handbell ringing endurance. Beyond warm-ups and stretches, ringers need to develop a healthy attitude toward daily exercise. A daily walk is free, easy, and greatly helps both with attitude and stamina for ringing. Walking at least half an hour daily will make a difference at each rehearsal.

Set a pace well within your comfort zone. For maximum endurance, work your way gradually to a 30-45 minute brisk walk, which will increase your heart rate and push your metabolism. Swing your arms; they become the pistons that move your legs. You will see gradual improvement in your endurance and strength. The results are worth all the effort.

Healthy Ringing

SECTION TWENTY

RESISTANCE TRAINING

Review *Understanding Resistance*, page 109.

Developing hand, arm and upper body strength

Although you can create natural resistance within your own body, many athletes create even more resistance by exercising with free weights. A *free weight* is anything that has weight and can be easily held in the hand; a good example of a free weight is a standard 9-ounce can of soup. Athletes use hand-held weights called *dumbbells* that place equal amounts of weight at each end.

Basic resistance training involves free weights held in each hand, used to build up muscle strength and endurance.

Sets and repetitions

To get the maximum results of a resistance program, exercises must be done in groups of repeated motions, called *repetitions*. These repetitions (or *reps*) are combined into a *set*. Generally, a set includes 10-12 repeated motions. You *must* repeat the initial set at least once. The first set warms the muscles; the second allows the muscles to elongate and stretch. This second set of repetitions will be more difficult, especially during the last few motions, but it is absolutely necessary to finish if progress is to occur.

Procedure

Unless otherwise stated, an exercise is done as follows: a set of 10 repetitions (reps); pause for 10-20 seconds; repeat another set of 10 additional reps.

Start with a 3 pound or 5 pound weight. If you feel muscle fatigue during the final few reps in the second set, then you are stretching correctly with the correct weight. Slowly build up your endurance and muscle strength. If you can finish the second set of reps without muscle fatigue, add a heavier weight or add more repetitions. Each time you add a heavier weight, back off the number of reps to 8. Work back up to 10-12 reps. If you're unable to complete the last set of reps, decrease the repetitions or the weight being used.

Developing grip strength

Begin by using a comfortable weight. After a few weeks of strengthening and after you can comfortably repeat your exercises many times without fatigue, add a heavier weight. These exercises are effective only if there is no pain. If you feel any "ouch", stop immediately! Try a lighter weight until you feel resistance without irritation to the muscle.

SECTION TWENTY

 Guidelines for using free weights

- Free weights should be used only every other day, so the body recovers from the workout.
- Warm-up with at least five minutes of aerobic exercise prior to resistance training.
- Create resistance from your body (as if you were pushing an object through water).
- Tighten your abdominal muscles when lifting any weight.
- Keep your shoulders pressed back and down.
- Start with a 3-5 pound weight; increase this weight when repetitions become too easy.
- Control the free weight – lift with a slow and steady movement.
- Concentrate on the muscles you use.
- Work each muscle independently. Counting will help to determine progress.
- Alternate your hands – this will help you concentrate on your body's movement.
- A sitting position is recommended. Your elbow needs to be placed in a static position by using one of the following positions:
  – by leaning forward and resting your elbow on your leg;
  – by touching your elbow to your side.
- Breathe deeply and slowly:
  – exhale when lifting the free weight (on the exertion)
  – inhale when returning the free weight to its neutral position.
- Pause between repetitions.
- Do not lock any joint during exercise, because it causes unnecessary stress on that area.
- No pain should be felt before, during, or after exercise.

important!

The following exercises are done with the arm straight out and supported. Rest your arm on a table, arm of a chair, on your thigh, etc., holding the weight comfortably in your hand. Start this set of exercises with your palm up; the wrist and hand are unsupported.

Hand and wrist

 WRIST CURL (figure 20a)
(*flexing* – palms up)
Without moving your forearm, *slowly* lift your wrist ***toward*** you and then return it slowly to its starting position. Repeat 10 times. Pause. Repeat this exercise using your opposite hand. Relax.

figure 20a

 WRIST CURL (figure 20b)
(*extending* – palm down)
Without moving your forearm, slowly lift your wrist toward you and then return it slowly to its starting position. Repeat 10 times. Pause. Repeat this exercise using your opposite hand. Relax.

figure 20b

Healthy Ringing

RESISTANCE TRAINING

 WRIST ROTATION (figure 20c)
(*pronating and supinating* – wrist rotated sideways)

Without moving your *elbow's* position, *slowly* **rotate** your hand from palm up to palm down, using your full range of motion. Always return your hand to the starting position. Repeat 10 times. Pause. Repeat this exercise using your opposite hand. Relax.

figure 20c

Arms

 BICEPS PULL (figure 20d)
- Keep your elbow positioned at your side. Your arm is out in front with your palm facing toward your body. Bend your arm only at the elbow (avoid flexing your wrist); slowly move your hand toward your shoulder.
- Right arm reps – 10 reps. Pause. Repeat.
- Left arm reps – 10 reps. Pause. Repeat.

 LATERAL RAISE (figure 20e)
- Use two matching weights. Stand with your knees unlocked and abs tight. Hold your arms down at your sides with elbows slightly bent to avoid locking. Your palms will face inward toward the side of your body.
- With your arms still in resting position, slowly inhale.
- Slowly extend your arms upward (no higher than your shoulders) and exhale as weights are lifted. Pause. Inhale as the weights are once again returned to the resting position at your side.
- Do a set of 10-12 reps. Pause. Repeat. Relax.

TIP: To avoid strain, keep palms facing floor throughout exercise.

figure 20d

 **Healthy Hint**
Work the weight – don't let it work you! Concentrate on moving slowly and evenly.

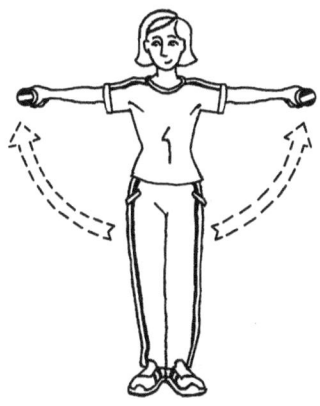

figure 20e

SECTION TWENTY

AN AFTERTHOUGHT!

The exercises in this publication don't begin to cover all the important aspects of stretching and strengthening. Only basic *Level I* exercises have been discussed and illustrated. In general, training all the major muscles is important in proper weight training as well as for cardiovascular health and endurance. I hope this book's contents will become a springboard for further study.

If *Healthy Ringing*® has whet your appetite for additional training information, visit a library or book store and pick up a book on stretching and resistance training. (Also see Resources in this publication for a list of recommended titles.) Joining a health center (a YMCA or a private health club) under the supervision of a trained staff can be the best way to develop a healthy body. Contact a sports trainer or sports physiologist in your community and find out if a personal training session is available. A personal workout and fitness program can be customized for you.

Bring in a personal trainer to develop a program for you and the other ringers – someone who can teach, guide, watch, and advise as your group "pumps bronze".

Care of Your Body

PART FOUR

- Ears
- Eyes
- Voice
- Stress Management
- Nutrition
- Moving Handbell Cases and Tables
- Gloves
- Support Devices
- Medical Concerns

SECTION TWENTY-ONE

EARS

Noise/music exposure

Excessive noise and/or loud music exposure can be harmful to your ears. Whether you're a construction worker, a pilot, or a classical musician, the environment that you work in may, over time, damage your hearing. As an example, woodwind players in orchestras often routinely deal with ear irritation, as the penetrating sound of the brass and percussion sections pushes past them to reach the audience. Some enterprising professional orchestras, realizing that the hearing of their musicians is an important asset, position a clear plastic shield between the brass and woodwind sections to help reduce the problem. A handbell ringer's situation seems remarkably similar to these beleaguered woodwind players; however instead of sitting in front of loud brass instruments, you stand among bronze ones – and the vibration happens close to your ears.

Three problematic situations come to mind:

- Rehearsing for a lengthy period of time in a small rehearsal room, with a low ceiling, hard walls, a tile floor, or all these together.
- Ringing for an extended period of time in a large handbell festival surrounded by many handbells.
- Ringing handbell literature with loud dynamics – shaking, rapid eighth-note passages, continuous sections marked forte or fortissimo.

Excessive shaking or sustained sounds (especially with the clappers turned to their hardest settings) emit higher decibel levels; these loud sounds can irritate your ears or those of a neighboring ringer. Upper fourth and fifth octave handbells have high frequencies that excite higher overtones, which can also sting your ears. The main symptom – a ringing in the ears – begins in rehearsal and may last for just a moment or may remain through the entire rehearsal. This ringing in the ears varies between individuals; some are more susceptible to low pitches, while some are more susceptible to high ones.

Ringing in the ears is fairly common in situations that feature loud noise and is not something to be ignored. One possible solution is to check the setting of the clapper mechanism (ask your director first) and adjust to a softer setting. Use the hard clapper settings only for special situations – large concert halls, performances with brass, etc. Rehearse the music on soft, and change to the brighter setting only during the dress rehearsal and the concert.

Hearing protection devices

DISPOSABLE EARPLUGS

One type of ear protection to reduce sound impact is an over-the-counter disposable earplug that is obtainable from your pharmacy. Available in soft pliable foam or in a wax-covered cotton, most brands claim to reduce the impact of sound on your ears by 20-30 decibels (the level of noise reduction is marked on the package). For many people, these earplugs are not exceptionally comfortable and usually diminish **all** sounds – including the handbells you must hear around you. Nonetheless, they are sometimes a good, inexpensive choice for some people.

CUSTOM HEARING PROTECTORS

Hearing protectors are by far the best choice for musicians who need to hear certain musical cues without reducing all sounds. Originally developed to aid instrumentalists in an orchestra, this special product can be advantageous to handbell ringers. Hearing protectors have a special filter that lets in mild to moderate sounds and general speech patterns but block out the high and loud levels of sound that cause irritation to the ear. The decibel level of any loud, damaging and piercing sounds will be reduced, and you'll still be able to hear the cues from the director and most of the sound from the handbells.

Hearing protector devices must be custom-made by a hearing aid specialist to fit your ear. The one drawback: a pair (including consultation, examination, fitting, etc.) can cost over $150. This may, however, be the best possible solution to a chronic problem.

If ear irritation regularly occurs, you should consult a physician or an audiologist – professionals who can best diagnose the problem and offer suggestions. It may be a combination of things unrelated to handbell ringing – an ear or sinus infection, a cold, wax in the ears, etc. If no medical problem can be diagnosed, a hearing care provider can steer you in the right direction toward protecting your hearing.

SECTION TWENTY-TWO

EYES

General Eye Care

The issue of eye care is important to consider as you ring handbells or handchimes. A good vision environment is a major factor in the overall success of any bell player.

Imagine the handbell ringer who is asked to read music at an awkward angle at a distance of two feet away while having to watch the director ten feet away for proper cues. This handbell ringer may have grand enthusiasm, may have an extensive music background, and may know how to ring with exceptional finesse and ability – but if vision is impaired, optimum performance is reduced and frustration will appear. Modern eyecare technology gives many options that makes it easier to read and perform.

Ringers, especially as they age into their forties, may require special eyewear that improves the *intermediate range* (also called *mid-range*) necessary in reading handbell music. Standard eyeglasses for distance or close-up reading may not correct this intermediate range! Each person makes his or her choice on what type of eyewear to use, based on the doctor's examination as well as desired comfort and lifestyle. Here are several options, both in eyeglasses and contact lenses:

Eyeglasses
BIFOCALS AND BLENDED BIFOCALS

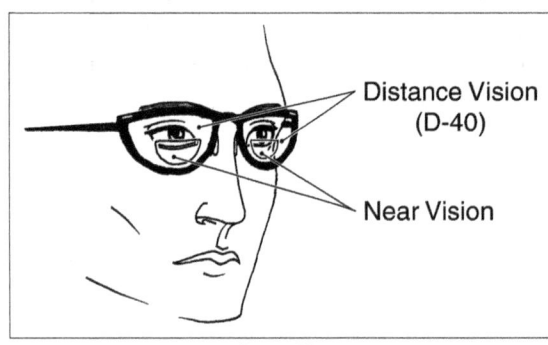

figure 22a

A special pair of glasses can be made with two prescriptions combined for intermediate range and for long distance (see *figure 22a*). With proper fit, you should not have to lift your head to change focus from distance to mid-range, since your glasses will force your eyes to adjust automatically.

Ask your eyecare provider for the lower area of the lenses to be prescribed for mid-range reading with a D-35 or D-40 segment. This wider lens opens your field of vision, which is helpful when trying to look at your director, read a handbell score, and pick up an assortment of handbells all at the same time.

Selecting standard or blended bifocals is a choice for every individual, as is the adjustment period the glasses will require. You will then need an additional pair of glasses for up close reading or short-range work when necessary. There may be a period of adjustment.

TRIFOCALS AND PROGRESSIVE LENSES

Trifocal and progressive lenses cost more than bifocals but may be a convenient way to cover all three necessary distances – to read music, to see your director, and to view the audience as well. The big advantage of trifocals is that you won't have to switch glasses to accomplish different tasks. There may also be a period of adjustment.

"HALF-EYES"

Half glasses (in the style of reading glasses) also work wonders and can be customized for mid-range reading. They are lighter than full-size glasses and take up less space in a pocket or purse.

Contact lenses

For successful contact lens wearers, switching to glasses is not an option! With the introduction of bifocal contact lenses, ringers now have a choice when making close and mid-range vision changes. When mid-range reading becomes a factor, special contact lenses must be worn; proper fitting by a qualified doctor is important, so stay away from mail-order companies that cannot offer this service.

GLASSES OVER CONTACTS

If you already wear contacts and do not want to give up the convenience, wear a pair of glasses *in addition* to your contact lenses. Your eyecare professional can prescribe mid-range lenses (or any other range) for handbell or computer use.

Distance range is normally not affected; the upper portion of eyeglass lenses can be made with no prescription so the contact lenses underneath will do the work. The necessary mid-range adjustment will be made on the bottom portion of each lens.

MONOVISION LENSES

Which is your dominant eye? With one hand, make an "OK" sign with your index finger and thumb. Select any object at a distance from you, and look at it through this circle. Close your left eye, then close your right. Whichever eye positions the object inside your finger and thumb is your dominant eye.

Monovision offers contact wearers a satisfactory way to utilize all ranges of vision. Each eye is fitted with its own lens: your dominant eye is treated for distance and your non-dominant eye is treated for mid-range. Together, both eyes function as a team and provide satisfactory vision without the use of prescription glasses.

Monovision contact lenses may take a period of adjustment with feelings of imbalance, lack of focus, or increased eye fatigue. These symptoms are usually temporary, and a trial and error period is the only way to find out if you are able to wear different strength contacts.

NOTE: Occasionally a monovision patient will need to wear a separate pair of reading glasses over contacts for extended close-range tasks. Some contact wearers will also "throw in the towel" and switch over to regular contacts. With the wide array of choices

available from several manufacturers, a ringer can usually find the correct fit. A good eye care provider will experiment until you are happy with your choice.

BIFOCAL CONTACT LENSES (figure 22b)
With bifocal contacts, a series of concentric rings offer two ranges of vision – far away distances centered in each lens and a close-up/middle range located around the perimeter. As you open and shut your eyes,

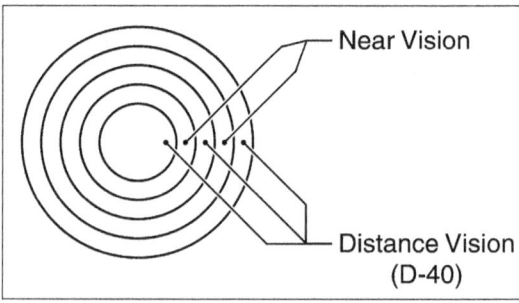
figure 22b

the lens rotates easily in the eye, creating an immediate vision adjustment. Many handbell ringers are choosing this option. If interested, discuss this with your eyecare provider.

CONCLUSION
Only you can make the final decision on which contact lenses are comfortable! Each person's comfort zone and vision needs are different – there is no steadfast rule. Your ophthalmologist or optometrist will listen to your needs, test your eyes, and find a solution to enable you to see in the special ways a ringer must!

Visual Aids
We can't always pick the optimum conditions for ringing handbells. Rehearsals are often held in the evening in a sanctuary with poor lighting conditions. Any high ceiling with widely spaced lighting can increase vision impairment; rehearsing during the evening without natural lighting can also be a factor. The following suggestions will improve visibility and avoid eyestrain:

USE A SIGHT RISER
A necessary piece of equipment for almost any handbell ensemble, a sight riser gives a better view of the director while reading music. This riser also reduces neck and shoulder strain. For anyone wearing bifocals or trifocals, a sight riser is a must!

USE A FLOOR STAND
A standard band/orchestral floor music stand will give a bass ringer a better sight line when lifting a bass bell, reading the music and watching the director simultaneously. Adjusting the height and reading angle of the stand is a bonus and will help reduce eyestrain when reading music at mid-range.

A floor metal stand will also help the neck and shoulders maintain proper body alignment and reduce potential strain when lifting a heavy bell.

USE A TABLE LIGHT

Ceiling lights, especially in older facilities, may not give ideal light! Lighting in sanctuaries and classrooms often provides no direct light – and may cause dark spots and shadows on the music.

Direct light source from a table stand is the best solution; there are several electrically powered brands available. Some of these require a fluorescent bulb; others use a halogen or incandescent bulb. Find one that gives optimum direct light for your ringing situation; one with an adjustable neck can also be advantageous. Avoid the inexpensive, battery-powered lights (e.g. a little book light), since they are too dim to help you read the music effectively. Although excellent for use with a metal floor music stand, avoid heavy metal clip-on music lights if you read music from a tabletop stand – the extra weight will cause your music stand to tip over!

Visual support

COLOR-CODING

A system of color-coding is often used with beginning ringers, where individual notes within a position are highlighted with different colors corresponding with different hands, helping the ringer quickly discern specific notes they must play. Highlighting is an effective system for teaching the basics of handbell ringing, and can be phased out after a few weeks of playing when a ringer has progressed. Color-coding works most effectively when used on a consistent basis, with two contrasting colors (one for notes played with the left hand, and one for the right).

Color-coding is often necessary for older and younger ringers alike and can become an important tool to help clarify notes – especially for a person who reads music fluently but has lost a percentage of his or her sight! This becomes more apparent for elderly ringers – color-coding provides a visual aid that allows them to see the upcoming note clearly and to anticipate the ring. Accuracy will improve dramatically with this simple procedure!

ENLARGING MUSIC

Increasing the size of the music by 20-25% will enable a ringer with a visual impairment to see the music with less strain to the eyes. This suggestion is even more beneficial in rooms where there is little natural light.

However, strict copyright laws must be observed. For your protection, the publisher must be contacted for permission to enlarge, and the original page should be placed in the folder near the copied music as proof of purchase.

SECTION TWENTY-THREE

VOICE

For the director

Voice problems occur with handbell directors who must clearly project instructions to the ensemble when rehearsing, exceeding the normal comfort range of the voice. Handbells are acoustically bright, musical instruments (especially in the upper octaves) and can easily overpower this comfort range. Raising your voice in large open areas – a classroom, a sanctuary, or a performance hall – can also cause vocal strain. Any director may experience hoarseness, a slight tickle in the throat, a loss of vocal range, or neck and throat discomfort; when these signs occur, don't ignore them!

Vocal Concerns

VOCAL PRODUCTION

- Start with a few gentle vocal warm-ups before rehearsal, such as humming or ascending and descending scale vocalises.
- Start with gentle announcements to your choir, speaking softly before actually ringing the bells or chimes.
- Work on projecting your voice. Focus your speaking voice toward the front of your head, not the back. A few voice lessons with a professional singer, lecturer or speech therapist may put you quickly on the right track.
- Speak clearly and always in a comfortable range. Avoid shouting; use amplification if at all possible.
- Do not talk for extended periods of time when the bells or chimes are ringing.
- Avoid yelling at your ringers! Instead, learn to speak slowly and calmly. This will help not only your voice but your group's nerves as well. If you need to stop the rehearsal, use a nonverbal cue by clapping or tapping your music stand. Perhaps create a special signal (for example, a hand held in the air) that will cue your ringers to stop and receive further instructions.
- If you feel irritation, suck on a non-menthol throat lozenge. Avoid excessive coughing or clearing your throat.

PHYSICAL FITNESS

- Maintain good posture – keep your head level and straight.
- Maintain good physical shape. Proper exercise extends vocal endurance.
- Maintain good breath support as you speak. When speaking over the sound of ringing bells or chimes, take in a deep breath before beginning.
- Get plenty of rest, especially before a day-long rehearsal, choir tour, or retreat.

Healthy Ringing

VOICE

PROPER HYDRATION
- Drink adequate water. This does not include coffee, tea, or soda, which contain caffeine and carbonation! Drinking plain water is the best remedy of all – it clears the throat, removes phlegm from the *vocal folds* (often called "vocal cords") and reduces any vocal irritation that may occur from dryness.
- Avoid caffeine! Caffeine is a diuretic that can aggravate the condition of acid reflux which is a common cause of vocal fold irritation, inflammation or swelling.
- Drink warm non-caffeinated liquids (e.g. lemon juice and sugar in heated water).

This will soothe your voice.

UNHEALTHY CHOICES
- Don't smoke!
- Avoid alcoholic beverages; alcohol is a diuretic that causes dehydration and aggravates the condition of acid reflux.

Amplification
- If possible, project your voice by wearing a portable microphone. There are those on the market that only require a small boom-box source for the amplification of sound. In a large room such as a sanctuary or auditorium, you may need custodial or office staff to help set up a sound system readily available for your rehearsal needs.

If strain or hoarseness continues, seek medical advice from a professional trained in otolaryngology.

CARE OF YOUR BODY

Healthy Ringing

SECTION TWENTY-FOUR

STRESS MANAGEMENT

Controlling stress

Chill out! Stress is a self-induced problem. If this rehearsal or performance isn't perfect, don't let it affect your composure. Your best tool for fighting stress is breathing deeply. Bell ringers can learn to breathe deeply, focusing their concentration on the job at hand. This is one thing that meditation, yoga and T'ai Chi teach so effectively – relax and breathe slowly, always from the diaphragm, and let the stress melt away.

Feeling stressed?

HERE ARE A FEW STRESS RELIEVERS:

- Breathe deeply a few times and consciously let your shoulder and neck muscles relax. Feel the tenseness flow from your body.
- Relax your facial muscles, especially your jaw and forehead muscles.
- Slow your breathing and concentrate on breathing deeply (see SECTION 3, BREATHING).
- To relieve stress and to calm nerves, exhale through your mouth.
- Exhale slowly and methodically, as if blowing up a balloon.

A NEW SITUATION

If you are a brand new ringer, avoid letting this new situation overpower you. Take it in a bit at a time. If you become overwhelmed and can't keep up with the ringing, realize that everyone started just like you. Don't be intimidated by those around you. A handbell choir is made up of a *team* of ringers – you are all in it together.

PROPER ATTITUDE

- **Stay positive!**
  Empower yourself with a proper attitude.
- **Think cup half-full, not half-empty!**
  Positive thinking and speaking will always reflect in your playing!
- **Have fun as you ring!**
  Laughter is a wonderful stress reliever. Enjoy the company of those around you. *Greet everyone with a smile!*
- **Think positive thoughts!**
  You want to do your best. Worrying may cause you to ring with less confidence and perhaps make more mistakes. The best remedy is to realize that if you make a mistake, let it pass. The note is gone forever – and you can't retrieve it – so move on! This doesn't diminish the need for excellence but rather tries to move you into forward thinking. Worry is counterproductive. If you mess up, grin and forget it!

Healthy Ringing

Prior to performance

- **Watch your caffeine intake!**

If caffeine has a negative effect on your system, avoid it prior to performing. Caffeine may raise your heart rate, and cause jittery nerves. Some people thrive on caffeine (even enjoying the *edge* it gives in a performance), so this is a personal choice. Just be aware that caffeine will change you for better or for worse, and deal with it either way.

- **Drink plenty of water**

Drink before you are thirsty. Dehydration can cause fatigue, which you certainly want to avoid. If possible, drink some fruit or vegetable juice – it will give you a lift.

- **Know your music well**

The three stages in proper preparation are: learning the notes, playing the notes, and then ringing beyond the notes. If you know your music well, most of the physical ringing becomes automatic. Then, if your mind wanders from the music, if you lose your place, if your stand falls off the table, if you turn two pages instead of one, etc., you'll be fine. This will also allow you to focus on the *music* instead of just the notes.

- **Know where you are going**

If you're not ringing at your normal location, have a plan of action for getting where you need to go. Lack of preparation creates anxiety that may transfer into other aspects of your performance.

- **Arrive early**

Arrange your thoughts, position your bells and equipment on the table, create some time for fellowship, and then most importantly, warm-up!

Dealing with pre-performance anxiety

- **Relax**

Take in a few slow, deep breaths. This will slow down your heart rate and reduce anxiety.

- **Spontaneous stretches**

A few gentle stretches at the table will help relieve tension in your body. A neck stretch, a shoulder roll (people tend to feel a lot of stress in their shoulder muscles, and this will help to alleviate this tension), as well as a few arm stretches will help. If possible, stretch areas throughout your entire body. The time spent stretching will be well spent – it will take your mind off the pending performance and loosen those tight muscles.

- **Gentle meditation**

Find a private spot and take in a quiet moment by yourself. Socializing can be a spirited event but can also play havoc on nerves before a worship service or concert. A little bit of inner peace can go a long way.

Spend a few minutes using the relaxation exercise found on the next page. You should try to find a quiet place where you will not be interrupted by noise, musical instruments, telephones, voices, or other distractions.

SECTION TWENTY-FOUR

During performance

For most people, some stress is actually good for a performance. It gives us an *edge* to keep us on our toes. However, uncontrolled stress can reveal your anxiety to the audience, through your body language. You are on stage, so it's often best to internalize your emotions until the final curtain, unless that emotion benefits your musicianship.

Think tall, think relaxed, and show control and command. The adrenaline will flow and you'll finally ease into the ringing. By the second piece you should settle into the performance, stress free.

For those few unfortunate individuals whose adrenaline flows abundantly even when well prepared, there are prescription drugs called *beta-blockers* that counteract the effects of the excessive adrenaline yet do not have any sedative effect. If you are in that category, see a physician familiar with this problem.

Healthy Hint
Muscle Relaxation Exercise

In a seated position, place your hands and arms comfortably on your thighs. Close your eyes. Slowly start to breathe in and out. Every time you exhale, think about letting go of all your troubles. Try to bring a sense of inner peace and serenity into your body.

As you relax, let your breathing slow down and deepen.

Direct your awareness to any tense muscle within your body. Focus your attention on that particular muscle, then gently stretch and then relax it. Move on to the next muscle, working your way up from your toes to all the muscles used in ringing (see SECTION 1, MUSCLES). Flex and hold each position for at least ten seconds, and feel tension leave your body.

If possible, spend a few additional minutes, still with your eyes shut, relaxing and feeling the quietness surround you.

General stretches in cramped quarters

Sometimes your body signals that it's time to take a good ol' stretch. You can feel your adrenaline starting to pump. You feel a bit anxious – ready to move *now*. But unfortunately you can't – you are sitting in worship or performing in a concert!

Rather than starting an internal *scream*, think in terms of acting on, rather than reacting to, your body's signs! You'll relieve a bit of your tension and make the remainder of your situation at least tolerable. These small acts don't take a lot of time and probably will not be noticeable to anyone around you. They are private stretches that focus your energy toward a particular muscle and force it to work for you. It's that simple!

Healthy Ringing

STRESS MANAGEMENT

DO A FEW SIMPLE STATIC STRETCHES THROUGHOUT YOUR ENTIRE BODY:

A few basic stretches are listed below. After a while, revise the list to develop your own customized routine.

REMEMBER: Isolate the muscle you are working to stretch; hold each stretch for at least 10 seconds. Relax following each stretch.

- Press your shoulders back.
- Bend your neck forward and gently stretch your neck.
- Clasp your hands together. Press.
- Place hands on your thighs. Press hands into leg muscles.
- Tighten your abdominals and your quads and firmly press your buttocks into your seat. For added support place hands on your thighs.
- Facing forward, gently rotate your torso (including shoulders) to the right. Hold. Rotate your torso to the left.
- Press your toes into the floor and raise your heels toward the ceiling. Hold. Press your heels firmly into the floor; raise your toes toward the ceiling. Hold. Point your toes to the right, then to the left. Hold.

Remember – a simple stretch feels good!

SECTION TWENTY-FIVE

NUTRITION

Ringing handbells is a physical activity requiring enough energy to last through a rehearsal, a concert, or even longer ringing activities (like a festival). We must be aware of what proper diet can do to give ringers that necessary boost. *Healthy Ringing* recommends:

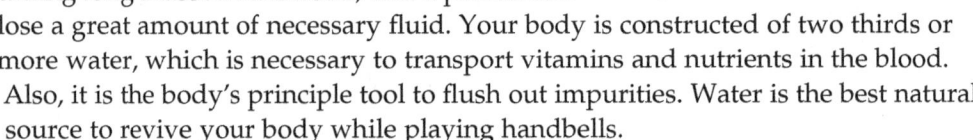

Water – the essential ingredient!

- Body fluids are naturally lost when ringing through sweating and breathing. To this, add the stress of exercise and increased body heat during long massed rehearsals, and a person can lose a great amount of necessary fluid. Your body is constructed of two thirds or more water, which is necessary to transport vitamins and nutrients in the blood. Also, it is the body's principle tool to flush out impurities. Water is the best natural source to revive your body while playing handbells.

- Drink water during active ringing. Many ringers now carry water bottles and drink often, replenishing their bodies during individual rehearsal breaks at festivals and prior to and following concerts. Drink water before you are thirsty! Thirst is the body's reaction to a water deficiency, so by the time you feel thirsty, you are probably already lower on water than you should be (dehydration). A better gauge of your body's water level is your lips; if they feel a little dry, drink some water.

- A tickling in your throat can be helped by various soothing drinks prior to ringing. An example of such a drink combines a mug of boiling water, a tablespoon or so of lemon juice (or juice from half a lemon), and a teaspoon of sugar or honey. You'll have an instant hot lemonade.

- Juices – fresh, natural fruit or vegetable drinks – will give you a refreshing lift prior to a rehearsal, concert, or during a ringing break. For an extra treat, have a frozen fruit bar.

- Reduce your caffeine intake. Tea, coffee, or soda can over-stimulate your nervous system, creating a quick *fix* of energy. When it wears off in the middle of a concert or rehearsal, however, you will find that you really have less energy than before, right when you need it most. Caffeine also acts as a diuretic, creating increased urinary production that unnaturally stimulates the kidneys.

- Avoid alcohol, which is both a diuretic and a depressant – neither of which you need while performing!

NUTRITION

Eating prior to a concert is important!

- Fruits and vegetables are energy boosters that give energy without adding too many calories. Carbohydrates (found in breads and grains, and sugars) give that extra boost of energy that comes in handy during a lengthy concert. Avoid fatty foods or spicy dishes that may cause indigestion.

- Having a quick snack prior to or during a rehearsal break is not only acceptable but should be encouraged. Here is a list of healthy snacks you might incorporate into your day prior to a rehearsal or concert:

Fresh fruit	Chewy dried fruits
Cheese	Pretzels
Popcorn	Raw vegetables
Nuts or seeds	Dry cereal
Graham crackers	Fruit and vegetable juices

Light peanut butter on low-fat rice cakes or crackers

- To take on extra fuel, a high performance energy bar is another excellent choice; it's a quick (and portable) source of energy-related nutrients. In order to be totally effective, an energy bar should be eaten with an 8-oz. glass of water 30-45 minutes prior to ringing. Energy bars are available at most sports shops and food stores that carry snack bars.

Avoid empty calories – sugar-based foods commonly called "junk food" – prior to a performance. These can quickly raise your blood sugar level, but then drop it just as quickly. This condition, known as *hypoglycemia*, can create a feeling of instant tiredness or weakness in your body. These simple carbohydrates include sugar as a primary ingredient, and are found in quick fixes such as candy bars, donuts or cookies.

Please check with your health-care provider if you question the consumption of any foods due to a previous medical condition (e.g. allergies, high blood pressure, migraines, etc.).

SECTION TWENTY-SIX

MOVING HANDBELL CASES AND TABLES

Most instrumentalists have a single case of equipment to transport from place to place, like a violin or trumpet. An exception to this is a percussionist, who must often move a mountain of equipment to and from every concert and rehearsal. With a *handbell* percussionist, this equipment tends to be very bulky and heavy, in the form of several massive cases and portable tables. Moving handbell equipment is a major undertaking!

The task of bending, lifting and carrying this equipment creates a perfect situation for muscle strain. Lifting all of this heavy equipment, sometimes in and out of a vehicle, up on to a table, or carrying it up flights of stairs, can be strenuous. Without proper physical warm-ups, unconditioned people suddenly ask their bodies to do more than they can normally handle, and they often end up hurting themselves.

When band/orchestral musicians have a large instrument to transport (such as a double bass or harp), they tend to move the instrument with the aid of wheels or a dolly. Unless a handbell choir has wheels on their cases or has access to a dolly (which is highly recommended), handbell equipment will need to be lifted and carried by individuals. Therefore, the practice of *Healthy Ringing* must also include the lifting and moving of bell-related equipment!

The Basics of lifting

Your entire body works to effectively lift a case of handbells or handchimes. Obviously, your arm muscles must work hard, but the rest of your body contributes as well. Leg muscles support you (your quadriceps in particular) and are perhaps your most essential lifting muscles. Your shoulder muscles (your deltoids) raise your arms, and your upper back and chest muscles keep everything steady. First, however, you should pay attention to your

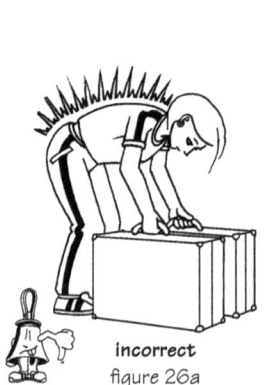
incorrect
figure 26a

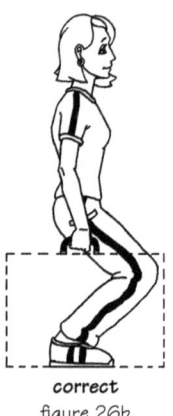
correct
figure 26b

lower back muscles (the erector spinae); they stand to be abused the most from lifting.

This abuse happens when ringers begin lifting handbell cases by bending at the waist, grasping the handles, then standing upright by contracting their lower back muscles. Their legs remain mostly straight and do not absorb much of the stress of lifting, transferring this stress to the smaller (and weaker) lower back muscles (*figure 26a*).

MOVING HANDBELL CASES AND TABLES

The principal rule in lifting any large, heavy object is to lift with your legs. The correct way to lift is to bend your legs at the knees, keeping your back straight and your head right above your body (*figure 26b*); lift by straightening your legs, keeping your back and abdominal muscles contracted as well. Don't twist your torso!

You may have to squat to lift a case and this takes some leg strength. Avoid compensating for lack of muscle strength by bending over! If you have ever lifted a handbell case and felt your back protest (e.g. a sharp pain or tingling sensation), it's probably because you weren't lifting correctly. Many ringers have injured their backs this way – you will not want to be one of them! If you can't comfortably lift a case, don't! Find somebody else to do it for you (like that hefty bass ringer nearby, for example). There's no shame in asking for help!

When lifting handbell cases and tables (as well as other heavy objects), keep these pointers in mind:

BEFORE LIFTING...
- ALWAYS stretch and warm-up before lifting!
- Think about the lift in advance!
- Keep your head straight and look forward, with good posture.
- Look out and not directly down at your feet (unless you are using stairs).
- Keep your shoulders back.
- Imagine a skewer connecting your entire body from head to toe.
- Keep your back straight and head up.
- Plant your feet securely on the floor, your heels aligned directly below your shoulders.
- Stand *directly* next to the case you are lifting. Don't lean to reach the case.
- Place your feet shoulder-width apart, since feet close together create poor leverage.
- Bend your knees, not your waist; let your legs take most of the stress, not your lower back.
- Don't lock your knees or elbows.
- Don't twist your torso!

WHEN YOU LIFT...
- Breathe deeply! Exhale as you exert the energy to lift. *Don't hold your breath.*
- Consciously lift slowly and evenly; avoid a quick, strained motion.
- Use your shoulder and arm muscles as well; keep your shoulder blades back and pressed together. Let your entire body lift as a total unit; avoid depending on any one region (like your lower back muscles).
- Keep your elbows in toward your body.
- If you feel pain anywhere, put the case back down immediately.
- Avoid leaning over sideways as you lift the case. This places too much stress on your opposite side and you could strain your neck or your shoulder muscle.
- Avoid lifting an unbalanced load. Lifting and carrying a handbell case with one hand and a music stand or purse with the other will cause back strain. If possible, balance your load and carry weight that is comfortable.

SECTION TWENTY-SIX

Questions about moving handbell cases

WHEN DO YOU KNOW THE CASE IS TOO HEAVY?
- If you can't lift the case more than an inch off the floor with your arms.
- If you drag a case.
- If you sense a muscle strain, especially near the elbow.

HOW SHOULD I LIFT A CASE UP AND DOWN THE STAIRS?
This is a tricky procedure unless you are strong enough to handle the weight. If you start to lose your balance, let the case go! It's not worth causing an accident – cases and handbells can be replaced, but you can't.
- In order to balance your load, carry two cases at once, if possible.
- If you can't comfortably carry two cases, use the security of the handrail for your unoccupied hand.
- If the case feels too heavy and unstable, slowly move one step at a time and rest before proceeding.

HOW SHOULD I LIFT A CASE TO THE TABLE?
- Avoid torso twisting! If possible, position the case directly in front of you, then lift.
- Keep your head up and eyes forward, not down at the table surface.
- Be careful not to strain elbows and neck when clearing the top of the table.
- Use the buddy system; lift with a partner. This goes for all lifting of cases when possible.
- If no partner is available, lift the case from directly in front of you.
- The best option may be not to lift the case to the tabletop at all; open it on the floor instead.

Alternatives to lifting heavy handbell cases
- Remove handbells from their cases and carry them individually or in manageable bunches to the table, up the stairs, or to your vehicle. With heavy bass bell cases, this is often a necessity, and you can carry the lighter empty cases afterward.
- A two-octave set of handbells is usually carried in two rather tall and heavy cases. Four smaller alternative cases are now available which make lifting a lot easier. For transporting single bass bells, purchase an individual case; or use a padded drawstring pouch, a sports bag, or a small piece of luggage.
- Find someone to assist you.
- Create a custom-designed storage cabinet (see description on page 163).

MOVING HANDBELL CASES AND TABLES

A *Healthy Ringing* STORAGE CABINET

If your organization has funds available and space in the rehearsal room, consider a professionally-made custom cabinet for the handbells, handchimes and all equipment. With a bit of ingenuity and detailed planning, a unit can be crafted that will be functional and save labor.

A possible design is a bureau-type cabinet, with shelves and drawers that pull out for easy access. The following type of cabinet allows a group to remove handbells and handchimes easily and efficiently without lifting a single case:

Full-length cabinet doors are constructed on the outside of the unit to hide the inside shelves and drawers. On the inside, each case has its own pull-out shelf. More standard slide-out drawers are used for storing smaller items, such as gloves, mallets, and music binders. When ringing handbells, pull out a shelf, open the case, and remove the bell – the case never needs to be removed from this storage unit except for a group outing.

In advance of contacting the cabinet company, measure each case and every piece of bulky equipment (tables, pads, music stands) to be included in the cabinet. Make a guess of the extra space needed for future equipment as well, and be generous with your measurements.

Suggestions:

- Upper section: to avoid the need to lift heavy items, store the lightweight objects (such as table padding, covers, and gloves) at the top, and keep a safe footstool nearby.
- Bottom and center section: store bell and chime cases.

> **Healthy Hint**
> The maximum lifting load (in general) for women is 30 pounds and for men is 50 pounds. If the weight of a case (or two) exceeds either amount, consider getting a "buddy" to assist you, or move this ringing equipment with the aid of a cart or dolly.

- For easy access: each pull-out shelf storing bell or chime cases should be constructed without sides and without a significant front lip. This becomes especially important when cases are often removed for outside concerts and festivals.
- Drawers: must be able to withstand the weight of all cases, easily slide out from the back of the cabinet with strong safety catches, and allow enough room to open each case fully for easy bell or chime removal.
- Full-length doors: must open easily and allow maximum room to remove all equipment from the building. A lock on each outside door is essential. If space is an issue, construct the external doors to easily open and wrap around the unit, similar to the accordion cover on an antique desk or pipe organ.
- Prior to building this unit, contact the company and meet with the builder. Show all the equipment, tell about your program, open a case or two, and remove a few of the bass bells. This will be a unique cabinet, and the builder needs to understand its use before the project can begin. Furnish some simple sketches of ideas you and other members may have, and review the plans on paper prior to construction. Remember, to avoid confusion, get a written contract!

SECTION TWENTY-SEVEN

GLOVES

The type of gloves used when ringing can affect your overall playing. Depending on the weight and size of the casting – and the width of the bell's handle – gloves can either help or hinder your ability to ring and damp effectively.

Thirty years ago, many handbell choirs preferred nylon gloves over cotton gloves because they stretched, fit the contour of almost anyone's hand, and washed easily. Nylon gloves were therefore considered the "performance glove of choice". However, following the development of new techniques that required quick changes and also facing increased technical difficulty of the music, the general handbell world discovered nylon gloves were slippery in use and warm to wear (especially in humid climates).

Cotton gloves then became the standard. A cotton glove absorbs moisture, especially appreciated in warm, humid climates or by a ringer who is nervous in performance. There are currently several styles being used:

- "one size fits all" glove
- plain cotton performance gloves
- cotton gloves with plastic grip dots on the palms
- gloves with Velcro® wrist straps (and even reinforced fingers)
- gloves with padding on contact areas, such as the palm
- sports gloves, such as weight-lifting, or bicycle gloves

WHAT GLOVE IS BEST FOR YOU?

You must wear a glove that works between you and the handbells you ring. Try on several types, and make your selection based on what gives you the best overall performance. A glove must have a comfortable fit, provide a secure grip, allow ease of movement from one bell to another, and not cause any stress or strain. Some ringers like to rotate glove styles to avoid the wear and rubbing on the hand from any one style. Only you can be the judge of your hand comfort.

Below is a list of choices used by handbell ringers, from least to most expensive:

- **"One size fits all" gloves**

    Advantage: Cheap

    Disadvantage: Because there is no reinforced stitching on the back of the hand, there's no curved shape to the glove; therefore, it doesn't adhere to the contour of the hand. This may cause the glove to slip during ringing and perhaps be pulled off when bell changes are made.

- **Standard cotton performance gloves**

    Advantage: Makes handbell switching easier, especially in the upper bells. Removing the secondary handbell is an easy transition.

    Disadvantage: Bass ringers feel a lack of security when picking up the heavier bells. Because there is no grip, page turning is often difficult.

Healthy Ringing

- **Cotton performance gloves with plastic dots on the palms**

    Advantage: Page turning is easier than with standard cotton gloves. The layer of plastic dots on the palm of the hand gives added grip security and traction. These gloves seem to hold shape better than standard cotton gloves. Bass bell table damping is more secure.

    Disadvantage: New gloves will stick to bell handles, thus making passing, switching or table releasing more awkward. TIP: Wash gloves several times before use.

- **Grip gloves with a Velcro® wrist strap added (and perhaps reinforced fingers)** (commonly used by flag carriers in drum corps)

    Advantage: The additional padding along the fingers and thumb helps avoid rubbing between the hand and the bell's parts. The Velcro® wrist strap keeps the glove from pulling off when switching from bell to bell.

    Disadvantage: May give a false sense of wrist support. Some brands include a thicker reinforced area around thumb and palm; this added friction may make quick changes from a normal grip to a mallet grip awkward. Also, warmer to wear than other types.

- **Bicycle gloves**

    Advantage: Available at any sport or bicycle shop, bicycle gloves are available from several manufacturers. The construction is generally a crocheted nylon or a stretch Lycra® with leather palm. The Lycra® tends to be cooler.

    Great for page turns! The fingers are open (cut off at the first knuckle), which gives plenty of room for flexibility when gripping handbells; normally bicycle gloves have elastic or Velcro® wrist straps.

    A real advantage to bicycle gloves is the soft padding on the palm (available in gel or foam). Look for the gel – it has a more natural feel. It also tends to hold its shape better than the foam.

    Disadvantage: It's difficult to find black bicycle gloves, so they may not blend well with a formal outfit. Cost is also a disadvantage – at $20-25, a ringer must make certain that this type of ringing glove will be useful and beneficial.

- **Weightlifting gloves**

Many brands are available – some are leather, and some are made from neoprene with leather trim and nylon mesh.

Leather weightlifting gloves are normally worn by men and women who lift or push heavy iron or lead barbells. This type of glove, with extra padding on the palm and with additional material around the wrist, is used in the controlled environment of weight-lifting. The bars with the added weights on each end are heavy and often have rough ridges embedded in the metal where the lifter's hands are positioned. Weightlifting gloves, with the extra padding on the palm of the hand, help prevent the athlete from

> **Healthy Hints**
> - For added protection, try wearing a double set of gloves – plain on the inside and plastic dot on the outside. The double set helps prevent potential blisters caused by rubbing during extended ringing in long rehearsals, festivals or recording sessions.
> - To avoid stiffness or binding, break in your gloves before wear.
> - Prewashing plastic dot gloves will help reduce them from sticking to the handles.

developing calluses and blisters on the palm of the hand. Weightlifting gloves are normally open from the second joint of the thumb and all fingers. The open tips of the fingers are necessary in order to execute a secure and safe grip.

Advantages: Open fingered gloves makes page turning easier; the added leather creates a more secure grip.

Disadvantages: May actually hinder the movement of the hand and fingers needed for ringing multiple bells. The handle may stick to palm of your hand, and they do not breathe like cotton gloves. The extra padding may hinder the direct contact with the handle, thus reducing hand and finger flexibility. The tightness of the leather and the extra finger padding around the second joints will constrict the ease of finger movement, so necessary in handbell ringing. When gripping the handle of a bell, the fingers may not bend and wrap correctly, thus causing muscle strain and a potential slip of the grip.

Some brands of weightlifting gloves may have added reinforcement with Velcro® that can be wrapped several times around the wrist. Added to the underlying strength of the weightlifter's arm and body, this glove reinforcement will *not* give extra support for the hand and wrist. As a preventive measure only, its advantage is to help keep the hand and wrist from over-extending; an athlete can feel when the hand is starting to over-extend.

However, it will be *false security* if a handbell ringer purchases a weightlifting glove with this wrist reinforcement and believes it will help strengthen and secure the grip. Only with initial muscle strength will the gloves be useful.

Avoid any weightlifting-type glove that contains reinforced metal pieces at the wrists. Lack of hand and arm flexibility could cause injury while ringing. Again, **Healthy Ringing** is the key! One must first strengthen the body prior to ringing.

Basic care

The simplest recommendation is that you wear the same type of glove at all times. Although differences from glove to glove may seem slight, switching from one style to another may have an effect on your overall performance. It's also recommended that you purchase your own pair of gloves. Having a bag of *community* gloves at your rehearsal is not the best solution for several reasons:

- At times a ringer may sneeze or cough into a glove. Individually-owned gloves will avoid the transfer of cold or virus germs from ringer to ringer.
- Proper hygiene is needed because hands sweat! Gloves feel clammy when previously worn by someone else (e.g. in back-to-back rehearsals).
- Responsibility is important in a handbell choir. Even children and teens can learn to take care of their own gloves.
- Gloves stretch somewhat to the shape of your hand. Overuse by many persons will create floppy gloves that will be difficult to wear.
- Time is wasted when selecting gloves from the community bag or box. Gloves get turned inside out and mismatched.

Gloves also wear out easily or get lost, so buy a second pair for backup. New cotton rubber dot gloves tend to be sticky during initial use – they may take a few washings to break them in.

WEARING NO GLOVES AT ALL

Advantages:
- The handbell (or handchime) and its motion can be felt more directly. There's a connection between body and instrument that is hard to duplicate when gloves are worn.
- Basic grips are more easily controlled.
- Bell changes can be more exact.
- Solo ringing may be easier.
- Gripping handchimes is more secure.

Disadvantages:
- Thumb damping leaves oil residue on the bell that must be removed following the rehearsal or performance.
- Chafing and blistering can occur from the direct contact of the handle rubbing against your thumb, palm and fingers.
- Perspiration can cause the bell to slip from your hand. This is of special concern to a bass ringer.

SECTION TWENTY-EIGHT

SUPPORT DEVICES

In the handbell community, support bands and braces have become increasingly popular for avoiding handbell-related injuries. Alarmingly, this trend often accompanies a lack of other forms of prevention: a handbell ringer with a brace usually substitutes it for a program of exercise and resistance training, relying on the brace for complete support. On the other hand, since a brace does lend extra support, why should it not be used, in the right conditions? Read this section to make your own educated decision!

Muscle overuse

Overworking muscles until damage occurs often takes the form of a mildly pulled or strained muscle. Minor injuries like these will usually self-heal with a day or so of rest, but as we get older it takes more like 2-5 days of rest. What happens when this occurs during a festival or right at the beginning of an important rehearsal? Such a situation may prompt a handbell ringer to "wrap up"; a muscle begins to hurt, and the ringer merely throws a brace around it. Then he/she continues to ring, expecting the brace to fix the problem.

This is a common misconception. It's not that your muscle doesn't have enough support; you are simply working your body beyond its current capability! A brace does not provide extra power (it won't make that bell any easier to lift) if your muscles aren't developed sufficiently. A brace may provide enough support to allow you to ignore a strained muscle, but you are *still using the muscle*. Your body is telling you to stop and to rest! If you do not rest a strained muscle, you risk a more serious injury, resulting perhaps in swelling, pain, and inflammation to the muscles and other soft tissues (tendons, ligaments). Then you'll be *forced* to rest and not ring at all.

When a strain or direct injury does occur that doesn't subside in a day or two, consult your physician, and temporarily *stop ringing handbells* until you address the problem causing the pain. This isn't a situation that you should take into your own hands and certainly not by merely applying a brace.

Support bands or braces

Support bands or braces often function like crutches, creating a false sense of security. It may seem more secure when ringing, but you may be damaging yourself by using one. There's a tendency to over-exert vital arm joints while they are artificially supported – ringers with incorrect ringing position or form can continue to hurt themselves. Some bands or braces inhibit flexibility in the joints and may cut off vital circulation if tightly or improperly applied.

Healthy Ringing

SUPPORT DEVICES

Unless you strengthen the hand and arm muscles that provide support for your wrist and elbow, strain is still highly likely! A wrist or elbow band may temporarily eliminate the hurt, but it doesn't solve the problem. When wearing a wrist or elbow brace, the wrist or elbow continues to absorb the strains of ringing. When you least suspect it (picking up a grocery bag, twisting your hand to open your car door, or throwing a rubber ball to your child, for example), a disabling joint problem may occur.

Occasionally directors buy wrist supports for their *entire choir*. These choirs don wrist braces just like handbell gloves without regard to the individual needs of the ringers and without any sort of muscle pre-conditioning. There is no worse method of injury prevention! Wrist-guards are often advertised as necessary products to help maintain normal hand motion during activity, and to give needed support to all bell ringers. Handbell articles frequently mention wrist guards as a means of applying "pressure" around the forearm for added support, but there is no evidence that simple pressure provides support or aids in injury prevention.

> **Healthy Hint**
> Always consult with your health-care professional. Think carefully before purchasing a wrist or elbow support, and don't rely on bands or braces continuously! If your physician recommends using a brace, then he or she will discuss its proper use regarding your particular case.

Weightlifters and bodybuilders may wear certain apparatuses to support their *already developed* muscular body. These athletes have developed their physiques over many years; even for them, a brace on the waist or arm only gives a warning of potential muscle strain. These devices help athletes know when they're pushing their bodies beyond current ability and long experience has taught them to recognize early warnings.

In addition, a weightlifter is constantly considering how far his body can go and studying body signs. A bell ringer, on the other hand, is more intent on listening to the music than to the body. Certainly a handbell ringer doesn't focus directly on every muscle movement, as a body builder would. Weightlifting is a controlled sport of focus, determination and concentration. In comparison, handbell ringing consists of quick body movements and often jerky arm motions as bells are moved around over the table. Between the two sports of bodybuilding and handbell ringing, little is similar except that heavy objects are being lifted and lowered; perhaps handbell ringers have something to learn from bodybuilders.

Wrapping up is not the cure or solution for ***Healthy Ringing***! Act to improve your fitness, posture, position and style – none of which necessarily improves with the use of "support" braces.

SECTION TWENTY-EIGHT

IF YOU DECIDE TO USE EITHER A WRISTBAND OR ELBOW BRACE

- Talk to a physician, a physical therapist, or another trained professional before purchasing any support band.
- A brace must fit correctly. It should not be so tight that it cuts off your circulation, or limits your normal range of motion. It must give you a constant friendly reminder not to over-bend a joint.
- Use the least amount of support necessary. A soft elastic band with a Velcro® edge to secure the fit is all that's necessary. *No bell ringer should wear a rigid arm support*, made with a hard plastic or metal insert.
- Avoid depending on this support. It can become a crutch. Instead, you need to condition and strengthen your muscles.
- After healing from an injury, "wean yourself" from any support braces and start to use your own muscle strength. Take the time to heal!

WAIST BRACES

Lower back strain is often a concern to bass bell ringers. If a muscle is incorrectly used, the body reacts to protect the area surrounding the muscle by creating a *muscle spasm*, or tightness surrounding the injured area. If a ringer is in good physical shape and has exercised properly, the body usually returns back to normal in just a few days with rest, application of heat or cold, and (if prescribed) an anti-inflammatory drug.

> **Healthy Hint**
>
> If you are serious about protecting your back and wish to know more about preventing an injury, contact a local health club with trained sport physiologists or a clinic with trained physical therapists. You can schedule an appointment to have your body assessed. Ask them to help you create an individual workout schedule for strengthening your back muscles (and the rest of your body as well).

However, to avoid a muscle spasm or even a more serious injury, handbell ringers will often purchase a waist support belt, commonly called a *waist brace*. Interviews with several weightlifters and personal trainers reveal that the main reason for wearing a waist brace is mental.

A tightly wrapped band around the waist reminds the brain: "be careful and lift correctly." The brace helps caution the athlete from overstraining when lifting heavy weights. Although a waist brace does give a minimal amount of support as the weight is lifted or pulled, it doesn't compensate for the individual's underlying body strength. An athlete who chooses to use a sport brace tends to *already* be in shape. It's a personal preference, not one based on popular demand!

Healthy Ringing

SECTION TWENTY-NINE

MEDICAL CONCERNS

This section has been written following the advice given by the medical advisors to *Healthy Ringing®* to help the handbell community with a growing concern about hand and arm strain. Not all healthy issues have been covered; only the "basics" are included.

If you believe you have any of the following general symptoms, contact your health-care provider for more detailed information, proper diagnosis, and possible treatment.

Common problems

Repetitive Strain Injury (RSI)

Repetitive strain injury is a general term used to describe several disorders caused by overuse of the hand or arm, generally attributed to poor work habits on the job or at home. *Healthy Ringing* is not a medical publication with detailed information on the subject of RSI, but the following brief explanation of a few general symptoms might be useful:

TENDINITIS

Injuries to the tendons are usually the result of overuse during daily activities, in sports, or even when ringing handbells. Often caused by over-exertion when a strong or repeated movement occurs, a tendon may become inflamed and causes discomfort, even pain. Irritation to the flexor and extensor tendons of the forearm is a common symptom. Apply ice, elevate, rest, and if necessary, visit your doctor for medical attention.

Tendinitis can creep up on you if you are not careful, so avoid bad habits early on. A ringer who lifts and rings a bass bell without adequate preparation in warm-ups, breathing, and proper lifting technique may create the perfect situation for increased irritation to the tendons near the elbow – tennis elbow (*lateral epicondylitis*) or golfer's elbow (*medial epicondylitis*). If the handbell is too heavy or the grip is too tight, the tendon in the shoulder (biceps tendon) could also be affected.

A strong, forceful martellato without correctly positioning the bell prior to hitting the table padding may also cause strain to the muscles. Remember to use the muscles throughout the upper body, and avoid *snapping* the wrist.

If any sharp pain causes you to say "ouch," and comes from a localized area near the elbow or shoulder, cease ringing immediately. Rest, and if the problem continues, seek medical advice.

Ulnar nerve

The *ulnar nerve* in your arm may develop a problem from the continued flexing and extending of your elbow that is necessary in ringing.

Called *cubital tunnel syndrome*, the symptoms include numbness and tingling in the little finger side of the hand and the ring and small fingers. There may also be associated medial elbow pain, and the sensation is often described as hitting your "funny bone". With continued soreness, ache, or discomfort, seek medical advice.

Healthy Ringing

SECTION TWENTY-EIGHT

deQUERVAIN'S DISEASE

deQuervain's Disease (also called *deQuervain's tenosynovitis*) is caused by overuse of the hand and predominately affects the thumb and wrist area nearest the thumb – the tendon moves with great difficulty, causing acute pain. Activities that involve motions such as twisting or wringing out a washcloth, strong gripping, or abrupt, jerky movements cause this painful RSI to recur.

For handbell ringers, deQuervain's disease can be caused by a continuous incorrect flick of the wrist while ringing a handbell. A solo or a multiple bell ringer who excessively rings one or two bells in one hand without warming-up, taking a break, stretching, or developing finger strength and hand strength is a potential candidate for this trouble.

A non-steroidal anti-inflammatory medication is often recommended to reduce inflammation. The treatment may include rest with a thumb splint, a gentle massage to the thumb and wrist, ice massage or ice packs (or mild heat or contrast baths), injections, or (as a last resort) surgery. Sometimes an alternative remedy (medically called *iontophoresis*) is the use of electrical current that drives medication into the painful tissues.

Strong medical advice is necessary to those active handbell ringers that have been diagnosed with deQuervain's tenosynovitis: **no matter how much you love to play handbells – don't ring! Rest is essential!**

CARPAL TUNNEL SYNDROME (CTS)

The accelerated use of computers in the home and office has caused an increased number of individuals to acquire a painful (and often chronic) hand and wrist condition known as *carpal tunnel syndrome*. This condition is also caused by constant repetitive handiwork (cross-stitching, needlepoint, woodworking, typing, painting, etc.). The principle warning sign is a numb

> ### Healthy Hints
> - Always precondition your body before any intensive ringing.
> - Warm up prior to **every** rehearsal and concert. Cool down your muscles afterward.
> - Don't lift a handbell that you're not able to support and control.
> - Take mini-stretches during every rehearsal. Avoid any tension in your ringing.
> - If an injury occurs, **stop ringing** and seek medical attention immediately.

sensation along the thumb, index, middle and ring fingers, and perhaps into the forearm. Sometimes, in more serious conditions, circulation is effected and basic movements, such as picking up a pencil, are difficult to accomplish. If any of these symptoms occur on a regular basis it would be a very good idea to contact a physician.

Many handbell ringers attribute their carpal tunnel syndrome to handbell playing. Unless a ringer does hours of repetitive practice without taking a stretch break, more than likely the symptom is related to another activity. If someone already has sore hands or inflammation in the joints caused by a work or home activity, then playing handbells might add to the already existing problem, but most likely will not be the cause of it.

If you are concerned about carpal tunnel syndrome, check your daily habits for repetitive motion. Keeping a record of the hours spent on the computer or in a handcraft will help. If symptoms aren't alleviated after rest or anti-inflammatory medication, then you may have cause for alarm.

Healthy Ringing

Drug pain relievers

Since *over-the-counter* (OTC) drugs are readily available and most of us use them at least occasionally, the following information has been included in *Healthy Ringing*. It is intended to supplement, not replace the expertise and judgment of your physician. For healthy persons who don't take regular medications, there is very minor risk in taking over-the-counter drugs per direction on the bottle. Otherwise, you should consult your health care provider, especially if considering taking high doses.

The following OTC drugs are available in multiple brand names at most pharmacies, groceries and convenience stores.

NSAID (NON-STEROIDAL ANTI-INFLAMMATORY DRUGS)

All NSAIDs provide the effects of pain relief, lowering fever, decreasing inflammation, and mildly decreasing blood clotting. The amount of each effect varies from one drug to another. These drugs may be purchased over-the-counter in strengths weaker than the prescription size. All NSAIDs share the potential side effects of causing stomach problems, which can often be avoided by not taking the NSAID on an empty stomach.

Ibuprofen

Ibuprofen is probably the most commonly used NSAID for pain associated with inflammation. While the pain relieving effect is present with each dose, the anti-inflammatory effect is attained with repeated, regular doses. When taken up to an hour before a strenuous activity such as a marathon mass ring, a single dose has a definite preventive effect.

Ibuprofen also has analgesic (pain relief) and antipyretic (fever reducing) properties, and is commonly used to treat muscle aches and athletic injuries associated with joint inflammation. Taken before or following a handbell rehearsal, ibuprofen can be an excellent way to alleviate tenderness in muscles especially associated with bass or upper multiple bell ringing.

Although quite effective with repeated, regular doses, care must be taken whenever using this drug. Ibuprofen has side effects, with stomach upset being the most common. Large continued doses of ibuprofen have been documented to cause stomach ulcers and gastro-intestinal bleeding, and should be taken with milk, with food, or with an antacid. Check with your doctor regarding any side effects you may notice.

Aspirin

Other over-the-counter medicines are standard aspirin and acetaminophen. *Aspirin* is the first-discovered of all NSAIDs and is a rather potent anti-inflammatory drug as well as a good pain reliever that will also reduce inflammation.

If you are a *free-bleeder* or are taking blood thinners, do not take aspirin except on specific directions of a physician.

Naprosyn

Naprosyn has many of the properties of ibuprofen, but its effects last a bit longer. For many, it is easier on the stomach than ibuprofen.

Other NSAIDs

There are many other NSAIDs. Most are dispensed only by prescription, but others are sold over the counter in lower strengths. All of these NSAIDs have the same side effects (to a greater or lesser extent) as ibuprofen, from gastric upset to ulcers.

Taking an anti-inflammatory drug is a choice that is yours, and there is a good medical rationale for preventing pain and inflammation. The two cautions apply: always read the label, and always check with your health-care provider if you have other medical problems or take other medications (serious drug interactions can occur).

ACETAMINOPHEN

Acetaminophen is a pain killer and fever reducer that **does not** significantly reduce inflammation. There are very few serious side effects or problems as long as the directions are followed. One exception is that repeated large doses can seriously (even fatally) damage healthy livers.

For additional information and advice, consult with your health-care provider.

Non-drug pain relievers

Icing-down and heating-up

Placing ice onto a sore muscle is the best immediate relief available. It slows blood flow, reducing immediate inflammation. When icing an area with the ice directly on the sore muscle, the ice must be kept moving; if not, then there may be a tendency for frostbite in the area. The ice can be applied until the area is numb. This usually takes about 3 to 5 minutes for areas in the hand and elbow and about 5 to 7 minutes for the shoulder (since shoulder tissue is thicker).

Effective icing options

Avoid frostbite with any of the following applications by placing a thin towel or a thin layer of mineral oil, or both, between the skin and the ice.

- Fill several small 2-oz. bathroom paper cups with water, and store them in your freezer until they are needed. When you have a sore muscle, place the open end of the ice directly on the sore muscle. Hold the cup on your skin for approximately 30 seconds, then take it off and reapply as needed to avoid skin irritation or freezing. As the ice starts to melt, peel the top off the paper cup as necessary.
- Use a frozen package of peas or other vegetables. This is an easy way to cool a sore muscle if you need a cold pack quickly.
- Use an ice pack or ice gel pack, which can be found at any drug store and at many grocery stores. These store easily in a freezer.
- Simply fill a freezer storage bag with crushed ice cubes.

MEDICAL CONCERNS

- Purchase an instant cold compress in advance for a potential emergency. It's convenient and portable for that one-time use (e.g. following a concert, on a tour) when ice is not available.
- Use plastic cling wrap (or an elastic wrapping) to hold an ice pack in place around the sore joint or muscle. Occasionally check the area for potential skin freezing caused by this direct contact.

Effective heating options

Mild heat can be applied for a period of 20-30 minutes when ice is no longer helpful. On following days, alternate ice with heat (see "contrast bath" below). It will help improve recovery time.

- Microwave pack – place dry rice in a cloth-sewn bag: microwave 1-2 minutes.
- Towel warmed in a microwave oven – the towel should be warm to the touch but not uncomfortable to pick up.
- Use a heating pad as a last resort; use it on the lowest setting.

Hot and cold combination

If a cold or hot method is not effective, a *contrast bath* is recommended.

The contrast bath may be used to help decrease pain and minimize the effects of swelling that may be increased with the use of heat alone. The cold immersion part of a contrast bath will help to minimize the possibility of increase swelling that may be produced from heat alone.

The temperature of the hot water should be set at 100–110° Fahrenheit and the cold water should be set at about 55–65° Fahrenheit. A good sequence to use is 10 minutes initially in the hot water followed by 1 minute in the cold water; then the sequence is 4 minutes in the hot water and 1 minute in the cold water. Alternate back and forth until a 20–30 minute treatment has been done.

Hand and wrist bath

Sometimes a contrast bath is effective for hands and wrists. Alternate from hot to cold water, for about 20 to 30 minutes. Follow the sequence above (contrast bath).

Foot bath

For those individuals who may have problems with sore feet, a contrast bath can be helpful. Follow the sequence above (contrast bath).

PART FIVE

The Massed Ring

- The Director
- The Ringer

SECTION THIRTY

The Massed Ring

A massed ring (sometimes called a festival, a conference, or simply a "ring") is a gathering of two or more handbell choirs ringing under one or more directors for at least a full day. These choirs rehearse pre-selected music together, intending to play it in a grand, combined performance at the end of the event. Extended rehearsals, with maximum playing time and minimum attention to ringers' (and directors') bodies, can be quite taxing. Therefore, it's a good idea to keep *Healthy Ringing* issues in mind, to not just make beautiful music but to make the massed ring a more enjoyable and comfortable experience.

THE DIRECTOR

PREPARATION

At home

Similar to any athlete, a massed handbell director must *train* for a festival. If you prepare with a daily exercise routine (like walking combined with gentle stretches) you may have the endurance necessary to direct a whole festival without fatigue. Imagine walking away after directing a festival, without any arm, back, or leg discomfort.

Build up the endurance necessary by daily stretches and strengthening exercises several times a week. Get into the habit of daily exercise: walking, cleaning, climbing stairs, dancing, attending a health club, playing a sport, doing anything to build up your stamina for a festival.

Prepare your upper body for directing

Directing a large massed festival that lasts several days can be a challenge for any director. Even directing a one-day event can be quite taxing if you have not adequately prepared your body for the challenge. You may have all the conducting skills necessary to be a great conductor, but your hands and arms may pay the price if you do not consider the many factors associated with directing *prior* to the initial downbeat. To avoid soreness during and after the ring, you *must* develop a workable plan of action.

If you belong to a health club, use the arm and rowing machines to help develop upper torso and arm strength. Using hand weights will also help create hand muscle strength and grip control so necessary in long periods of conducting. What seems difficult in a workout will have great benefits when you are up on the podium for extended periods of time.

AT THE RING

You must find a quiet place away from the festival site where you can prepare yourself physically, mentally, and emotionally.

Physical

You *must* warm-up your **entire** body prior to stepping onto that podium. The blood needs time to work its way throughout your circulatory system, well before the initial downbeat. Create a short stretching routine that you can easily remember and will use often. (see PART III, EXERCISES FOR RINGING). Start with your upper torso, head, and work your way down to your feet. Spend at least 10-15 minutes preparing your body for the ring.

It's even more important *and necessary* that you focus much of your warm-up on fingers, hands, arms, and shoulders. Start with small muscles of the hand and work into full arm motions. Initially do static stretches and end with full arm and shoulder rotations. To avoid cramping (even before picking up your baton) do a few simple hand grip exercises (see SECTION 15, FINGERS, HAND AND WRIST).

SECTION THIRTY

To prevent fatigue, maintain your own body's proper energy level with proper nutrition. Continually drink water and if possible during a rehearsal break, eat something that will stabilize your energy (e.g. a piece of fruit, a handful of nuts or a high-energy bar (see page 159 for a list of healthy snacks).

Mental
Check to see that your music is in order and supplies (water bottle, baton, pencils, etc.) are ready. Glance over your music one last time and know which piece you'll use for the initial ringing warm-up. Make any last minute revisions to your rehearsal lesson plans.

Emotional
To control pre-festival jitters, inhale and exhale a series of deep, slow breaths to focus your energy. Think of your overall goals and the good performance that you will be supervising. Formulate a pace that you can keep throughout the day without burning out, and stick to it.

If you have a few extra minutes, spend them using the relaxation exercise found on page 156. It can be an effective warm-up for you and can even be an effective tension-reliever (with you as the facilitator) for an entire group of ringers.

Care of your voice
Directing a festival tests the leader's voice. These suggestions should be taken to heart for any massed festival director:

- Drink water! Projecting your voice to a large group will create additional dryness in your throat and around your vocal folds. Drink water before dryness occurs; this will help avoid hoarseness or a ticklish cough. Avoid replenishing your thirst with liquids like soda, tea, or coffee. They're not a good substitute for the real thing! In addition, while conducting you'll lose body fluids from perspiration and rapid breathing. Water will help keep your energy level high, avoiding any drop in stamina from dehydration.

- Under no circumstances should you direct a large gathering of handbell choirs without a microphone! You are asking for vocal problems by the end of the day. Contact the event planner or festival coordinator and send a message that a microphone is a must! Request a lavaliere-type microphone rather than a floor-stand microphone. A floor microphone inhibits your overall movement, and if it is not properly positioned in front of you, neck and shoulder strain may occur as you bend or twist to use it.

- Avoid the feeling of running a *marathon*. Your body – especially your voice – needs a few minutes every hour or so to replenish itself. If necessary, shorten the massed rehearsal by a few minutes so that you are able to take a rest. Your ringers can use the same break time to stretch, relax, and interact.

- If you direct a lot of massed events, seek individual counseling from a professional trained in vocal projection. Universities and hospitals with departments in otolaryngology or speech pathology often have small clinics that offer one-on-one counseling. Another

Healthy Ringing

good source is a college music or theatre department; trained vocal and drama teachers make excellent coaches and can give you invaluable information. There will sometimes

Healthy Hint
Finding periods of voice rest in between more demanding voice intervals can be helpful. A vocal break every forty minutes of continuous vocal use is recommended.

be a fee for such an evaluation (especially for a formal hospital visit), but the result will be well worth the expense. (For additional information, review SECTION 23, VOICE.)

Breathing

Proper breathing is as important to handbell ringing as it is to every other athletic activity, and time must be taken in your rehearsal to ensure that everyone is breathing deeply as a group. Setting aside a brief moment with a slow series of breathing patterns will help solidify all the individuals into a cohesive ensemble.

Following the introduction and/or instructions for the day, have the entire group take a series of slow, sustained breaths. You will immediately have the eye contact and attention of every person in the room, and they will all follow you as you demonstrate this simple breathing pattern. (For additional information, see SECTION 3, BREATHING.)

REHEARSAL WARM-UPS WITH THE RINGERS

It's absolutely necessary that a day-long ring start with at least a ten-minute warm-up prior to ringing. The massed director should coordinate a sequential series of static stretches and breathing exercises with the entire ensemble to ensure that all participants are properly warmed up and ready to ring. A group warm-up is a great way to develop instant rapport with the ringers. You'll also earn the respect of the entire group because they'll appreciate the fact that you treat handbell ringing seriously and want to establish a healthy day of ringing.

I've observed massed handbell events where the initial warm-up consisted of a movement sequence set to music. While this activity is an ice-breaker and raises the ringers' heart-rates, it tends to be more a crowd-pleaser than beneficial to *Healthy Ringing.* Slow, individual static stretches are still the best preparations for ringing.

I've also observed festivals where the director had the ringers face the back of an adjacent person, massaging their neck and shoulders. While this activity is fun and breaks the ice, unless the person applies the massage correctly (gently and attending to the correct muscles), it can cause strain.

The normal warm-up of a ballet class provides a useful example for the massed director. Before starting basic dance steps, the dancers perform exercises in a standard sequence as an entire group. The instructor creates a series of stretches that prepares all the muscles of the dancer's body as a preliminary to each practice or performance.

This preparation is also useful for handbell ringers. Expecting participants to stand and ring in a massed setting for hours usually takes more endurance than they have available. A normal weekly handbell rehearsal lasts for one or two hours, while massed

festivals tend to last three to four times that long. This makes warm-ups even more important and is a responsibility that a massed director must take seriously.

Address the importance of proper posture. Proper posture prevents muscle strain, backaches, and general fatigue.

General stretching

Create a simple stretching routine for the entire group: briefly explain each stretch, do the stretch, take a brief pause, then move on to the next.

- Start stretching the upper muscles first: begin with the neck and shoulders, the arms, and work downward toward the feet. Then stretch the hands and fingers. Have the ringers hold each position in a static position for at least 10 seconds.

- When stretching, explain and simultaneously show a basic shoulder or arm stretch so that everyone can clearly see what you want them to accomplish.

- Caution the ringers not to bounce in any warm-up or stretch, mentioning that it can strain their body. For maximum results, stretches must be slow and controlled. Each person must feel and sense his/her own body waking and warming up for ringing.

- Mention if any ringer feels pain, they should stop immediately. In a festival setting, exercise space will likely be at a premium. Use effective stretches that aren't awkward in limited space. Once you are familiar with basic stretches and are comfortable with teaching them, you'll be able to adapt easily and develop a standard sequence of exercises that you can follow each time.

- Avoid using any stretch that requires bending over and touching the toes. If not done correctly (knees locked, etc.), this will place excess stress on the lower back which can cause strain, especially for a ringer with existing back problems. One ill-considered bending exercise could ruin a participant's entire day!

Other useful warm-ups

- *Conducting:* Demonstrate to the ensemble a basic beat pattern of a 3/4 or 4/4, and have everyone conduct with you. Communicate verbally as well as physically. You may even have to turn around and direct above your head with large gestures. Vary the tempo; add a few ritards. To tie into the actual rehearsal, you might select a meter used in the first massed number. This simple warm-up will help reinforce rhythm and beat to the ringers, work as a dynamite aerobic activity prior to ringing, and teach a skill that can be applied to the day's event. This is a great beginning to a festival! It forces the group to follow you immediately and helps develop instant rapport.

- *A simple run-through:* Pick up handbells and begin one of the easier festival pieces at a slow and gentle tempo. Let the ringer's muscles start to work without strain. The ringers should underplay marts, shakes, ring-touches, etc.

— THE DIRECTOR

SPONTANEOUS GROUP STRETCHES
During each rehearsal
- Include a brief stretch break during each rehearsal (e.g. hands over the heads, circular motions, hand stretches, calf stretches; any simple stretch will do).
- When rehearsing a difficult section in the bass or treble, encourage idle ringers to stretch any muscles that feel overworked. Most minor irritations can be alleviated with a simple stretch.

important!

Following each rehearsal
- Finish with stretches. A simple hand stretch (*Praying, figure 15j* for example), a shoulder roll, or a neck stretch will help loosen muscles before departure. Select stretches as needed. Your instruction and encouragement will affect the ringers long after they have left the ringing site; leave on a positive **Healthy Ringing** note. Do some stretches on your own as well – you'll thank yourself later!

Prior to the final concert
- A group warm-up is essential, but you may be changing clothes or may be offstage waiting to be introduced! In advance, ask one of the directors to be responsible for a set of simple stretches prior to the concert. Three to five minutes will be adequate. It's important for this assistant to create a general stretch sequence focusing on the arm, shoulder and back muscles. This warm-up is of utmost importance – it will focus everyone's physical and mental energies and prepare them for action from the initial downbeat.

important!

BE A GOOD COACH
- It's your responsibility to inform the group if you spot incorrect ringing. You may not be able to jump off the podium and give direct teaching assistance, but you can reinforce good ringing habits, even at a distance. If you see ringing that could cause an injury, mention your concern. However, avoid focusing on one ringer or one group; teach to the entire mass of choirs.
- Expect accuracy in entrances *immediately*, starting on the first downbeat of the first selection! As always, breathing together is the key! If all ringers in the massed choir watch and breathe together on the first downbeat, "splatter chords" will be avoided.

Healthy Ringing

SECTION THIRTY-ONE

THE RINGER

Are massed rings hard on your body? Do you walk away from a ring musically content but physically spent, with your entire body sore? This state of affairs is common among handbell ringers, unless they make a conscious effort to ring the *Healthy Ringing* way. A massed ring is a wonderful way to meet people, immerse yourselves in handbells, and have fun playing great music in a unique setting (often with dramatic results). On the other hand, a massed ring is much more handbell ringing than most handbell ringers are accustomed to doing. Just as a once-a-week runner will have trouble finishing a marathon, a ringer who rehearses once a week will have trouble making it through a massed ringing festival. A festival of this sort is definitely not something to take lightly, especially for bass ringers.

PERSONAL PREPARATION

At home

- You must *train* for a massed ring before the event. Under normal circumstances you ring for one or two hours and usually only once a week. During a festival, however, you may ring way beyond your normal endurance level.
- Maintain a good fitness program! I've mentioned developing strength and endurance in previous chapters. Unless you prepare your body with daily stretches and a walking routine (perhaps even developing a resistance training schedule at a nearby gym or sports facility), you may not have the endurance necessary to make it through a day (or perhaps a several day) ring.

Before the ring

- You must warm-up your entire body before the initial downbeat of the first rehearsal. This is important to avoid muscle strain! The blood needs time to work its way throughout your body, well before the ringing commences. The massed director should take you through basic warm-ups, but if this doesn't happen, you should be prepared to do a few simple stretches and warm-ups on your own.

During the Ring

- Practice gentle stretches throughout the day as well. Hand and upper torso cool-down stretches are a good idea after *every* rehearsal. When a break in the rehearsal occurs (perhaps when the director addresses another section of the room, or provides a break), give your body a rest. If a muscle feels tired or sore, stretch or massage it lightly. Focus on the fatigued muscle; if it seems a little tight, gently stretch and hold it for a few moments, then relax. If done correctly, you should feel a pleasant, soothing sensation. This will only take a couple of minutes and is well worth your time.

- When you are rehearsing and start to feel pain, *stop immediately and rest!* Continued ringing will only aggravate the problem. Even if the rest of the choir is still ringing, have a quick stretch break. If nothing seems to alleviate the pain, stop ringing altogether.

Proper dress and footwear

Comfort is the key! Wear clothes during the day that give you a full range of motion. Layering may be advisable – ringing sites are somewhat unpredictable and may be too warm or cold. The final concert may require more fitted clothing, but even properly fitted tuxedos will allow adequate movement. Since most festival concerts are now less formal (many choirs wear matching t-shirts), you can probably get away with wearing comfortable clothes the entire time.

Avoid shoes without arch supports. Cross-trainers (athletic shoes) are great, and made for endurance and movement. Avoid thin-soled shoes; you'll end up paying for them with sore arches and calf muscles by the end of the day, as standing for several long rehearsals can add strain to your lower back, leg muscles, and feet.

Foot fatigue may be minimized with the following suggestions:

- Wear comfortable shoes that allow foot expansion (not pumps or high heels).
- Keep your knees relaxed.
- Shift your weight from one foot to another. If able, occasionally raise one foot up on a small, low footstool.
- Stand on carpet squares or on an interlocking foam puzzle mat (purchased at an educational supply store or through a pre-school supply catalog).
- Do a static stretch.

SPONTANEOUS STRETCH BREAK

Learn to take brief stretch breaks. Do one simple stretch, or do several. With practice you'll learn to work a muscle that feels fatigued.

Here are a few easy stretches to use (others may be found throughout PART III):

Stretch	figure	see page
SHOULDERS		
• Shoulder roll	13c	111
• Shoulder squeeze	13e	112
• Hug	13f	112
NECK		
• Neck Stretch	13h	113

Healthy Ringing

SECTION THIRTY-ONE

Stretch	figure	see page
ARM		
• Forearm stretch	14d	116
• Upper arm stretch	14e	117
• Praying	14f	117

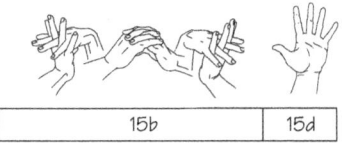

HAND		
• Flexible snake	15b	119
• The fan	15d	119
• Finger play	15f & 15g	120

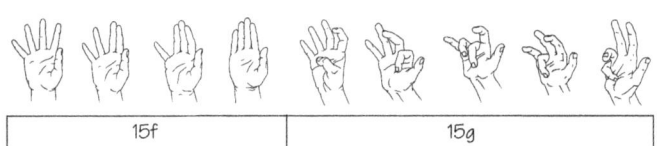

BACK		
• Shoulder raise	16f	127
• Bell hug	16g	127
• Gentle forward bend	16i	128
• Torso twist	16L	129

LEG		
• Tip-toe stretch	18b	135
• Leg raises	18d	136

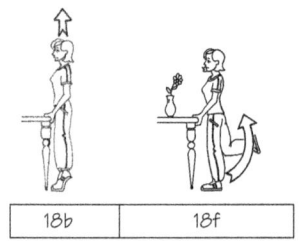

FOOT		
• Tired toes	19b	138
• Tired ankles	19c	139

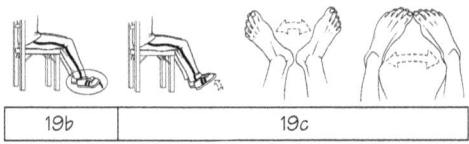

Healthy Ringing

Your sight line
You must be able to see the director easily. Position yourself in a comfortable location that will not cause any back strain (from twisting to see the conductor) or neck strain (from looking up because you are too close to the podium). If you are not able to adjust your ringing location, notify your director or one of the ringing-site coordinators. Your ensemble's tables may need to be moved slightly or placed in a different area of the room altogether.

Band/orchestral floor stands are essential for bass bell ringers. Adjustable in height and music-reading angle, a floor stand gives the bass ringer the extra table room for proper placement of the large bells, and allows the ringer to correctly position the stand in front of table for a better sight line of the massed conductor.

NUTRITION
Drink water! Replenish your fluids throughout the day. Water will refresh you, help keep you from feeling lightheaded, and not allow a drop in energy level due to dehydration. Although there are alternative liquids (pop, coffee, etc), avoid them during rehearsal. Water is still the best source to satisfy your body.

Have healthy snacks on hand. When you start to feel your energy drop, eat a piece of fruit, a handful of nuts, a granola bar, etc. to give you enough stamina until your next meal. Don't forget to eat natural sugar and protein, both important ingredients nutritionally to give you the energy necessary when ringing. (For additional information, see SECTION 25, NUTRITION.)

AVOIDING STRESS
When you start feeling anxious about a section in the music as you near concert time, take a series of deep breaths and try to relax. You want to do your best, but worrying may cause you to ring with less confidence and make more mistakes. The best policy is to tell yourself that if you make a mistake, go on. The note is gone; you can't get it back, so move ahead. This doesn't diminish the need for excellence but rather tries to move you into forward thinking. Worry is counterproductive.

Laughter is a wonderful stress reliever – have *fun* at a festival! Enjoy the fellowship – meet new friends, and smile. If you are attending your first festival, absorb as much as you can, but just take it in a bit at a time. If you become overwhelmed and can't keep up with the ringing, take a moment and catch your breath. Sit down or *air-bell* your part until you've regained your confidence and energy. Remember that everyone, including the massed director, is on your side. Relax and enjoy the day.

SECTION THIRTY-ONE

AFTER THE RING
To avoid unnecessary muscle soreness, you should do a short series of stretches to allow the muscles and ligaments to return to normal. However, it will be difficult to schedule at this time. Everyone will want to leave for break, for lunch, or pack up to return home.

Protect your own investment (your healthy body) and spend just a few minutes doing some gentle stretches. You may be surprised – some of your fellow ringers may even join you!

If muscle soreness still continues following the concert, get some rest, and if able, take an anti-inflammatory drug, such as ibuprofen or aspirin.

DEPARTURE
This is when most injuries from lifting cases occur. You are in a hurry to load equipment into the van and leave before all those other groups get in the way. However, you should slow down and think carefully about how you will pick up that heavy equipment. Moving cases, bending over to put bells away, twisting to move foam off the table and into a vehicle, etc., all contribute to body strain, especially following an active concert when you've spent much of your reserve energy. Remember, slow and steady wins the race! Always plan ahead when moving equipment – a thoughtful plan of action can save you unnecessary discomfort.

Healthy Ringing

RESOURCES

Health and fitness

Alexander Technique Workbook, by Richard Brennan, (Element Publishing Company; ISBN 1-85230-346-8)

Carpal Tunnel Syndrome and Overuse Injuries, by Tammy Crouch and Michael Madden, D.C., (North Atlantic Books; ISBN 1-55643-135-X)

Human Body, an illustrated guide to its structure, function, and disorders, edited by Charles Clayman, MD; (DK Publishing Book; ISBN 1-56458-992-7)

Mayo Clinic, guide to self-care: (Mayo Clinic; ISBN 0-9627865-7-8)

Repetitive Strain Injury, a computer user's guide, by Emil Pascarelli, MD, and Deborah Quilter; (John Wiley & Sons, Inc.; ISBN 0-471-59533-0)

Stretch and Strengthen, by Judy Alter, (Houghton Mifflin Company; ISBN 0-395-36263-6)

Stretching, by Bob Anderson, (Shelter Publication, Inc.; ISBN 0-936070-01-3)

Workout for Dummies, by Tamilee Webb; (IDG Books Worldwide, Inc.; ISBN 0-7645-5124-8)

Handbells and handchimes

Bell Basics, a training videotape, Susan Berry and David Weck, (Hope Publishing Company; HP 1274)

Director's Manual, from the "Learning To Ring" series, Susan Berry and Janet Van Valey, (The Lorenz Publishing Company; HB200)

Handbell Notational Guide, (guideline published by The AGEHR, Inc.; R 100)

Using Handchimes, from the "Learning To Ring" series, Susan Berry and Janet Van Valey, (The Lorenz Publishing Company; HB215)

INDEX

A
Abdominal breathing, 28
Abdominal press, 133
Abdominals, 28
   exercises, 132-133
   muscles, 132
      control with, 32
   stretches, 132-133
Acetaminophen, 174
Achilles tendon, 29-30
Action hand exerciser, 46
Adhesive bandage, 86, 88
"Air-bell" warm-up, 116
Alternative ringing set-ups,
   bass bells, 84
   beginning ringing, 53
Amplification of voice, 153
Anatomy, see Muscles
Ankle spins, 139
Arm
   muscles, 24, 115
   resistance training, 141
   stretches, 116-117
   warm-ups, 115-116
Arm rotation, 111, 115
Aspirin, 173
Assignments, alternative, 54
Attitude, stress and, 154

B
Back
   muscles, 27-28, 125
      sore, damping, 58
      spasm, 170
   relieving strain with abdominal
      muscles, 32
   stretches, 126-129
Back care, 130-131
   bass bells, 85
   with lifting, 160-161
Back strain, 131
   avoiding, 130-131
Banana stroke, 49
Bass bells, 77-86
   allowing weight to control
      the ring, 53
   alternative set-ups, 84
   back care, 85
   body damp, 81-82
   custom-built table, 84
   damping, 56, 81-82
   floor rack, 84-85
   grip, 42, 79
   gyro, 75
   learning to ring with, 53-54
   lifting, 79-81
   lifting and ringing, 78
   LV, 83
   martellato, 69-70, 83
   mart-lift, 83
   matched grip, 44
   plucking, 68
   ready-to-ring position, 48, 80
   rehearsal warm-ups, 78
   ring-hook, 84
   ringing upward, 81
   ring-touch, 72, 83
   shake, 83
   shimmer, 75
   support bands, 86
   table damp, 60, 82
   thumb damp, 82
   toll, 83
   warming up for, 77-78
   weaving, 67, 81
   weight training, 77-78
Bass handchimes
   damping, 101
   grip, 97-98
Bass ringers
   breath support, 78-79
   director's responsibility, 86
   posture, 79
   preventing chafing and blisters,
      85-86
   protecting, 86
   uniqueness of ringers, 77
Beginning to ring, using extended
   octaves, 53-54
Bell hug, 112, 117, 127
Belltrees, 75-76
   stands, 76
Beta-blockers, 156
Biceps, 24
Biceps pull, 143
Bicycle gloves, 165
Bifocals and blended bifocals, 148
Blisters, bass ringers, preventing,
   85-86
Body damping
   bass bells, 81-82
   handchimes, 99-101
   multiple bell techniques, 90-91
Breaking the wrist, 52
Breathing, 34-38, 49
   abdominal, 28
   as a synchronized group,
      34, 37, 183
   awareness, 35-36
   chest, 28
   combined with ringing, 37
   conducting and, 38
   cues for director, 38
   from diaphragm, 34-35
   disruptions, 36
   exercises, 35-37
   for handbell choir, 37
   with martellato, 71
   massed ring director, 181
   preparatory breath, 37-38, 70
Bubble bell, 46

C
Cabinet, storage, 163
Calf muscles, 29
Calf stretches, 135
Carpal tunnel syndrome, 172
Casting
   leading with, 53
   rolling during damping, 57
Chafing, bass bells, preventing,
   85-86
Chest
   muscles, 27
   sore, damping, 58
Chest breathing, 28
Circle of support, 42, 45
Chest breathing, 28

Healthy Ringing

INDEX

Clapper adjustment, 51
    for shaking, 74
Claw, 121
Clothing, massed ring, 185
Color-coding, 151
Combo-ring, 94-95
Conducting
    breathing and, 38
    as a group warm-up, 182
Conference, see Massed ring
Contact lenses, 149-150
Contrast bath, 175
Cool-down, 108
    stretches, 124
Cotton performance gloves, 164
    with plastic dots, 165
Cubital tunnel syndrome, 171
Custom-built table, bass bells, 84

D

Damp, 55-60
    accuracy, 55-56, 59-60
    bass bells, 56, 81-82
    body, bass bells, 81-82
    concerns, 57
    double, 57
    effect of shape and size of bell, 56, 59
    finger, 58
    handchimes, 99-101
    hand position, 55
    multiple bell techniques, 90-91
    shoulder, 55-56
    sore back muscles, 58
    sore chest, 58
    sore elbow, 58
    sore neck, 58
    sore wrist, 57
    table damp, 69, 82
    too far down your body, 57
Deltoid, 27
deQuervain's disease, 172
Developmental stretch, 107
Diaphragm, 28
Diaphragm breathing, 34-35

Director
    breathing cues, 38
    massed ring, 179-183
        breaks, 180
        breathing, 181
        emotional preparation, 180
        mental preparation, 180
        physical preparation, 179
        physical warm-up, 179-180
        rehearsal warm-ups with ringers, 181-183
        voice care, 180-181
        protecting bass ringers, 86
        voice problems, 152
Door pushups, 129
Double damping, 57
Double gloves, 86
Drug pain relievers, 173-174

E

Earplugs, disposable, 146-147
Ears, 146-149
Eating, prior to a performance, 159
Elbow, sore, damping, 58
Elbow brace, 170
Emotional preparation, massed ring director, 180
Enlarging music, 151
Epicondylitis, 44, 171
Erector spinae, 28
Exercises
    abdomen, 132-133
    abdominal press, 133
    "air-bell" warm-up, 116
    ankle spins, 139
    arm, 115-117
    arm rotation, 111, 115
    back, 125-131
    bell hug, 112, 117, 127
    biceps pull, 143
    breathing, 35-37
    claw, 121
    door pushups, 129
    fan, 119
    finger play, 120

    fingers, hand and wrist, 118-124
    finger spread, 120
    flexible snake, 119, 124
    foot, 138-140
    forearm stretch, 116
    full shoulder rotation, 114
    gentle forward bend, 128
    grip strength, 46
    habit of, 104
    healthy hands, 122
    hug, 112
    keyboard press, 119
    lateral raise, 143
    leg, 134-137
    leg lean, 136
    leg raises, 137
    neck stretch, 113
    multiple bell techniques, 87
    oblique stretch, 132
    OK knuckle bend, 121
    pelvic tilt, 133
    praying, 117, 121, 128
    putty play, 119
    putty press, 119
    quadriceps lift, 137
    rag doll bend, 128
    resistance training, 141-144
    shoulder and neck, 110-114
    shoulder pull, 127
    shoulder raise, 127
    shoulder roll, 111, 126
    shoulder shrug, 111
    shoulder squeeze, 112, 126
    shoulder stretch, 113
    sitting leg raises, 136
    staircase stretch, 135
    step to the side, 136
    sunshine stretch, 127
    swaying branch, 127
    table press, 124
    tip-toe stretch, 135
    tired ankles, 139
    tired toes, 138
    torso twists, 129
    upper arm stretch, 117

INDEX

warm-ups, 106-109
for weight shifting, 61
wrist curl, 123, 142
wrist rotation, 123, 143
see also Stretching; Warm-ups
Exhaling, 35-36
Extensors, 26, 30
Extrinsics, 26
Eye care, 148-151
Eyeglasses, 148-149
over contacts, 149

F

Fan, 119
Fatigue
avoiding, 33
breathing and, 36
Festival, see Massed ring
Finger damp, 58
multiple bell techniques, 91
Finger play, 120
Fingers
cool down stretches, 124
muscles, 118
muscle strain, avoiding, 118
stretches, 119-121
Finger spread, 120
Flexible snake, 119, 124
Flexor muscles, 26, 30
Floor rack, bass bells, 84-85
Floor stand, 150
Floor surface, proper, 140
Foot
contrast bath, 175
muscles, 30
protection, 139-140
stretching, 138-139
Footwear, see Shoes
Forearm, muscles, 26
Forearm stretch, 116
Four-in-hand, 93
Free weights, 45
exercises, 142-143
guidelines, 142
Full shoulder rotation, 114

G

Gentle forward bend, 128
Gloves, 164-167
bass bells, 86
care, 166-167
choices, 164-166
double, 165
wearing none, 167
Gluteals, 29
Golfer's elbow, 44, 171
Grip basic, 40-46, 49
adjustment, 43-44
balance, 40
bass bells, 42, 79
belltrees, 76
four-in-hand, 93
handchimes, 97-98
incorrect, 42
martellato, 70
matched, 43-44
multiple bell techniques, 88-89, 91
picking up handbell, 41
proper, 40-42
proper hand fit, 43
shake, 73
shelley, 92
tension, 44-45
thumb damp, 69
thumb placement, 41-42
too tight, 57
Grip aid products, 46
Grip gloves with Velcro wrist strap, 165
Grip strength, 45-46
developing, 45-46, 141
exercises, 46
Gyro, 75

H

Half glasses, 149
Hamstrings, 29
stretching, 136
Hand
contrast bath, 175
cool down stretches, 124
muscles, 26, 118
muscle strain, avoiding, 118
resistance training, 141-143
stretches, 122-124
Handbell
assessing fit of bell in ringer's hand, 43
picking up, 41
placement on table, 40
substitutes, for practicing, 46, 67
Handbell cases
alternatives to lifting, 162-163
carrying up and down stairs, 162
lifting to table, 162
moving, 160-163
too heavy, 162
Handchimes, 97-102
bass
damping, 101
grip, 97-98
damping, 99-101
grip, 97-98
multiple techniques, 102
ready-to-ring position, 98
ringing, 98-99
special techniques, 102
table damping, 101
weaving, 101
Hand exerciser, 46
Hand position, damping, 55
Hand strength, multiple bell techniques, 89
Head, position, 32
Healthy hands, 122
Hearing protection devices, 146-147
Heating up, as pain reliever, 175
History, handbell ringing, 18
Hug, 112
Hydration, 158
massed ring, 180, 187
voice problems and, 153
Hypoglycemia, 159

INDEX

I
Ibuprofen, 173
Icing-down, 174-175
Icons, listing, 22
Inhaling, 35
Intercostals, 28
Intrinsics, 26

K
Keyboard press, 119
Knees, keeping unlocked, 32

L
Laissez vibrer, 75
  bass bells, 83
Lateral raise, 143
Latissimus dorsi, 28
Learning to ring, using extended octaves, 53-54
Leg lean, 136
Leg raises, 137
Legs
  muscles, 29, 134
  stretches, 135-137
Let vibrate, 75
  bass bells, 83
Lifting
  after massed ring, 188
  basics, 160-161
  bass bells, 79-81
  belltrees, 76
  maximum load, 163
Light, table, 150-151
Locking your wrist, 52
Lower leg muscles, 29
LV, 75
  bass bells, 83

M
Mallets, 72-73
Martellato, 69-72
  after shaking, 74
  bass bells, 69-70, 83
  small bells, 70
  variations, 71-72
Mart-lift, bass bells, 83

Massed ring, 178-188
  director, 179-183
    breaks, 180
    breathing, 181
    emotional preparation, 180
    mental preparation, 180
    physical preparation, 179
    physical warm-up, 179-180
    rehearsal warm-ups with ringers, 181-183
    voice care, 180-181
  ringers, 184-188
    clothing and footwear, 185
    departure and injuries, 188
    nutrition, 187
    preparation, 184-185
    sight line, 187
    stretches after the performance, 188
    stretching break, 185-186
Matched grip, 43-44
  malleting, 73
  martellato, 70
Medical concerns, 171-175
Meditation, pre-performance, 155
Mental preparation, massed ring director, 180
Molefoam, 86
Moleskin, 88
Moving, handbell cases and tables, 160-163
Multiple bell techniques, 87-96
  adhesive bandage, 88
  combo-ring, 94-95
  damping, 90-91
  elbow position, 91
  exercise and stretching, 87
  four-in-hand, 93
  grip, 88-89, 91
  hand strength, 89
  moleskin, 88
  picking up secondary bell, 89
  portable ringing, 96
  primary bell, 88
  proper alignment of grip, 89

  range of ringing, 87
  ringing, 89-90
  secondary bell, 88
  shelley, 92
  six-in-hand, 95-96
  table damping, 91
Multiple chimes, 102
Muscles, 24-30
  arm, 24, 115
  back, 27-28, 125
  chest, 27
  diagram, 25
  foot, 30
  forearm, 26
  hand, 26, 118
  large, bearing weight, 32
  leg, 29, 134
  neck, 26-27, 110
  overuse, 168
  respiration, 28
  shoulder, 27, 110
Muscle spasm, 170
Music exposure, 146

N
Naprosyn, 173
Neck
  care when ringing, 110
  muscles, 26-27, 110
  sore, damping, 58
  stretches, 111-114
  warm-ups, 111
Neck stretch, 113
Noise exposure, 146
Non-drug pain relievers, 174-175
Non-steroidal anti-inflammatory drugs, 173-174
Non-stopped techniques, 73, 76
  belltree, 75-76
  gyro, 75
  LV, 75
  shake, 73-74
  shimmer, 75
  toll, 74
NSAIDs, 173-174
Nutrition, 158-159
  massed ring, 187

INDEX

O
Oblique stretch, 132
OK knuckle bend, 121
Over-extending wrist, 52

P
Pain relievers
    drug, 173-174
    non-drug, 174-175
Paintbrush stroke, 53
Pectoralis major, 27
Pectoralis minor, 27
Pelvic tilt, 133
Performance
    eating prior to, 159
    stress management, 155-156
Performance anxiety, 36, 38, 155
Physical fitness, voice problems and, 152
Plucking, 68
Portable ringing, 96
Posture, 31-33, 49
    bass bells, 79
Practice "bells", 46, 67
Praying, 117, 121, 128
Preparatory breath, 37-38
    for martellato, 70
Pre-performance anxiety, 155
Primary bell, 88
Progressive lenses, 149
Putty play, 119
Putty press, 119

Q
Quadriceps, 29
    stretching, 136-137
Quadriceps lift, 137

R
Rag doll bend, 128
Ready-to-ring position, 47-48
    bass bells, 80
    handchimes, 98
Rebound, 50
    with jerky action, 52
Repetitions, 141
Repetitive strain injury, 171-172

Resistance, understanding, 109
Resistance training, 141-144
    developing grip strength, 141
    free weight guidelines, 142
    hand and wrist, 142-143
    procedure, 141
    repetitions, 141
    sets, 141
Respiration, muscles, 28
Rhomboids, 27
Ringers
    massed ring, 184-188
        clothing and footwear, 185
        departure and injuries, 188
        nutrition, 187
        preparation, 184-185
        sight line, 187
        stretches after the performance, 188
        stretching break, 185-186
    new, stress management, 154
Ring-hook, bass bells, 84
Ringing, 47-54
    allowing bell's weight to control the ring, 52
    basic ring, 48-49
    basic stroke, 49-51
    beginning, using extended octaves, 53-54
    clapper adjustments, 51
    controlling energy, 48
    handchimes, 98-99
    history, 18
    leading with casting, 53
    locking your wrist, 52
    over-extending wrist, 52
    paintbrush stroke, 53
    quickly, 51
    ready-to-ring position, 47-48
    rebound, 50
Ringing circle
    size, 50
    while shaking, 73
Ringing motion, combined with breathing, 37

Ring-touch, 72
    bass bells, 83
Rotator cuff, 27

S
Secondary bell, 88
Sets, 141
Shake, 73-74
    bass bells, 83
    into martellato, 74
    stretching after, 74
Shelley, 92
Shifting weight, 32
Shimmer, 75
Shoes, 33, 139-140
    massed ring, 185
    proper support, 140
Shoulder
    muscles, 27, 110
    posture and, 32
    stretches, 111-114
    warm-ups, 111
Shoulder damp, 55-56
Shoulder pull, 127
Shoulder raise, 127
Shoulder roll, 111, 126
Shoulder shrug, 111
Shoulder squeeze, 112, 126
Shoulder stretch, 113
Sight line, massed ring, 187
Sight-reading, bass bell ringers, 78
Sight riser, 150
Sitting leg raises, 136
Six-in-hand, 95-96
Slider, 57
Small bells
    martellato, 70
    plucking, 68
Space, around you, 33
Special techniques, 68-76
    non-stopped, 73-76
    stopped, 68-72
Spine, keeping erect, 31
Spontaneous break, 183, 185-186
Sport tape, 85

INDEX

Stage fright, 36, 38
Staircase stretch, 135
Stairs, carrying cases, 162
Standing up straight, 31
Static stretch, 107, 157
Step to the side, 136
Sternocleidomastoids, 26
Stopped techniques, 68-73
    mallets, 72-73
    martellato, 69-72
    plucking, 68
    ring touch, 72
    thumb damp, 69
Storage cabinet, 163
Strength
    developing, for carrying a belltree, 76
    grip, see Grip Strength
Stress
    avoiding, massed ring, 187
    controlling, 154
    relievers, 154
Stress management, 154-157
Stretching
    abdomen, 132-133
    after massed ring, 188
    after shaking, 74
    arm, 116-117
    back, 126-129
    benefits, 106
    calf, 135
    cool down, 124
    in cramped quarters, 156-157
    developmental, 107
    foot, 138-139
    gentle, 106
    guidelines, 107
    hamstring, 136
    hand, 123
    how to, 107
    massed ring, 182
    multiple bell techniques, 87
    pre-performance, 155
    prior to lifting, 161
    quadricep, 136-137
    reminders, 111, 118, 126, 133-134, 138
    repetition, 107
    routine, 108
    shoulder and neck, 111-114
    spontaneous break, 183, 185
    wrist, 123
    see also Exercises; Warm-ups
Stroke, 49
    basic, 49-51
    paintbrush, 53
    rebound, 50
Sunshine stretch, 127
Support bands, 168-170
    bass bells, 86
Support braces, 168-170
Support devices, 168-170
Swaying branch, 127
Swing, 74
    bass bells, 83

T

Table covers, 60
Table damp, 59-60
    accuracy, 59-60
    bass bells, 60, 82
    handchimes, 101
    multiple bell techniques, 91
Table-less ringing, 96
Table light, 151
Table padding
    necessary for martellato, 70
    table damp and, 60
Table press, 124
Tables
    custom-built, bass bells, 84
    lifting case to, 162
    moving, 160-163
Tendinitis, 171
Tennis elbow, 44, 171
Tension, grip, 44-45
Thumb damp, 69
    bass bells, 82
    multiple bell techniques, 91
Tip-toe stretch, 135
Tired ankles, 139
Tired toes, 138
"Toasting", 50
Toll, 74
    bass bells, 83
Torso twists, 129
Tower swing, 74
    bass bells, 83
Trapezius, 26-27
Triceps, 24
Trifocals, 149

U

Ulnar nerve, 171
Upper arm stretch, 117

V

Visual aids, 150, 151
Voice, 152-153
    care, massed ring director, 180-181
    production, 152

W

Waist braces, 170
Walking, 140
Warm-ups, 19, 106-109
    arm, 115-116
    bass bell ringers, 77-78
    before ringing, 108
    during ringing, 108
    fingers, hand and wrist, 119
    following ringing, 108
    importance, 106
    massed ring
        group conducting, 182
        group stretches, 183
        prior to final concert, 183
        simple run-through, 182
        stretching, 182
    massed ring director, 181-183
    prior to lifting, 161
    rehearsal, bass bell ringers, 78
    shoulder and neck, 111
    see also Exercises; Stretching
Water, 153, 158
    massed ring, 180, 187

INDEX

Weaving, 61-67
    bass bells, 67, 81
    bell set-up, 62
    four-bell, 66
    handchimes, 101
    home for each bell, 62
    process, 62-66
    three-bell, 64-65
    weight shifting, 61
Weightlifting gloves, 165-166

Weight shifting, 32
    weaving, 61
Weight training, bass bell ringers, 77-78
Wrist
    avoid locking, handchimes, 98
    contrast bath, 175
    cool down stretches, 124
    locking, 52, 98
    muscles, 118
        strain, avoiding, 118
    over-extending, 52
    resistance training, 142-143
    sore, damping, 57
    stretches, 123
    twisted, 57
Wristband, 170
Wrist braces, 169
Wrist curl, 123. 142
Wrist rotation, 123, 143

About the Author

Susan Berry is best known for her work in "the basics" of ringing. A nationally-known handbell educator, she has taught at local, area, and national workshops and conferences, and has directed massed festivals throughout the United States. She has written articles for professional journals, including Overtones, the official monthly publication of The American Guild of English Handbell Ringers.

Susan received her musical training at Michigan State University, Wayne State University and Oakland University. A music educator since 1970, she has served in Detroit, MI as an organist, choir director, handbell director, and classroom teacher. Certified in Orff-Schulwerk, she also taught general music at the Center for Creative Studies in Detroit.

Susan has co-authored two other major publications: *Bell Basics*, a beginning instructional training videotape published in 1986 by Hope Publishing, Carol Stream, IL, and the *Learning To Ring* curriculum, containing instructional manuals, music, skill-building exercises, and charts, published by The Lorenz Corporation, Dayton, OH, in 1988.

Her company, Handbell Services (established in 1991), publishes **BELLS**, a gift catalogue of products created by artists from all over the United States. HSI also operates the **BELLfry**, a retail music and gift store in Dearborn, MI, and hosts a variety of training workshops, reading clinics, concerts, and festivals for directors and ringers each year. She has developed hundreds of beginning handbell and handchime programs in churches, schools, community centers, senior communities, and hospitals in Michigan.

Susan has directed handbell choirs in Detroit area churches since 1974. She founded and directed the Classical Bells of Metropolitan Detroit (1982-89) and the Detroit Handbell Ensemble (since 1991), both choirs of recognized excellence. Susan has represented Malmark, Inc., Plumsteadville, PA, in the state of Michigan since 1979.

About the Illustrator

Allan Berry earned his Bachelor of Fine Art degree in 1999 at the University of Michigan in Ann Arbor, with a specialty in painting and drawing. Allan has created many illustrations for Handbell Services'® **BELLS** gift catalog, and has designed many retail products for the handbell community. Allan created the Bellman© in 1997, which has become an icon for handbell ringers worldwide.

Since he was young, Allan has been drawing – on restaurant napkins, homework assignments, and anything else he could get his hands on. This has allowed him many interesting experiences and pedigrees, from designing a nationally aired commercial for MTV while in high school, to winning awards in numerous art shows. Currently Allan intends to focus his talent in illustration, and may eventually enter a career in fine art conservation, illustration, or art education. Always with a new project on his plate, *Healthy Ringing* proves to be just one in a long line of creative endeavors that Allan continuously finds himself embroiled in, and usually loving every second of it.

NOTES

NOTES

www.ingramcontent.com/pod-product-compliance
Lightning Source LLC
Chambersburg PA
CBHW080542170426
43195CB00016B/2652